THE
MEANING
OF SOUL

REFIGURING AMERICAN MUSIC

A series edited by Ronald Radano, Josh Kun, and Nina Sun Eidsheim

Charles McGovern, contributing editor

THE
MEANING
OF SOUL

BLACK MUSIC AND RESILIENCE
SINCE THE 1960s

EMILY J. LORDI

DUKE UNIVERSITY PRESS *Durham and London* 2020

Designed by Matthew Tauch
Typeset in Arno Pro by Copperline Book Services

Library of Congress Cataloging-in-Publication Data
Names: Lordi, Emily J., [date] author.
Title: The meaning of soul : Black music and resilience since
the 1960s / Emily J. Lordi.
Other titles: Refiguring American music.
Description: Durham : Duke University Press, 2020.
Series: Refiguring American music | Includes bibliographical
references and index.
Identifiers: LCCN 2019057426 (print)
LCCN 2019057427 (ebook)
ISBN 9781478008699 (hardcover)
ISBN 9781478009597 (paperback)
ISBN 9781478012245 (ebook)
Subjects: LCSH: Soul music—History and criticism. | Soul
musicians. | African Americans—Music—History and
criticism. | Music and race—United States—History—
20th century. | Popular music—United States—History
and criticism.
Classification: LCC ML3537. L67 2020 (print) |
LCC ML3537 (ebook) | DDC 781.644—dc23
LC record available at https://lccn.loc.gov/2019057426
LC ebook record available at https://lccn.loc.gov/2019057427

Cover art: Minnie Riperton poses for a studio portrait,
USA, 1975. Photo by Gilles Petard / Redfern

To Anthony, Stokely, and Nelson — my loves

CONTENTS

ACKNOWLEDGMENTS

A lot has happened since my last scholarly book appeared in 2013: marriage, two kids, a short book, freelance work, and then, recently, a new job, home, and city. This book was, consequently, written in pieces, and it came together through invitations and inspirations from people I know, love, and respect.

Several scholars lit the way with their own writing on soul music and culture, including Mark Anthony Neal, Gayle Wald, Charles Hughes, Farah Jasmine Griffin, Ed Pavlić, Margo Crawford, and GerShun Avilez. I am grateful to Mark, Tanisha Ford, and Lloyd Pratt for organizing panels through which I developed key facets of this work, and to everyone who helped me think with and through soul—at Columbia College, the University of Georgia, George Mason University, Columbia University, Yale, Bard College, Amherst College, UCLA, the University of Michigan, and Dartmouth. Thanks to the scholars who made my visits to those institutions possible: Gianpaolo Chiriacò, Ed Pavlić, Paul Smith, Tiana Reid, Josef Sorett, Pete L'Official, Colleen Daniher, Lynnée Denise, Marcus Hunter, Manan Desai, Donald Pease, and Eric Lott. Thanks to all my friends at the Pop Conference (MoPOP) for making my life in music writing a joy. I miss Rashod Ollison, who was a bright star within that circle and one of the most beautiful "soul folks" I've known.

I am grateful to several editors for soliciting and helping me refine various pieces of this work: the collective at *Women and Performance*; John Drabinski and Grant Farred for *New Centennial Review*; Jeffrey Ogbar for *Keywords in African American Studies*; Tanisha Ford for the *Feminist Wire*;

Jason Parham at the *Fader*; Rebecca Milzoff and Nick Catucci at *Billboard*; Lenika Cruz at the *Atlantic*; Michael Agger at the *New Yorker*.

I was also fortunate to share parts of this work, at early and late stages of the writing process, with two wonderful groups of scholars: the Black Feminist Sound Studies colloquium organized by Daphne Brooks at Princeton, where my primary interlocutor was Imani Perry; and the Post45 Workshop organized by Merve Emre at Worcester College, Oxford, where I received helpful feedback from several readers, including Sarah Chihaya, Jane Elliott, Summer Kim Lee, and Nijah Cunningham. Thanks as well to everyone at the 2014 New England Americanist Collective workshop, and to Courtney Thorsson, Michael Gillespie, Salamishah Tillet, Barry Shank, Joshua Clover, and Robert O'Meally for smart questions and encouragement along the way.

Zandria Robinson and Mark Anthony Neal: You are dream readers. Thank you so much for "getting" this project and for embodying both brilliance and soul. It has been such a privilege to work with my editor Ken Wissoker, whose advocacy for his authors is unmatched. I also thank Nina Foster and Lisl Hampton for guiding this book through production.

Thanks to my fantastic former colleagues in the English and Afro-American Studies Departments at UMass-Amherst, where I had the pleasure of working from 2011 to 2019. Thanks to my new colleagues at Vanderbilt, especially Dana Nelson and John Geer, for making me and my family welcome here too. I am also grateful for the spiritual sustenance provided by Pastor John Faison, Alethia Faison, and the community at the Grove.

Thanks as ever to my family—Mom, Dad, Jeff, Joe, Catherine and the kids—for their boundless support, kindness, and humor. Big love to Ed, Tameka, Nia, Soleil, and Deborah Reed. Stokely and Nelson, without idealizing any of us, I can say that you are my miracles. Being your mother is the wildest blessing of my life. Anthony Reed: You are my secret weapon and my best friend. Through all the changes, here we are: soul to soul. I love you.

I hope this book will honor, in particular, the memory of Aretha Franklin, Donny Hathaway, Minnie Riperton, and Lucille Clifton—guiding lights, all.

INTRODUCTION KEEPING ON

> Our bright revolutionary generation. And its fantastic de-
> sires. Its beauty. Its strength. Its struggle. Its accomplish-
> ment. Its legacy. What will that be?! AMIRI BARAKA, 1996

The song opens with a demonstration of soul swagger—propulsive bass
guitar and drums followed by piano, horns, strings, and the voice of Gladys
Knight:

> *I've really got to use my imagination*
> *To think of good reasons to keep on keepin' on*
> *Got to make the best of a bad situation*
> *Ever since that day I woke up and found that*
> *You were gone.*[1]

Gone, gone! go the Pips as if keening, albeit efficiently. There's no time to
keep from keeping on and moving up: Knight soon hauls the lyrics up an
octave amid ascending strings. Still, her words start to betray new depths
of sorrow:

> *Darkness all around me, blocking out the sun . . .*
> *Emptiness has found me, and it just won't let me go*
> *I go right on living*
> *But why I just don't know.*

Luckily, the Pips are on hand, and they do more than just repeat Knight's words in their stylish falsettos; here, at the song's lyrical nadir, they sing their first and only original response: "You're too strong not to keep on keepin' on!" "Yes I am!" Knight fires back, as if the truth was never in question but she just wanted to hear it. Still, the Pips repeat their reassurance to boost her into the next verse. The song builds relentlessly though multiple counterpoints and intensified dynamics, insisting on affirmation against the undertow of despair.

Released in 1973, "I've Got to Use My Imagination" both describes and enacts the kind of resilience for which Knight and the Pips were, by then, rightly famous. The group enjoyed their greatest success in the early 1970s, at which point it was about a decade overdue. They had formed at a birthday party in Atlanta in 1952, when Knight and her brother Merald (a.k.a. Bubba), eight and ten, joined forces with their sister Brenda and cousins Eleanor and William Guest (the girls were later replaced by Edward Patten). The ensemble cut its teeth singing in church; then played for segregated audiences throughout the South ("white in the day, black at night"); then moved to New York, where for a time Merald packed boxes in the Garment District to pay the bills, and even the best gigs were grueling: six shows a day from 11:00 a.m. to midnight at the Apollo Theater in Harlem.[2] The group could have been forgiven for thinking they had made it when, in 1966, they signed with Berry Gordy's Motown Records and released the smash hit "I Heard It through the Grapevine" (1967). But even Motown underrated them, prioritizing stars like the Supremes and Marvin Gaye.[3] So it was not until Knight and the Pips left Motown for white-owned Buddah Records, where they were given control over song production, that they enjoyed sustained commercial and critical success. Their best-known hit, "Midnight Train to Georgia," topped both white and black charts in 1973, and by the time "Imagination" was released three months later, the group was, in *Ebony* critic Phyl Garland's estimation, "possibly the best soul group of the day performing at its peak."[4]

The group's trajectory registered the historical changes of a people in transition: from the segregated Jim Crow South to the exploitative urban North, from the ambivalent gains of the civil rights movement to the ongoing struggle of Black Power. "Imagination" runs on the mixture of energy and world-weariness one might expect of a group that had broken into formerly white-only venues (in Reno, Miami, Las Vegas), but still needed to tour eleven months of the year.[5] Nonetheless, it's the energy that wins out, as Knight's labored yet surefire vocals attest. It's "such a sad, sad season when a good love dies," she sings, but seasons like this one have produced the knowledge Knight is turning to by the end of the couplet: "Not a day goes by when I don't realize . . . I've really got to use my imagination." Pains both past and present have produced a determined resilience—tight, stylized, and, thanks to the Pips, collective. Despite the song's interracial production (hit makers Barry Goldberg and Gerry Goffin wrote it, and white musicians played the instrumental track), its sound and sentiment are coded as black, due to a mix of racial signifiers: Knight's textured, church-raised voice; the gospel drive and intensification;[6] the blues-like lyric that seeks solace not in God but in oneself; the Motown polish; and the economical string arrangement typical of upwardly mobile soul—lush enough to appreciate, but not to luxuriate in. Here, struggle yields black resilience. This is the logic of soul.

That logic shaped a cultural sensibility that was bigger than soul music but that was especially audible in the music due to the commentary that shaped its social life. Early-1970s accounts of Gladys Knight and the Pips in both the black and white press constantly stressed the group's unbroken two-decade run, and, by extension, the payoff of collective struggle. That narrative of unbroken striving, if somewhat overstated (neglecting as it did some personnel changes and Knight's brief departure from the group to raise her children), was central to the group's story about itself and, in particular, to its political self-fashioning. As Merald told a *Washington Post* reporter in 1972, the group often discussed the importance of "giving young black kids and some of the older ones, too, an opportunity to see a black organization stay together throughout its life span. . . . If we don't make a penny," he added, "I want to go down with the same people."[7] This was the group's answer to the splintering of black communities, which had as its industry counterpart the breakup of house bands like Motown's Funk Brothers and the peeling off of solo artists from the groups in which they had started out: Sam Cooke from the Soul Stirrers, Curtis Mayfield from the Impressions, Eddie Kendricks and David Ruffin from the Temptations, Diana Ross from the Supremes. Gladys Knight could have easily followed suit. She was a child prodigy who had debuted at Mount Moriah Baptist Church in Atlanta at age four, studied classical voice and won the nationally televised *Ted Mack's Amateur Hour* by age eight, and started touring with the Pips by age nine. "People have been trying to steal me for years," she told *Ebony* in 1973, "But we are all *one*—a unit."[8]

That commitment to unity does not result in anything like the conformity or masculinism so often associated with soul; on the contrary, in musical terms, the group dynamic enables Knight's standout performance. I mean this not just in the obvious sense that the Pips back her up, but more precisely in that their timbral smoothness and melodic faithfulness create a taut canvas against which Knight's vocal colorings and innovations can pop. Those innovations are crucial to filling in the portrait of resilience to which the lyrics only allude. Whether as a matter of privacy or pride, Goffin's lyrics reveal next to nothing about the doomed love affair; it's just a "bad situation" about which there's nothing more to learn or say: "our misunderstanding is too well understood." Neither do we hear much about Knight's recovery—what her "good reasons to keep on keepin' on" might be. We suppose the song itself becomes one of them, thanks in part to the camaraderie of the Pips. But Knight's other reasons will be supplied by an imagination that is her surest source of security and, in a way, her biggest secret.

That imagination is manifest, however, in her technique. Knight is a powerhouse minimalist with a meticulous sense of the small variations one might play on a lyric or melody. (These choices, again, are thrown into relief by the Pips' right-on-the-money approach.) At first, Knight's variations are slight microtonal shifts through which she lifts the words at the end of each line ("my imaginatio-on," "keep on keepin' o-on," "you were go-one"). The next verse features more changes, with Knight jumping up the octave and switching the word *misunderstanding* to the cleverer, more syncopated "missed understanding." Characteristically sparing with her ad-libs, in the last verse Knight implements several other small but potent changes, changing the phrase "keepin' on" to the more propulsive "pushin' on" and briefly poring over the fact that her lover is "gone gone gone gone." Knight's minimalist, gradualist approach to performance is just as important as the song's composition and arrangement. In the context of "Imagination," her vocal embroidery enacts the many *ways*, if not the *reasons*, that she will keep on keeping on. Her attention to detail and craft exemplify the song's otherwise elusive imaginative will.

Knight and the Pips seldom figure in scholarly discussions of soul music, which tend to privilege charismatic men such as James Brown and unimpeachable movement anthems like Sam Cooke's "A Change Is Gonna Come" and Nina Simone's "Young, Gifted and Black." Fundamentally resistant to paradigms that treat soul music as a mere vehicle for civil rights messaging, the group embodied a wonderfully unruly set of signifiers by the 1970s: righteous problackness; unhip respectability and uplift politics;[9] a queer sounding of gender (high male voices backing a deeper female lead); straight hair for Gladys, naturals for the Pips, cool bellbottoms for everyone; a traditional focus on hard work. They didn't sing anthems. Yet the group, in its very complexity, embodies the story of soul that I tell in this book—where the stylization of survival is conditioned by pain, often led by women, and driven by imagination, innovation, and craft. Again, this is not only a story about soul music; it is also about the logic of soul that the music enacts. This logic opposes that of liberal subjecthood and neoliberal individualism by articulating a resilience that is collective, that is about staying with the band. And, despite the way that soul has been remembered, the "band" as I describe it featured a range of women's, femme, and queer voices.

I argue that, whereas the term *soul* had evoked a deep spiritual-racial consciousness at least since W. E. B. Du Bois's theorization of *The Souls of Black Folk* (1903), in the 1960s, soul came to signify the special resilience black people had earned by surviving the historical and daily trials of white supremacy.[10] At a moment when it was becoming possible to describe oneself as "spiritual but not religious"[11]—a moment when, according to Amiri Baraka, religious concepts such as faith and conversion "expanded past religion" to "permeate the entire culture"[12]—soul discourse reimagined the Judeo-Christian ideal that suffering might be worth something. But what it earned you was not a heavenly afterlife in which the last might be first, but worldly gifts such as emotional depth and communal belonging. To have soul was to have developed a kind of virtuosic survivorship specific to black people as a group. And soul musicians, through a series of practices drawn from the black church, modeled virtuosic black resilience on a national stage. Soul was not, then, an inherited essence black people held in common. Nor was it simply a genre of music. It was a logic constituted through a network of strategic performances—musical, literary, journalistic—meant to promote black thriving, if not liberation.[13]

This understanding of soul weaves together the many valences Gayle Wald describes when she writes, "That one can *have* soul, *be* soulful, and play *soul music* demonstrates soul's compass over varied terrains of style, politics, ideology, subjectivity, and spirituality."[14] I use an archive of literature, theory, and journalism to illuminate live and recorded performances from the late 1960s and early 1970s, showing how artists and intellectuals of Baraka's "bright revolutionary generation" articulated soul logic and how the music called soul enacted that logic right down to its performative details—the showstopping ad-libs and ethereal falsettos, but also the missed cues, signs of exhaustion, admissions of strain. In short, I draw together soul's conceptual and aesthetic registers to show how an overarching theory of soul might bridge the nuances and contradictions yielded by close readings of soul music as well as the idiosyncrasies of individual artists. In so doing, I advance a holistic and complex view of the subject that contests most histories of black popular music (that see soul music as simply transmitting political content); mass-marketed representations of soul music (which sideline black women and mystify musical craft); and theories of "post-soul" black art, which reduce soul itself to an essentializing, heteropatriarchal monolith that later, more enlightened "post-soul" artists must overcome. I will have more to say about the circumstances that give rise to post-soul theory. But I will note here that post-soul's field-shaping assumption that art created during the 1960s reflects a repressive program of compulsory unity explains why scholars, despite having provided rich accounts of blues, jazz, hip-hop, and post-soul aesthetics, have not yet theorized the aesthetics of soul. Despite the crucial work of Portia Maultsby and other scholars who have codified the musicological components of soul music, scholarship on black expressive culture tends to assume that soul as a concept does not have an aesthetics, but only a *politics*— one coded as a short-lived radical energy, at best, and an outmoded essentialism, at worst.[15] In my view, however, soul's logic of overcoming encompasses a diverse and experimental set of aesthetics, which themselves express a range of ways of being black together in a perilous age. This new understanding of soul, finally, recovers past aspirations for a better future than the one in which we ended up.

....

The term *soul* rose to national consciousness at a moment of crisis, which is also to say, at a time of community building and breaking. Maultsby explains that the term became a household word among black people during "the inner-city uprisings (labeled 'riots' by the media) of 1964 (Harlem), 1965 (Watts), and 1967 (Detroit and Newark)," when black business owners, hoping to prevent black residents from looting and destroying their establishments, put signs in their windows reading "soul brother."[16] So soul was fundamentally linked to black solidarity, to the kind of togetherness forged under siege. In an era when poor black people were so desperate for national visibility that they set their own cities on fire, the language and logic of soul served as flares of a different kind—signs of encouragement, belonging, and critique sent up to fortify the group. The term *soul* helped to organize black people's process of self-redefinition in the 1960s, a process that was most clearly reflected in the lexical shift from *Negro* to *black*. Soul was also, at that time, used as a general modifier to describe and advertise things created by and for black people: soul food, the television show *Soul Train*. And of course, soul denoted a genre of music rooted in the gospel tradition.

The most determined efforts to unite soul's diverse musical and socio-historical meanings were made during the soul era itself, when black critics hastened to claim the newly codified, and incredibly lucrative, genre of soul music as the province of black people whose historical suffering it both registered and worked to overcome. Still, these early efforts reflected a disjuncture between historical and musical understandings of soul that has persistently marked its theorization. In the introduction to her landmark book *The Sound of Soul* (1969), Phyl Garland drew a straight line from the field hollers of the enslaved to the agitated energy of contemporary soul singers; the rest of her book collected interview-based profiles of blues and soul artists that Garland had originally published in *Ebony*.[17] The book's structure itself therefore raised the question of how the individual artists Garland profiled might represent the racial-historical charge of soul music. A. X. Nicholas, in his 1971 book *The Poetry of Soul*, followed Garland's lead (which was itself shaped by that of LeRoi Jones/Amiri Baraka, in *Blues People*) by framing soul music as a sonic reflection of black people's past and present in which all prior forms of vernacular music (work songs, field hollers, jazz) combined to express "the Black man's condition (in fascist Amerika)—his frustrations, his anger, his pride."[18] But Nicholas repeated Garland's bifurcated form: a historical introduction followed, in his case, by a collection of song lyrics reprinted as poetic verse, which Nicholas used to illustrate, though not exactly to support, his claim that soul music was "*the poetry of the Black Revolution*."[19]

That segregation of abstract and concrete, ideal and particular meanings of soul continues to shape recent scholarship. Most discussions of soul now emphasize either musical or ontological meanings. Paul Gilroy and Fred Moten venture performance-based ontologies of the concept, which Gilroy describes as an energy that "resists the reach of economic rationality and the commodifying process" and which Moten describes as a "will to proceed."[20] Scholars such as Mark Burford (writing about Sam Cooke) and Daphne Brooks (writing about Nina Simone) combine Garland's interest in biography and Nicholas's interest in composition with attention to the sound of soul music itself.[21] Yet their exemplary discussions of musicians' techniques do not yield theories of soul per se. Maultsby, William

Van Deburg, Mark Anthony Neal, and Brian Ward have all offered rich, in-depth discussions of soul as ideology, commodity, and musical practice, but without advancing a theory of soul that would bind these dimensions together.[22] The same is true, finally, of Monique Guillory and Richard C. Green's anthology *Soul: Black Power, Politics, and Pleasure* (1998), which represents both the most extensive and the least conclusive theorization of the concept to date. In an effort to respect what they call "the chameleon-like nature of soul," the editors seek only "to grasp soul in some of its many guises and articulations."[23] That approach, while suited to both the genre of the anthology and the 1990s focus on the vagaries of subject formation, is too expansive to constitute a useful theory of soul—one that would reveal the visions of black struggle and survival the concept helped to create.

Writers and scholars have struggled to bridge the different valences of soul because they have mistaken it for a discrete thing instead of a habit of thinking, a logic. But the most consistent feature of soul discourse is the recuperative logic I have described, whereby suffering is made to pay off. Hence, linguist Geneva Smitherman, in her dictionary of black vernacular terms, defines *soul* as "the essence of life; feeling, passion, emotional depth—all of which are believed to be derived from struggle, suffering, and having participated in the Black Experience. Having risen above the suffering, the person gains *soul*."[24] Zadie Smith likewise later notes, more simply, soul is "an alchemy of pain."[25] People who had soul believed in—had to believe in—the value of pain, and they showed how it could be alchemized into artistic expressions of deep feeling. Both the belief and its creative expression secured one's place in a community of other black people who understood that suffering had meaning and who lived that understanding through a life-affirming style. What the discourse of soul gave people, then, was an assurance that even their most chilling experiences of grief did not isolate them but rather connected them—with their contemporaries, to be sure, but also with a procession of ancestors whose personal griefs were unknowable but whose historical traumas were rendered increasingly present through national discourse about slavery. "You think your pain and your heartbreak are unprecedented in the history of the world," James Baldwin told an interviewer in 1963; but it turned out "the things that tormented me most were the very things that connected me with all the people who were alive, or who ever had been alive."[26] Whereas Baldwin credited Dostoevsky and Dickens with inspiring that epiphany for him, soul discourse would, by the end of the 1960s, racialize that habit of thought, training black people to recuperate their past and present struggles into a narrative of belonging to and with other black people.

Sufficiently essentialist to keep white Americans from appropriating it and capacious enough to allow many black Americans to tailor it to their own lives, soul discourse developed alongside, yet independently of, the turn from civil rights–era models of peaceful protest and interracial alliance toward the more defiant praxis of black self-reliance signified by Black Power. Amid conservative retrenchment and spectacular antiblack violence (Nikki Giovanni recalled of the 1960s that, in light of the assassinations of Medgar Evers, John F. Kennedy, Malcolm X, Martin Luther King, and Bobby Kennedy, "You woke up every day being surprised that *you* were alive"[27]), soul helped to mark black cultural production as the desired yet inappropriable result of oppression while organizing a community's redefinition around the concept of stylized survivorship. At a moment when, as Imani Perry notes, the integration black people had worked so hard for seemed destined to fail, with black Northerners consigned to ghettos and black Southerners beaten and killed for claiming their civil rights, black people began, in Perry's words, "to reach even more deeply into their cultural repertoire to find what had kept the enslaved and their spirits alive."[28] In place of the peaceful energy needed to survive violent attacks—what King had termed "soul force"—arose a more generalized ethos of readiness and resilience in the form of soul itself: a belief that black people, having already overcome, were spiritually fortified for the necessity of doing so again.[29]

Underpinning this cultural logic was a theory of reading history similar to what Fredric Jameson advances through his engagement with Paul Ricoeur. In *Valences of the Dialectic* (2009), Jameson outlines an ideal mode of reading that could hold together "multiple dimensions of time": individual and national temporalities; past, present, and future.[30] When soul theorists such as Garland and Nicholas described soul music as synthesizing musical genres from all of black American history, they were advancing a similar hermeneutic. Soul fans should, these critics suggested, relate their personal trials to those described in the music, but they should also hear the music itself as the latest chapter in a "single great collective story" (to cite Jameson) in which they each played a role.[31] It was not unusual for writers, especially in the black press, to describe soul music in such all-encompassing terms. "Gladys, reaching back into time, pulled out the roots of black pain, black hope and black joy and described them with a revival-meetin' voice," wrote B. J. Mason of a concert in 1973; meanwhile, "the Pips, rocking to a motherland beat, sidestepped busted black dreams in a *danse de joie* like it was somehow the last gig in the world."[32] Such descriptions suggest that the language of "depth" that often attended discussions of soul was not merely an individual emotional depth but a *historical* depth—the sort that Langston Hughes had ascribed to the generic "Negro" who had witnessed all of human history and emerged to declare, "My soul has grown deep like the rivers"; and the kind that Black Aesthetic theorists of the 1960s (many of them indebted to Hughes) had in mind when they invoked "the racial memory."[33] Julian Mayfield defined that concept with particular clarity: as "the unshakable knowledge of who we are, where we have been, and, springing up from this, where we are going." "Where have we been?" Mayfield asked: "Up a hell of a long, hard road."[34] The language of soul encouraged black people to understand their own "long, hard road[s]" as part of a grand historical narrative of a people who had survived and arrived (as the title of Franklin's 1968 album *Aretha Arrives* declared she had)—and were ready to do so again. For Jameson, the practice of reading multiple vectors of history offers a glimpse of future possibility; the soul hermeneutic fostered a similarly open-ended readiness for whatever might come to pass—be it death, revolution, or more of the same.[35] This was its greatest gift to a people in transition.

To show how soul circulated in this way, I develop a vision of the concept that is capacious enough to encompass the term's racial-political meanings and sensitive enough to draw out the details of the music, as well as the less academically prestigious but equally crucial details of artists' biographies, and fans' habits of identification therewith. Soul's recuperative logic helps explain how, for instance, James Brown, the self-designated "Soul Brother No. 1," made the concept of being "the hardest-working man in show business" not a source of frustration or shame but a badge of honor. Soul logic illuminates Nina Simone's decision to cover a song from the rock musical *Hair* in which she declares she has nothing but "life," while mobilizing several musical idioms in a virtuosic display of life's musical richness and therefore enacting a flamboyant survivorship that, in light of murders and assaults on black people, could sound like a taunt or a victory. Through rigorous revival-style vocal and physical performances, singers like Brown, Simone, and Franklin performed a cultural logic by which racialized labor yielded ascendant style. In this sense, they embraced the charge that generations of black parents had given their children—to do everything twice as well as their white counterparts in order to get over as far—and turned it into an affirmative conceit. (*Yes, we have had to work harder; but one effect of having done so is that now we are better than you.*)

Although song lyrics were an obvious way to express such affirmation—"Everybody is a star!" Sly and the Family Stone sang out, on the brink of the '70s—I focus more on the musical techniques or practices through which artists enacted soul ethos. These practices include transformative cover versions of popular songs; vocal ad-libs and falsetto singing; and false endings that trick listeners into thinking a performance is over. While these practices did not all begin with, and are certainly not exclusive to, soul music, they did enact with particular clarity the logic of overcoming that was politicized and racialized in the soul era. By privileging the performative and biographical detail—an aesthetic category that, as Alexandra Vazquez notes, following Naomi Schor, has been gendered as feminine—I mean to destabilize and materialize the idealized category of soul, which has been figured as impenetrably masculine.[36] But whereas Vazquez privileges the detail, which she sees as "refus[ing] analytical capture," in order to puncture the myth of Cuban music's knowability (as anthropological object, colonialist fantasy, global commodity), I use the detail differently: to puncture the idea that soul *cannot* be known.[37] I resist the concept of soul's inscrutability ("If you have to ask [what it is], you'll never know," according to the popular dictum) by using the detail to concretize soul, to draw it closer, make it personal.

I also deploy a rather shamelessly presentist method of listening—by which I mean, one grounded in a moment-to-moment description of what is happening in the music. This mode of close listening, in addition to helping make soul a more knowable quantity, reflects the presentism of my artists, who often throw themselves into the moment of performance as if there might not be another—as if the time to say what needs saying is always, to cite the Pips again, about to be "gone, gone!"[38]

These efforts to detail and clarify soul, to draw us into its present, are important because the notion of soul's inscrutability, which was strategically advanced in the late 1960s for reasons I will explain in the following chapter, has since become a fetishized justification for simplifying the craft and politics of soul-era artists. Several biopics, documentaries, tribute albums, and histories of soul stars and major labels that have been released in the last two decades bear this out. The 2004 biopic *Ray* frames Ray Charles's music as the mystical expression of childhood trauma; James McBride unironically begins his book-length search for James Brown in a South Carolina field at midnight, "a land of a thousand ghosts";

the 2013 documentary *Muscle Shoals* features U2 front-man Bono crediting the sound of the music recorded at Fame Studios to the proximity of the Tennessee River: "It's like the songs come out of the mud."[39] These works exemplify the at times unbelievably obfuscating, atmospheric image of soul that drummer Uriel Jones critiques in *Standing in the Shadows of Motown* (2002): "People would always credit everything but the musicians," he notes. "They would say it was the [solo artists], the producers, the way the building was structured, the wood in the floor, even the food."[40]

Another problem with contemporary soul biopics is they tend to isolate soul stars from the communities that made them possible. These communities were often religious. Although the logic of soul develops, as I will explain in the following chapter, from cultural discourse about the blues, the *music* called soul might owe more to gospel. And it is those gospel roots—which, in addition to being gendered and classed, have not been subject to white revival or capture in a manner akin to the blues—that account for soul's relative illegibility, compared with the blues and jazz, in many scholarly circles.[41] To recognize gospel as a key force in soul music—not simply as a point of origin but as a "living tradition," which scholar Fredara Hadley calls "the greatest black conservatory"—is, moreover, to highlight the women and queer people who dominate black gospel spaces and are therefore crucial to the sound and meaning of soul.[42] The brilliance and work of these people is constantly obscured by texts of the twenty-first-century soul boom.

These texts betray one further, related problem: a subconscious cultural association of soul with a vague, essential masculine charisma. In an effort to dismantle that paradigm, I prioritize the creative innovations of women soul artists; I explore the gendered implications of men's and women's work; and I analyze the workings of patriarchal power in the music. This feminist approach calls attention, for instance, to *Simone's* role in catalyzing the political turn in soul music so often credited to men like Curtis Mayfield and Marvin Gaye; it means examining the gendered meanings of men's and women's falsetto singing; and it means highlighting the power dynamics between Isaac Hayes and his backup singers, as well as between Sly and Rose Stone.[43] What this book does not do is provide a comprehensive history of soul music that includes everyone's—or all of my own—favorite artists. Instead, it models a method of listening to and apprehending soul through especially salient examples of soul ethos and techniques. While I focus on solo artists, I try to maintain soul's communitarian ethos by describing the networks out of which soul stars emerge—networks, again, that are often religious and therefore gendered, sexualized, and classed. In the end, the most basic point I hope to make, in the midst of the soul boom in American culture, is that the *way* we represent soul, how we tell these stories, matters. It is not enough to celebrate soul icons if that celebration just remarginalizes women, remystifies soul artistry, and reduces soul's complex meanings to a single, easily digestible message.

While my ambition to shift the terms of soul's representation is broad, my specifically academic intervention is to challenge theories of post-soul art that create their own mystical versions of soul by framing soul as post-soul's vague yet racially essentialist, masculinist, heterosexist other. The term *post-soul* is used most neutrally as a historical marker; it helps scholars designate the cultural productions of black Americans born after 1963. However, scholars inspired by Trey Ellis's and Greg Tate's laudatory accounts of black aesthetic diversity in the late 1980s and abetted by Henry Louis Gates Jr.'s influential dismissal of Black Arts–era writing often frame post-soul as the liberated alternative to soul itself.[44] Their accounts conjure soul as a distant yet tyrannical mirage, a shroud covering all black people in the interest of coercive unification. Even Bertram Ashe, the most dedicated theorist of post-soul aesthetics, explains that his conception of soul simply "refers to a centuries-old, historical black tradition that post-soul artists somehow both extend and critique."[45] To the question of what soul actually is or who might represent its "set of traditional black expectations," Ashe cites but one thinker, Larry Neal, whose 1968 manifesto "The Black Arts Movement" exemplifies, in his view, the "prescriptive" attitude toward black art that post-soul artists such as Ellis and Tate refute.[46]

Now that several scholars have reduced soul to a mere shorthand for hegemonic forms of collective black politics that seem undesirable, we must again ask what soul actually is. To conflate it with the worst impulses of the Black Arts and Black Power movements—for instance, with the masculinism, misogyny, and binary vision of race that are indeed extant in Neal's Black Arts manifesto (though not in all Neal's work)—is insufficient.[47] Not only does that view reduce soul's complexity, but the uncritical embrace of post-soul also overemphasizes integration as a positive turning point in the history of African American aesthetics and, most misguidedly, reframes a set of movements explicitly tied to black liberation as the primary obstacle to black expressive freedom, thereby critiquing not the repressive state but the movements designed to defeat it.

The problem was not, of course, black radicalism but antiblack praxis; not black revolution but the world that made it seem necessary. If post-soul theory, at its best, critiques intraracial oppression in the interest of democratizing black critical discourse, at its worst, it conflates community with conformity and advances an individualistic, even consumerist, understanding of liberated blackness as the freedom to buy and identify with many different things—"both Jim and Toni Morrison," as Ellis famously put it.[48] I hope this book's mode of close reading and listening will show that soul-era work was just as beautiful, flawed, and complex as the artistic and political movements that followed it—and, more to the point, that soul-era artists were, at their best, co-conspirators in a vision of community that privileged not self-sacrifice but self-expression, not conformity but shared struggle and pleasure.

As a mode of thought and a way of being available to any and all black people who elected to practice it, soul was at once exclusively and nonessentially black. If by 1968 Aretha Franklin could offer a reporter what had to be the briefest definition of the era—"Soul is black"[49]—that did not mean that either soul or blackness was *rigidly* defined. Rather, what Margo Crawford writes of the Black Arts movement is true of the soul era as well: this was a moment when "black consciousness-raising and black experimentation [were] inseparable."[50] Few artists were as versatile as "High Priestess of Soul" Nina Simone, who mastered numerous musical idioms, or Donny Hathaway, who did the same. Few writers were clearer about the construction of racial and sexual identities than James Baldwin, or more committed to difference within unity than Audre Lorde. I see these artists as exemplary creators of, not exceptions to, soul aesthetics and ethics. But they will always be written out of accounts of soul so long as that formation is conflated with patriarchal versions of cultural nationalism. To disarticulate the two is to perceive soul's many nuances, as well as its continued resonance beyond the Black Power era. Each of my latter four chapters ends by examining contemporary echoes of a soul strategy—for instance, in the work of Prince and Solange Knowles—while showing how those strategies change in response to the Black Lives Matter movement and the neoliberal co-optation of narratives of resilience.

What I delineate in this book as the soul era proper—the period of the late 1960s through the early 1970s—describes a complex sociopolitical moment in which revolution vies with reform before the latter emerges as the dominant mode. As Lyndon Johnson's Great Society gives way to

Richard Nixon's enterprise zones, as the energies of Black Power are themselves neutralized by a focus on electoral politics, the cultural focus shifts from an emphasis on collective thriving toward a valorization of the enterprising individual on his/her hustle. That shift, while it does not spell the end of soul logic, does result in a perverse redefining of resilience, which now primarily connotes individual economic fitness, the ability to rebound from the blows of an inhumanely profit-driven global economy.

Overall, *The Meaning of Soul* recovers the promise and texture of the previous era by advancing a new understanding of soul: as a capacious narrative of black overcoming that illuminates an eclectic set of musical aesthetics and signals unexpected futures. This book therefore offers both a richer version of soul than one finds in most popular representations of the music and an extended critique of those scholarly paradigms that celebrate post–civil rights black cultural production in opposition to a reductive image of late 1960s black cultural politics. Against the deeply influential historiographical framework that pits Black Arts–era calls for black unity against post–Black Arts investments in intraracial diversity, I show how soul itself combined both: it was a general theory of black group vitality whose discrete manifestations were as flexible and mutable as the details of life and performance.

This revisionary reading relies on several sources: accounts of soul music and artists published in the black press in the soul era proper; writings about black music and politics by such figures as Baraka, Giovanni, and Baldwin; and, of course, recordings and performances, which, to my way of listening, contain their own arguments about and insights into soul and so serve to modify other commentaries. I am also deeply enabled and inspired by cultural studies of soul music published in the 1990s and 2000s by such scholars as Neal and Ward, and by two more recent bodies of scholarship: work in popular music studies on the regional and emotional nuances of soul music (Charles Hughes's *Country Soul* [2015], Mitchell Morris's *The Persistence of Sentiment* [2013]) and work in African American studies on the aesthetic and political complexities of Black Arts and Black Power (Gayle Wald's *It's Been Beautiful* [2015], GerShun Avilez's *Radical Aesthetics and Modern Black Nationalism* [2016], Tanisha Ford's *Liberated Threads* [2015], Ashley Farmer's *Remaking Black Power* [2017], Margo Crawford's *Black Post-Blackness* [2017]). I depart from these outstanding studies by disarticulating soul from the Black Power movement, which allows me to access the complexities of soul's musical, gender, and sexual politics; provide a stronger account of its female leadership; and offer a longer if gestural sense of its resonances beyond the 1970s.

My first chapter presents a genealogy of soul—as cultural logic, marketing category, musical genre—and, in so doing, sets the stage for my analyses of music in the following chapters. By situating the development of both soul and post-soul theory in relation to the blues, Black Power, and the Black Aesthetic, I crystallize soul's unique place and power within late twentieth-century American culture, and explain how and why post-soul theory has negated soul's complexity.

My second chapter reveals how Nina Simone, Aretha Franklin, Donny Hathaway, and Minnie Riperton (in her work with the band Rotary Connection) enact soul's logic of overcoming by covering white and black artists' songs. Several of their cover recordings reflect not only competitive attempts to unseat the original versions but the more intimate, intraracial forms of struggle and transformation that are also the focus of chapter 3. There I show how Sly and Rose Stone, Simone, Hathaway, Franklin, Prince, and Rosie Gaines use vocal ad-libs to revise and enforce conventional social scripts. Chapter 4 extends these meditations on experimental vocal performance by showing how Ann Peebles, Al Green, Isaac Hayes, Riperton, and Solange Knowles use falsetto singing to generate an expansive interiority that tests the boundaries of black creative expression and permissible social behavior. The boundaries my artists test in chapter 5 are more temporal; there I examine the practice of the "false ending," where an artist brings a song to a close and then strikes it back up. Tracing this strategy through live and recorded performances by Mahalia Jackson, James Brown, Otis Redding, Franklin, and Marvin Gaye, as well as through a music video by contemporary artist Flying Lotus, I show how these artists enact as well as complicate soul's message of black group resilience.

My conclusion treats the narrative of soul's death as its own kind of false ending. There I analyze twenty-first-century redeployments of soul to theorize a mode of black cultural production I call Afropresentism. Using the presentist method of listening I have described to reopen the present as a question, I show how Beyoncé, Erykah Badu, and Janelle Monáe revive classic soul artists' dreams of an alternate future that would have been superior to our present. My analysis challenges the progressive model of history advanced by Afrofuturism (as well as by post-soul), whereby the present improves on the past and becomes solid ground from which to launch imagined futures. Afropresentists, in contrast, excavate the dreams beneath our feet. They critique the ongoing *need* for black resilience, while trying to ensure that the soul generation's "fantastic desires" will keep on keeping on.

....

How and why those dreams get tamped down and need reviving is a subject for the next chapter, but here I will say that the historical shift from revolution to reform I have described, which is also a narrowing of imagined horizons of future possibility, explains why soul has been misremembered. The systemic failure to theorize soul is the product of a postrevolutionary conservative backlash—what Toni Cade Bambara, writing in 1980, called "the impulse to pronounce the Movement dead."[51] That backlash is the reason why Gates's derisive take on the Black Arts movement became the canonical version of that movement and why African American literary studies has embraced Ralph Ellison—that is, a conveniently conservative vision of Ellison as a democracy- and diversity-loving liberal—but not the more radical "militant" Baraka.[52]

In short, soul's misremembering is linked to a broader misremembering of the civil rights and Black Power movements. If one clear sign of that misremembering, in the academic context, is a self-aggrandizing version of post-soul as soul's more enlightened successor, then its sign in the realm of black politics is the representation of the Movement for Black Lives/Black Lives Matter. That movement is often framed, both from within and without, as the corrective to previous struggles for justice: more inclusive and nonhierarchical in its practice of leadership, more intersectional in its analysis of power. That view of Black Lives Matter—as an updated version of Black Power but with better politics—does not only betray a blinkered vision of the past; it also neglects a crucial body of scholarship being created right now, as historians such as Ford and Farmer highlight the feminist and queer nuances of the Black Power movement itself.[53] I hope to contribute to that project of historical revision by showing soul to have been much more inclusive than its current framing suggests. In fact, it is a consequence of our postrevolutionary moment that soul's diversity has been suppressed. So the close reading of soul I advance here is also a closer reading of American history.

If, as I have said, soul's gift to its own generation was a sense of resilience and readiness, its gift to us, as contemporary readers and listeners, is a richer sense of the past and the future. I do not claim that soul songs provided perfect models of togetherness, but I do think that the logic of soul, as a force of group encouragement, offers a crucial alternative to our current state of personal and political atomization. By seeing soul's complex beauty as a site of alternative futures, I refute suggestions from all quarters that what we have now—post-soul, the neoliberal hustle, the carceral state, electoral politics—is the best we could possibly get. Soul-era visionaries worked for and imagined more.

1 FROM SOUL TO POST-SOUL

A Literary and Musical History

Before it came to denote a musical genre or to encompass a cultural logic, soul was most often used to describe a quality of jazz performance. In a pioneering 1961 article about the subgenre of "soul-jazz," *Ebony* writer and editor Lerone Bennett explained, "Soul, to be sure, is not even a music. It is the feeling with which an artist invests his creation."[1] The techniques for expressing that feeling were honed in the black Baptist church, which Baraka described as "the wellspring of black music"; here was the fount to which soul-jazz artists like Horace Silver and Max Roach returned, in part to distinguish themselves from white "cool jazz" musicians.[2] By rooting the soul-jazz sensibility in the black church, which Bennett coyly described as "a never-never land from which [white musicians] are barred," Bennett and others framed soul as a technical and spiritual quality that white artists could not learn or appropriate.[3]

The "soul" of "soul-jazz" described the music's soulful feeling. It took about a decade for soul to become a categorical term for a genre of music, a process David Brackett meticulously traces in *Categorizing Sound* (2016). The fact that an extraordinarily diverse series of musical styles and subgenres—pop soul, neo–doo-wop ballads, psychedelic rock-funk-soul, and secular gospel—would come to be gathered under the banner of "soul" is a historical curiosity that, according to Brackett, reflects not only musical but also social transformations.[4] Brackett ultimately credits changes in black political thought, from the civil rights era to the Black Power era, with moving soul from an adjective to a noun—from a term used to describe a "soulful" jazz or R&B performance to an industry-codified genre of music. This naming process unfolded unevenly across a range of black and white media in the 1960s. In 1965, James Brown was called the "King of Rhythm and Blues"; by 1968, he was lauded as the embodiment of soul.[5] As late as 1967, *Billboard* magazine devoted an issue titled "World of Soul" to articles about blues artists.[6] But one key turning point in the meaning of soul came in 1969, when *Billboard* renamed its R&B chart the "Soul" chart.

Much of the music gathered under that capacious banner in the 1960s carried elements of gospel music onto a secular stage, channeling a revival-style performative energy and "towering [gospel] vocals" into nonreligious lyrical content.[7] "It's an old cliché," Baraka notes, "that if you just change the lyrics of the spirituals they are R&B songs."[8] When Etta James sang, "Something's got a hold on me / It must be love," she was riffing on a gospel song that had originally called the transfixing force "God."[9] Soul singers, like their soul-jazz predecessors, constantly cited their indebtedness to the church. As Al Green later noted, "Most of us, one way or another, hark back to the church as the cradle of our musical birth and of any ten soul stars you care to name, I'll guarantee that eight of them learned their licks in the choir loft."[10] Soul was both a feeling, then, and the homegrown techniques required to express it.

The bond between the church and racial feeling was so widespread by the late 1960s that it was a point of self-authentication for "High Priestess of Soul" Nina Simone to insist that her musical training had begun in the church. Eager to correct the misconception that she "first studied classical music and switched to jazz," Simone told Phyl Garland, "I played for *revivals* and I was *colored* long before *that*!"[11] Simone's origin story, in addition to shoring up her racial belonging, invested her music with the spiritual authority previously associated with black religious music. So too, of course, did her use of "musical and presentational devices drawn from a gospel idiom"—devices that, as Brian Ward argues, "enabled [soul music] to fulfill . . . psychological and social functions" previously associated with the black church at a moment when "the center of black political gravity [shifted] from church-based institutions toward secular [black nationalist] organizations."[12] The notion that soul music retained the political and religious authority of the churches from which it emerged was an extension of the logic enacted by civil rights protesters, who literally carried the moral authority of the church, via song, into streets, police cars, and jails. These processes made possible Aretha Franklin's declaration that, despite her decision to record secular music, she never left the church; she took it with her.[13] Through musical as well as rhetorical practices of rooting soul music in the church, black artists and fans carved out spaces apart from white appropriation and invested black music with the spiritual and political authority associated with black religious practice.

Once the term *soul* came to denote a massively lucrative genre of music, it also became a subject of national debate: mainstream and black press outlets in the late 1960s frequently asked what soul was, who had it, and whether or not white people might get it. At this point, black writers increasingly tied the "soul" of soul music not just to the church but more specifically to the oppressive historical conditions that had made the church a segregated crucible of black expression in the first place. Jack Hamilton's survey of soul discourse comports with my own sense that "the concept was almost always framed in terms both of blackness and of oppression. . . . To have 'soul' was to have suffered at the hands of an unjust white society."[14] So whereas everyone could claim to have suffered, it was only black people, as victims of racial oppression, who were invited to understand their pain as generative of soul. Clayton Riley, reviewing the TV show *Soul!* for the *New York Times* in 1970, maintained that, whereas white people might "suffer their special griefs," they would have to find another term for them; they couldn't use soul. "I mention this in the hope that no one will feel put down by the suggestion that something does indeed exist in the nation beyond the reach of those who really believe all things are theirs for the taking," Riley concluded.[15] Garland's *The Sound of Soul*, as I have noted, took a longer historical view of the connection between black suffering and soul. Dating soul to the arrival of the first enslaved Africans at Jamestown, Garland argued that, notwithstanding its popularity among white listeners, soul music was the "aesthetic property of a race of people who were brought to this country against their will and were forced to make drastic social adjustments in order to survive in a hostile environment"; thus, "the sound of soul has also been the sound of suffering."[16] The following year, Clarence Major advanced a similar, if more graphic, definition of soul, as "a sense of racial history or of the suffering of the thousands of black people killed or tortured or worked to death since the 1620s."[17] In these writings one can see that the work of historical recovery that characterized the black cultural revolution more broadly—the interest in African retentions, the construction of the South as the birthplace of black culture—was manifest, in soul discourse, as a recuperation of historical black struggle, which writers reframed as the medium of worldly grace, skill, and connection.[18]

Whereas soul music rechanneled the styles and techniques of the church into secular lyrical content, soul *discourse* performed a parallel move by rechanneling religious logic into a secular faith in collective redemption. "Continue to work with the faith that unearned suffering is redemptive," Martin Luther King Jr. advised his listeners at the 1963 March on Washington.[19] Suffering was conventionally understood as redemptive because it could strengthen one's faith in God's grace. As Al Green put it, "I believe that the Creator of this universe takes delight in turning the terrors and tragedies that come with living in this old, fallen domain of the devil . . . into something that strengthens our hope, tests our faith, and shows forth His glory."[20] In soul discourse, however, the payoff of struggle was soul itself, understood as unique resilience. In "rising above suffering," to recall Smitherman's definition, one "gains *soul*."[21] This was a collective and spiritual take on the traditional bond between personal pain and great art (a logic reflected in Marvin Gaye's conviction that his "pain could be converted into artistic statements of real worth," as well as Carolyn Franklin's understanding sense that "her sister's gift" was the ability to "transform her pain into extreme beauty"[22]). Because the language of soul invested the project of black group resilience with spiritual meaning, it offered a noninstitutional way to express faith in a divine benevolence that was on the side of justice.[23] One could call this divine force "God" if one wished, but it wasn't necessary to do so at a moment when religious concepts such as spirit, faith, conversion, and transformation were, to recall Baraka, "expand[ing] past religion" to "permeate the entire culture."[24]

While soul discourse was new, its recuperative logic was not. Rather, the language of soul democratized, politicized, and spiritualized theories of the redemptive value of black marginality—culturally specific versions of the Judeo-Christian belief in the value of suffering—that had animated black intellectual discourse for nearly a century. In 1892, Anna Julia Cooper ventured, "It may be woman's privilege from her peculiar coigne of vantage as a quiet observer to whisper just the needed suggestion or the almost forgotten truth."[25] A decade later, W. E. B. Du Bois asserted that black people's oppression had produced the "[gift] of second-sight," which had as its clearest manifestation the hard-won "gift of story and song" conveyed through the sorrow songs.[26] In discussing the sorrow songs, Du Bois hinted that the value of marginalization was not only epistemological, as it was for Cooper, but also expressive—a thread that Alain Locke picked up in the mid-1920s, when he claimed that "with [the oppressed], even ordinary living has epic depth and lyric intensity, and this, their material handicap, is their spiritual advantage."[27] But while Locke's concern was with how the art of the "cultured few" might express that "spiritual advantage,"[28] James Baldwin later distributed the expressive advantage wrought from racialized suffering to all black people. Locating the "freedom" of black music in "something tart and ironic, authoritative and double-edged"—something that white Americans, not having "been down the line," could not perform or comprehend—Baldwin posited racialized struggle as the source of an ascendant cultural style.[29]

This was the early 1960s, so Baldwin was discussing the blues, not soul. Yet his writings about blues resilience were instrumental to the development of soul discourse. "This ability to know that, all right, it's a mess and you can't do anything about it . . . so, well, you have to do something about it. You can't stay there, you can't drop dead, you can't give up, but all right, okay, as Bessie [Smith] said, 'picked up my bag, baby, and I tried it again'"— the sensibility Baldwin attributed to black people in his 1964 essay "The Uses of the Blues" prefigured precisely the logic by which soul commentators turned social exclusion to cultural exclusivity.[30] Comedian Godfrey Cambridge, for instance, when interviewed for a *Time* magazine cover story about soul in 1968, explained, "Soul is getting kicked in the ass until you don't know what it's for. . . . It's being broke and down and out, and people telling you you're no good. It's the language of the subculture; but you can't learn it, because no one can give you black lessons."[31] According to Cambridge's characteristically valedictory formulation, soul was produced by black suffering, but it manifested as an enviable style that nonblack people could not learn or claim. Both his and Baldwin's formulations subversively figured black oppression as an affective and aesthetic advantage while implicitly coding white "privilege" as a moral and aesthetic liability.

In fact, the same *Time* story on soul in which Cambridge was quoted featured the words of Baldwin himself. Alongside the cover story, the editors included a long excerpt from Baldwin's *The Fire Next Time* (1963) to illustrate what writer Chris Porterfield termed the "supercharged evangelist-gospel atmosphere of Aretha Franklin's childhood."[32] Baldwin moves swiftly, in that passage, from the "fire and excitement that sometimes, without warning . . . cause[s] the church . . . to 'rock,'" to the "ironic tenacity" of jazz and the blues, to a powerful definition of sensuality—which is not the unbridled sexuality white Americans might hear in black music, but instead the ability "to respect and rejoice in the force of life . . . and to be *present* in all that one does, from the effort of loving to the breaking of bread."[33] A year later, Garland would call that definition of sensuality "perhaps the most eloquent and concise definition of soul and all it entails ever to be set down on paper"—a claim that illustrates both the flexibility of soul discourse and Baldwin's centrality to its development.[34]

Although Baldwin was, for Garland, the patron saint of soul, there were other writers who had likewise set the stage for soul discourse through their writings about other forms of black music. For both Ralph Ellison and Amiri Baraka, the blues had been the primary language for discussing essential characteristics of black music and the richest crucible for theorizing the value of African American suffering. These writers' theories of the blues carry over into their later writings on soul; this movement reflects the industry shifts Brackett traces, whereby the music called the blues throughout most of the 1960s was gathered under the rubric of soul. When Baraka writes that "the terms *Soul* and *Soulful* . . . refer to the music's origins as an African-American cultural projection . . . [b]ecause what is being expressed in the music . . . is the existence of a particular people and their description of the world!," he is clearly extending the premise of *Blues People* (1963), that the blues is an index of black life.[35] "Soul music is music coming out of the black spirit," he told reporters when interviewed for the 1968 *Time* story, which described him as "the militant Negro playwright."[36]

Ellison, more neutrally identified as a "Negro Novelist," was also interviewed for the piece. Like Baraka, he tied soul to black life, but he accented its epistemological role over its spiritual roots. He suggested that soul music contained *information* for and about black people: "The abiding moods expressed in our most vital popular art form are not simply a matter of entertainment. They also tell us who and where we are."[37] Tell *us*, not *you*—to put the matter thus was to subvert the article's aim to let white America "in on" soul. Although Ellison rarely addressed the subject, by the 1960s, he had done as much as any writer to lay the foundation for theories about soul, especially through his assertion that the blues expressed a "rock-bottom sense of reality, coupled with our sense of the possibility of rising above it."[38] He explicitly linked such ideas with the discourse of soul in an essay, "What America Would Be Like without Blacks," that was itself published in *Time*, in 1970:

> Without the presence of Negro American style, our jokes, tall tales, even our sports would be lacking in the sudden turns, shocks and swift changes of pace (all jazz-shaped) that serve to remind us that the world is ever unexplored, and that while complete mastery of life is mere illusion, the real secret of the game is to make life swing. It is the ability to articulate this

tragic-comic attitude toward life that explains much of the mysterious power and attractiveness of that quality of Negro American style known as "soul." An expression of American diversity within unity, of blackness with whiteness, soul announces the presence of a creative struggle against the realities of existence.[39]

This passage does not revise so much as it condenses Ellison's signal tenets from the prior decades—about the "chaos" underlying any "plan of living," which might be managed by working with and against one's fellow improvisers in the manner he associated with jazz, and by developing the blues-shaped expressive technique to "transcend" painful experience "not by the consolation of philosophy but by squeezing from it a near-tragic, near-comic lyricism."[40] These familiar tropes, here recontextualized, again serve to contest the terms of the *Time* story, which sought to demystify (and remystify) soul for a white reading public. First, Ellison describes soul not as an essential quality of black life (or the "black spirit") but as a culturally specific "style" derived from an "attitude" one must possess the "ability to articulate." In other words, soul is about practice and technique. Moreover, while Ellison's contributionist vision of soul is at odds with my own sense that soul offered a means not of enhancing but of surviving America, his invocation of "American diversity within unity" anticipates my sense of the diverse expressions of blackness that soul encompassed.

Whereas writers' theories about the blues as an expression of black group resilience were drafted into theories of soul, the latter concept conveyed a more capacious, spiritual, and political understanding of the group and its survival. If the blues had been the province of Langston Hughes's "low-down folks" and Baraka's (poor and working-class) "blues people,"[41] soul was something that, according to television host Ellis Haizlip, all black people had, regardless of "economic or educational or social level."[42] In a 1964 article in *Negro Digest*, Sergeant Gerald Westbrook described soul as an essential sympathy that drew all black people—"princes and paupers, the bourgeoisie and bums"—into a "common secret."[43] Soul was available to them all, and it offered precisely "the consolation of philosophy" that Ellison's definition of the blues rejects.

The invitation to soul was, in a sense, extended even when writers and singers refused to define the term. "For those who don't understand / Soul, there is this word, / You never will," Barbara Simmons concluded in her 1967 poem on the subject.[44] "Soul defined is soul necessarily misunderstood," Riley claimed in the *Times*.[45] By the end of the 1960s, according to

Cameron Crowe, "every black person from the jugglers on the [Ed] Sullivan show to the politicians on the [Dick] Cavett show were asked their definition of 'soul'"—and yet, Crowe noted, "I still can't remember anybody answering the question without saying, 'Well, Mike, it's hard to say....'"[46] Musical references to soul only enforced this ambiguity. The Impressions' 1965 recording "Woman's Got Soul" gave no sense of soul's positive content, except to rate it more highly than good looks or "high society" charm.[47] Sam and Dave's hit 1967 duet "Soul Man" filled in the picture by portraying the title figure as a sexually insatiable yet faithful country man "coming to you on a dirt road" with "good lovin', I got a truckload."[48] But Sam and Dave's joint belting of the lyrics worked against the singular grammar of the chorus ("*I'm* a soul man") to suggest there were multiple ways to inhabit the soul man's role. In short, evasive or complex accounts of soul helped create a loose framework of black belonging, rallying people around a race-based sense of community without precisely defining that community's contours. In 1969, Giovanni insisted of soul music, "A people need to have something all to ourselves."[49] But what Giovanni's black "thing" was remained vague in order to keep the "ourselves" open.

Shaped as it was by claims to "know it when you see it," soul discourse also emphasized black people's capacity to not only create but also *apprehend* soulful expression. Even those who struggled or refused to define soul often claimed, as Tanisha Ford writes, "to be able to identify soul when they saw, tasted, or heard it."[50] When, in a 1968 *Esquire* feature on soul, Claude Brown defined the concept as "walkin' down the street in a way that says, 'This is me, muh-fuh!' . . . It's exhibitionism, and it's effortless," Brown implied that the strutter's soulful style would be recognized and applauded as such by other members of her community.[51] When, in another part of the same issue, Brown celebrated "The Language of Soul" (or "soul talk"), he explained that, although "spoken soul" might sound like improper English to outsiders, those in the know would understand "mah" (instead of "my") and "yo" (instead of "your") to be "the most communicative and meaningful sounds ever to fall upon human ears."[52] This focus on black reception resonated with the Black Arts ethos that the "community [was] both the essential source and the chief critic of the artists' work."[53] If, as Baraka claimed in "Black Art," black people "are poems & poets," they also had to be readers—able to perceive their own pain as a source of soulful resilience and to hear that resilience enacted in soul music.[54] It was this habit of thought, or of reading, that soul commentators were seeking to cultivate—even when they, like Westbrook, defined soul as an essential black characteristic. We can think of it this way: No such explanation would have been needed if soul had really been an inheritance about which "if you have to ask, you'll never know."

The theory of soul established a hermeneutic for understanding the artfulness of black life and, in so doing, performed a function akin to that of the Black Aesthetic. Black Aesthetic theorists advanced a similarly flexible view of the vitality of black art. Even Addison Gayle's *The Black Aesthetic* (1972), though later framed as a rigid, prescriptive project, actually refused to define its title concept. Larry Neal's contribution to the volume took the ironic form of a poetic chart; titled "Reflections on the Black Aesthetic," the chart worked against its own codifying impulse by including impressionistic, even oxymoronic thoughts on the subject: "Jesus as somebody you might like to know, like a personal deity," "Bobby Blue Bland wearing a dashiki and a process."[55] Echoing Baraka's insistence that "the content of The New Music, or The New Black Music, is toward change. It is change. It wants to change forms," Neal concluded his reflections by hailing "black love, conscious and affirmed. Change."[56] Don L. Lee (later Haki Madhubuti), after enumerating a particularly specific list of "starting point[s] for determining and categorizing the Black Aesthetic" (polyrhythm, irony, music), concluded, "Finally, the Black Aesthetic cannot be defined in any definite way. To accurately and fully define a Black Aesthetic would automatically limit it. . . . What most of the young writers are doing is taking the lead in defining that which is of value to them."[57] While the Black Aesthetic was an ever-evolving theory of black art making meant to establish criteria for the just evaluation of black artists' work, soul was a theory of life designed to fortify one's sense of belonging to a buoyant black collective.[58]

Soul Power / Black Power

As such, soul discourse had a broader purchase than did relatively academic conversations about the Black Aesthetic. But it also had a wider reach than did the discourse of Black Power. Although soul logic was fueled by that complex movement, it also predated it: Westbrook assessed "The Essence of Soul" for *Negro Digest* readers in 1964, two years before Stokely Carmichael issued his historic call for "Black Power." So soul was not simply, as other critics suggest, "a key expression of the Black Power movement"; soul also *animated* that movement's faith in black resilience, while also exceeding its formal purview and speaking to different constituents.[59] As James Brown noted, "Black Power meant different things to different people. . . . To some people it meant black pride and black people owning businesses and having a voice in politics. That's what it meant to me. To other people it meant self-defense against attacks like the one on [James] Meredith [in 1966]. But to others it meant a revolutionary bag."[60] This internally variegated movement did not determine either the logic or the sound of soul. Although Simone, for one, was proud to support the movement through message songs like "To Be Young, Gifted and Black" (1969), other soul artists affirmed black life in less orthodox ways, "summon[ing]," as Baraka wrote of Brown's music, "a [spiritual] place . . . where Black People move in almost absolute openness and strength."[61] Donny Hathaway, too, although he recorded few explicitly problack songs, nonetheless created a rich body of work that expressed what Baraka might have called "the freedom to want your own particular hip self."[62] That freedom is audible in Hathaway's celebration of "The Ghetto" (1969), in his call-and-response with his fans, and in his habit of cheering on every member of his band in live performance.[63]

We are talking, at the most basic level, about the revolutionary power and practice of black love—what José Esteban Muñoz would call the "transformative force of *eros* and its implicit relationship to political desire."[64] Black Arts poet Askia Touré theorized that relationship in a 1965 essay for the *Liberator* titled (after the Impressions' anthem) "Keep on Pushin': Rhythm and Blues as a Weapon." Positing the music then called *rhythm and blues* as the soundtrack to a revolution bound to "[sing] this Empire to the grave," Touré's essay culminates in this remarkable claim:

> EACH TIME a Black song is born, EACH TIME a Black Sister has another child, EACH TIME Black Youth says NO! to the racist draft board, EACH TIME someone remembers Brother Malcolm's smile, EACH TIME we write a poem or an essay as a Way into "things," EACH TIME we love each other a little more: THIS THING QUAKES![65]

Here was perhaps the earliest argument that soul music was a revolutionary project rooted in its capacity to foster black love. But Touré's conclusion also presaged the capacity of soul, as a *literary* subject, to expand a writer's own sense of who might be included in the "we" that might "love each other a little more."

Of course, even Touré's most inclusive passage was marred by a patriarchal logic that glorified black reproduction in service of revolution ("EACH TIME a Black Sister has another child . . . THIS THING QUAKES!").

That heterosexist logic also informed the work of Larry Neal, though Neal was likewise spurred by soul music to craft an evocation of "the people" that stretched beyond, without wholly transcending, his own familiar purview. Like Touré's "Keep on Pushin'," Neal's 1969 essay for *Ebony*, "Any Day Now: Black Art and Black Liberation," is inspired by a soul hit, Sam Cooke's "A Change Is Gonna Come" (1964), which Neal uses to articulate "a steady, certain march toward a collective sense of who we are, and what we must now be about to liberate ourselves."[66] Black Power needs the Black Arts movement, he explains, to nurture and sustain "the very thing we are trying to save along with our lives. That is, the *feeling* and *love-sense* of the blues and other forms of Black Music. The *feeling* of a James Brown or an Aretha Franklin."[67] Neal argues that James Brown affirms cultural memory through his hit song "There Was a Time," which "traces the history of a people through their dances" to create "a rhythm and blues epic poem," and that Marvin Gaye and Tammi Terrell "affirm the love that we have for one another, singing 'You're All I Need to Get By.'"[68] Neal's essay builds, like Touré's, toward an encompassing roll call of the people whom this love should free: "Black Liberation for all of the righteous sinners and hustlers . . . , for Cinque, for Bo Diddley, for Bobby Hutton . . . , for William T. Dawson, Albert Murray, Ralph Ellison, Margaret Walker . . . for our unknown Fathers and your Mammy's Mammy . . . , for all political prisoners everywhere."[69] This liberation has been prophesied, he explains, by an endless host of ancestors:

> Pimps and prostitutes . . . , college presidents and porters . . . , mucked up intellectuals and exploited workers . . . , high yellow debutantes and mulatto clarinet players. . . . [These ancestors] were . . . Seventh Day Adventists and Baptists and Methodists and Holy Roller and Sanctified. They wore wigs and day glow drawers. Moved to Lincoln Drive and to Mobile and to Chicago and to Harlem and to Paris. . . . They worked in the Post Offices and sent their daughters and sons to Negro colleges. And we love them. And we love them. And we will struggle and dedicate our lives to them (thank you Marvin Gaye and Tammi).[70]

For Neal, as for Touré, the very act of writing about soul music seems to affect, on a structural level, an opening out to a broader black public. Both essays therefore implicitly posit soul music not simply as a vehicle or a vanguard for the revolution (both common figurations of black music in this era) but as a prompt to extend the very contours of the revolutionary community.

This is not to say that soul catalyzed perfect equanimity—Neal's essay ends by declaring, "ALL PRAISES DUE TO THE BLACK MAN"—but it is to show how the discourse surrounding soul music, like the language of soul more generally, helped to expand one's sense of those included in the black "common secret." It was precisely this inclusive vision that Riley celebrated when reviewing Haizlip's *Soul!* for the *New York Times*. Encouraging readers to watch the show in color, he declared that to see "groups like the Delfonics or the Five Stairsteps dressed in the clothes and the sound of the 70s, blazing pastel blouses, trousers, hats, counterpointed by the lush traditional tones of the African clothing worn by the incredibly exciting troupe from Barbara Ann Teer's National Theater, is to know how urgent a thing is a people's sense of themselves as a reborn, spiritually awakened 20th-century tribe."[71] A theater critic who was himself enough of a radical to advocate that Broadway venues and Lincoln Center be razed to the ground ("make them memory, these freak palaces; let them burn") and enough of an establishment writer to review shows for the *Times*, Riley portrays soul as campy if not queer, woman-centered, and stylistically diverse.[72] His "tribe" is all over the map.

To be sure, Riley's inclusive vision of soul was unusual among mainstream accounts and early histories of both the concept and the music. A cutesy "Who's Got Soul?" chart of thirty-three "haves and have-nots" published in the soul issue of *Esquire* included only one black woman, Lena Horne (and two white women, Peggy Lee and Jackie Onassis Kennedy).[73] Michael Haralambos maintained that gender bias in his 1974 history of soul music, in which he cited only about a dozen women artists amidst hundreds of men.[74] Yet there was more gender parity within soul music itself than such accounts admitted. If soul was a court, it had a *King and Queen* (a 1967 Otis Redding–Carla Thomas record that predates Aretha Franklin's seizure of the latter's crown). More important than these honorifics, soul music modeled dialogue between men and women, most explicitly through the subgenre of the response song. It was as a feminist response to Hank Ballard's 1954 hit "Work with Me, Annie," that Etta James composed her first song, "Roll with Me, Henry" (1955).[75] Two decades later, Shirley Brewer would respond with contempt to a heartbroken Stevie Wonder in "Ordinary Pain" (1976), tearing into the song by calling Wonder "a masochistic fool" who "knew my love was cruel."[76] Earlier duets between Ray Charles and Margie Hendricks also staged male-female contests that challenged the misogyny and pimp logic of Charles's songs. Where Charles's hit song "I Got a Woman" celebrated the fact that his woman "gives me money," "saves her lovin just for me," and "knows her place is in the home," Hendricks (backed by the other Raelettes) instructed Charles to "Hit the Road, Jack," and traded lines with him across an improbably soulful version of "You Are My Sunshine" to admit that she'd done him wrong, too.[77]

Soul music not only staged, but also inspired these contests. In a 1969 essay for *Negro Digest* titled "Black Poems, *Poseurs*, and Power," Giovanni implied that songs by Smokey Robinson and the Miracles, like "You Can Depend on Me" (1959), were more radical than supposedly revolutionary poems by community-alienating male "poseurs."[78] "And if you ask, 'Who's Loving You?'" Giovanni wrote, referring to the Miracles' 1960 hit, "just because I say he's not a honky you should still want to know if I'm well laid. There is a tendency to look at the Black experience too narrowly."[79] Declaring Aretha Franklin to be "the voice of the new Black experience," she continued, "It's rather obvious that while 'Think' was primarily directed toward white America, Ted White [Franklin's then husband] could have taken a hint from it. We must be aware of speaking on all levels."[80] The personal might indeed bear on the political, but the reverse also had to be true: any politics worthy of the name would have to affect personal, intimate change. In addition to advancing the kind of hermeneutic that I have associated with soul (attention to "speaking on all levels"), Giovanni's essay offered further proof that soul music, as a literary subject, provoked reflection and debate about the reach of revolutionary participation and care.

Yet the sexual politics of soul music exceeded even Giovanni's black feminist framework.[81] A 1971 profile of Franklin in *Ebony* speculated that her shows were so well attended by women as well as by "boys who wear rouge and dresses—a contingent of about 50 [of whom] came to her Atlanta concert"—because Franklin expressed the truth of people's treatment by, love of, and desire for men.[82] Not only did Franklin appeal to gay fans; her sound was shaped by queer figures: by her mentor, the Reverend James Cleveland, and by her sister Carolyn, an openly gay woman who composed and sang backup on her songs.[83] The sexual politics of soul performance were so fluid that even male artists who styled themselves as "ladies' men" often did so in queer ways: think of the hysterical screams of James Brown and Isaac Hayes's gold chain "suits." Even the famously seductive Al Green stresses male vulnerability, homosocial bonds, and gender-bending fashion at every turn of his 2000 memoir, *Take Me to the River*. There Green emphasizes his superlative bond with producer Willie Mitchell (his partner in what *Ebony* called a "highly successful entertainment marriage") and describes how he developed his sartorial style by sharing clothes with his partner, Juanita: "I'm so very thankful I came up in a time when a man was free to wear feathers and furs, paisley prints and pastels," Green writes, "to be as outrageous as a peacock and let the whole world know that he was special."[84]

Of course, many soul songs, by Franklin and others, seem to defend male-female unions. But even these can be heard to create a homosocial if not queer community of women. If we must be aware of "speaking on all levels," we might hear some of these songs as offering safely familiar spaces in which to work out changing conceptions of black womanhood in relation to heterosexual domesticity. This dynamic is most apparent in "cheating songs" like Shirley Brown's 1974 "Woman to Woman," in which Shirley confronts "Barbara" about messing with her husband, and in Betty Wright's 1971 "treat-your-man-right-or-I'll-get-him" hit "Clean Up Woman."[85] There is a similar, if subtler, logic at play in Gladys Knight and the Pips' 1970 recording of "If I Were Your Woman," where Knight imagines the kind of woman she would be in relation to the kind of woman her lover's wife is.[86] These songs are as much concerned with the bonds between black women as they are with affairs between women and men.

As Gayle Wald points out in her masterful study *Soul!*, the "black power television" show featured a spectrum of gender and sexual performances by such artists as Green, Hathaway, and Labelle. Wald writes of Labelle's appearance on a 1972 episode that it refigures "black arts and Black Power—that is to say, masculinist political and cultural formations—as the sources of agency for feminist and queer projects."[87] We might go further, however, and say that the popularity of such performances calls into question the cultural dominance as well as the masculinism of these formations. There is a counternarrative encoded, for instance, in the very fact that Black Arts and Black Power architects embraced falsetto singers as their representatives. Touré singles out Curtis Mayfield and the Impressions, whose high falsetto singing paid tribute to the black church quartet tradition and whose hits "People Get Ready" (1965) and "Move On Up" (1970) were civil rights and Black Power anthems, just as Neal highlights Gaye and Terrell, and Giovanni applauds the Miracles.[88] To realize that the "Black Power era" also names the moment in popular music that enshrines the androgynous male falsetto, along with Al Green's feathers and furs and Labelle's proto-futurist aesthetic, is to see that Black Power is at once queerer and less determinative of popular culture than most theorists suggest. Soul music exceeds the logic of heteronormative patriarchy so often associated with black nationalism and so characteristic of US culture generally.

That the male falsetto sound only increased in popularity as the 1960s turned into the 1970s is one sign of soul music's changing aesthetics, its movement beyond Peter Guralnick's definition of soul as "frenzied spirit possession."[89] Al Green, for his part, frames the rise of the quieter falsetto sound as a succession; in the late 1960s, he writes, "the whole era of the blood-and-thunder soul shouter was fading away."[90] Most icons of 1970s soul—Green, Stone, Wonder, Gaye, Hayes, Minnie Riperton, Syreeta Wright, and Dionne Warwick—were not best known as belters. Instead, they united the mellow sensibility of singers like Smokey Robinson and Nat King Cole with innovations in psychedelic rock and innovative production techniques associated with Charles Stepney and Norman Whitfield to create longer, more elaborately orchestrated works—a turn that was initiated by Hayes's 1969 *Hot Buttered Soul* and that included such albums as Simone's *Emergency Ward* (1972).

These recordings' new musical textures, counterpoints, and overdubbed layers expressed what Mitchell Morris, in his analysis of "softer soul," calls a more "reflective sensibility"—a development that Morris relates to the promise of black bourgeoisification.[91] But the music's focus on interiority also indexed what Ed Pavlić calls "the energy borne between people."[92] One hears this turn toward intimate relationships in Minnie Riperton and Rotary Connection's 1969 cover of Otis Redding's "Respect" (1965). Whereas Franklin's more famous 1967 version of the song was clearly a feminist response to Redding's version, it was also widely heard, like "Think," as a demand to white America. But Riperton's intricate psychedelic cover of the song (which I discuss in chapter 2) does not readily invite the latter reading—this despite and because of Riperton's re-creation of the song as an interracial duet.[93] The political salience of Riperton's version lies in its suggestion that black love songs don't always have to double as commentaries on racial oppression. And in this sense, her recording draws soul music into yet closer alignment with soul logic by conveying a deeper sense of collective black self-sustenance.

Buying Power

Soul music's turn toward intimate relationships is inseparable from developments in black feminist thought and fiction in the early 1970s, when writers such as Audre Lorde, Toni Cade Bambara, Toni Morrison, and Alice Walker privileged the exploration of intraracial dynamics over the interracial contests often depicted by their male predecessors. It is ironic, if unsurprising, that male critics should date soul music's decline to precisely the moment of heightened cultural representation of black (queer) women—a moment when soul's musical aesthetics expand to better reflect the inclusiveness of soul discourse itself. This is not, of course, the way the story is explicitly told. Instead, discussions of soul's demise are coded as concerns about its mass marketization.[94] In a move that also typifies critiques of disco, historians displace anxiety about the power of black queer folks and women onto a more palatable, even righteously nationalistic, critique of commodification; stated concerns about dilution or absorption by the white market therefore screen anxieties about black gender performance.[95] These critiques retroactively figure soul as a straight and male formation instead of what it is: a capacious narrative of black overcoming with which black music is most closely aligned when it is most inclusive.

To blame soul's supposed decline on its marketization instead of on an antirevolutionary backlash—one marked by massive divestment from black communities and investment in a militarized police force and surveillance state exemplified by COINTELPRO—is to miss how the market reflects, and does not independently engineer, social shifts. That is to say, insofar as corporatization limited the range of black voices, it did so in a postrevolutionary context that rendered those voices unprofitable. James Brown was convinced that "Say It Loud" had "cost [him] his crossover audience"; the primary reason for Simone's post-1960s exile from the United States was her marginalization by the music industry and US society at large.[96] At the same time, however, the corporate consolidation of major labels made room for the very aesthetic diversification I have described; that diversity was often produced by the smaller independent labels (Philadelphia International Records, Buddah Records) that flourished as Stax, Motown, and Atlantic declined.[97] The recordings issued by these labels in the early 1970s (including work by Gladys Knight and the Pips) retain soul's fortifying capability even when they are not explicitly about social change; even when they are no longer called *soul* but rather pop, rock, rap, and, yes, disco.

To overstate the role of capitalism in soul's demise is, moreover, to misunderstand soul's abiding connection to commerce. I have noted how the term *soul* itself arose due to black business owners' efforts at self-preservation during urban uprisings. And although the story of overcoming that soul encoded was not primarily economic, neither was it necessarily anticapitalist or independent of the market. Successful soul artists did at times express resistance to market pressure ("I'm proud of myself because I'm self-owned," James Brown told the press in 1968; "nobody can tell me what to say or do") and in that way articulated a sense of self-possession that was obviously resonant for descendants of the enslaved.[98] But the notion that soul music expressed an essential sense of self that could not be bought or sold also played a key role in its marketization. "Even in its early years," as Ford writes, "soul style was always entangled with capitalism and the demands of the marketplace."[99] This was a point to which Garland was especially attuned: The "earthy Memphis soul sound" produced at Stax, she wrote in 1969, "does not rely on accident or sheer intuitiveness. It is the result of careful calculation that leaves to chance only the individual expressiveness of the artist."[100] The calculation behind the sound is "so well concealed that the music comes out with just enough strut and swagger to give it a feeling of inborn ease. . . . [It] gives the impression of being funky without being phony; catchy, but not gratingly commercial. It is fast enough for dancing and cool enough for foot-patting or leaning back and listening. And so much of this has been coolly thought out beforehand"[101]—by artists such as house organist and pianist Booker T. Jones, whose career at Stax was briefly interrupted by his pursuit of a degree in music (classical music composition and transposition) at Indiana University.

Insofar as black bohemianism and a nonmaterialistic sense of "inborn ease" were themselves stylish commodities by the 1960s, these values were in keeping with, not opposed to, soul artists' desire to get paid. As Lerone Bennett wrote of soul-jazz in 1961, white consumers' enthusiasm for the music meant that "Negro musicians for perhaps the first time in jazz history have been in a position to cash in on a commercialization of the Negro folk idiom."[102] Bennett quoted one musician from Chicago who described the situation "with cash-register bluntness":

> In the Thirties, Satch [Louis Armstrong] and Fletcher [Henderson] did the work, but Benny Goodman and Tommy Dorsey made the bread (money). In the Forties, Duke and Count did the work, but Glenn Miller and Harry James went to the bank. In the Fifties, Dizzy and Bird and Miles planted the seed, but Brubeck and Chet Baker harvested the crop. But now Ray Charles and Cannonball [Adderley] and Horace [Silver] are doing the work and, baby, *they're* out there making the bread.[103]

Anxiety about white artists profiting from black innovation would return as white artists caught on to the soul sound, a development that led Clayton Riley to note, in an extraordinary *New York Times* article titled "If Aretha's Around, Who Needs Janis [Joplin]?": "In order to write of whites who sing and play Black, it is first necessary to call the imitators by their rightful names. Thieves. Bandits. . . . Crooks. . . . They are good thieves or they are bad thieves. . . . Which is not meant to be personal, if you can dig it. Just a simple way of establishing a point of departure."[104]

Although Paul Gilroy is not alone in aligning soul with "the anticapitalist politics that animate the social movement against racial subordination," that view can obscure the fact that soul musicians relied on the market as much as their fellow activists did.[105] To the extent that black artists worried about the music's commodification, their fear was that the wrong people would reap its profits, cheating or crowding them out of their share. As Simone put it, "A little [black] group will get up a hit-tune album and then some white group comes along and takes the dress, the songs, the style and the next thing you know they're featured on television. . . . [We've] got to stop the white ones from stealing our stuff, getting the money and then influencing a thousand other white kids to think these were *their* ideas."[106] By the late 1960s, the notion that music created by black people should also be produced and otherwise represented by them had become an organizing force both within and beyond the music industry, uniting institutions such as the National Association of Television and Radio Announcers with several black political organizations, including Jesse Jackson's Operation PUSH, the Student Nonviolent Coordinating Committee, and the NAACP.[107] According to Brian Ward, these efforts produced "a steady, if slow and equivocal, expansion of black executive and managerial power" within the industry.[108] Whether or not artists and activists imagined that white enthusiasm for soul music could fuel egalitarian social policy (a dream that Wilson Pickett called "the Big Lie"), many argued that problack "communal and commercial" agendas could catalyze social revolution—or, at the very least, improve black life.[109] Several figures in this story were more concerned with getting proper credit and payment for their work than with thwarting the system altogether. This reality allows me, methodologically, to privilege their work within the music industry over anxiety about the fact that they were working in an industry. If, in the economic parlance I have deployed, the "payoff" of collective struggle was soul, one payoff of musical enactments of soul was supposed to be money.

Soul music's status as a commodity did not compromise its potential to restore one's sense of belonging to a community defined by resilience.

To see this, we might return to Haizlip's definition, cited above. Haizlip first calls soul a thing that "all blacks have." He then calls it "an experience" that only they, being a "suppressed, oppressed minority," can "express and understand." While his definition is typical of the era for how it associates soul with a socially oppressed group and strategically figures oppression as advantage, it is unique, and uniquely useful, for how it locates soul in the movement between a thing one might possess and an experience one might be touched, moved, or possessed by. The soul one "has," in this view, needs revitalizing through specific practices that might (to cite the Staples Singers) "take you there."[110] As I noted in the introduction, soul is not a static inheritance but a way of being that must be revived. As is true of any religious or spiritual practice, one must keep recharging one's soul—I think here of what Baldwin described as people's ability to "renew themselves at the fountain of their own lives"—and since books, records, and concert tickets were some vehicles for this renewal, this process was often related to consumption.[111] So while the racialized *struggle* to which Haizlip alludes could not be bought or sold, certain products could help one to experience and read that struggle as a source of collective strength. When the sales of such products made black artists rich, the commentators in this study were not dismayed but often thrilled, especially given the expectation that artists would channel money back to their communities— a view that assumed it was not wealth that compromised one's soul but white supremacy.

In short and at best, the discourse of soul and the music that enacted its highest principles helped to gather and sacralize black community—to generate a sense of belonging to Riley's "reborn, spiritually awakened 20th-century tribe." Capacious enough to hold what Wald refers to as "the misfit energies of the Black Power era" ("diversity, nonconformity, and freakishness"), soul was a "big tent" that could foster love of one's own and others' blackness, as well as what Richard Iton might call "black deliberative activity" about how best to live together.[112] This love and struggle, inseparable from commerce in a capitalist society, might not translate into political action. But it gave people a beloved "I" and a complex "we"—a sense of individual and collective mattering—that was the necessary starting point for political mobilization.

Post-soul Politics

The story of post-soul's development as a scholarly category is the story of that demobilization. I track that development here to show how soul's radical, inclusive logic yielded post-soul's male-dominated neoliberal paradigm, which recast the prior generation's vision of black collectivity as a roadblock to personal freedom. As noted in the introduction, recent scholarship on post-soul links soul itself to "Say It Loud" machismo, heterosexism, and a narrow view of what counts as a black aesthetic. So we must ask how it is that such an amorphous concept has been made to stand in for the most restrictive heteropatriarchal impulses of the Black Arts and Black Power movements. To be sure, the most visible representatives of those movements (Baraka, Ron Karenga, Huey P. Newton, H. Rap Brown) did advance heterosexist, misogynistic views, as Angela Davis, Michele Wallace, Cheryl Clarke, and Audre Lorde all attest.[113] Soul music at times registered those repressive dynamics.[114] But the critical practice of conflating the two, of mapping restrictive nationalist politics onto something called *soul*, is symptomatic of broader postrevolutionary trends within and beyond the US academy, including state divestment from and increased policing of the black poor and what Toni Cade Bambara, as I have noted, called "the impulse to pronounce the Movement dead."[115]

Nelson George coined the term *post-soul* in 1992 to describe not only a musical development but cultural, political, and economic shifts whereby the "we-shall-overcome tradition of noble struggle" was surmounted, in the 1970s and 1980s, by black materialism and group fragmentation.[116] George was not sanguine about this. Even when, in his landmark 1988 book *The Death of Rhythm and Blues*, he described the aesthetic diversification of black music in the 1970s and 1980s, he treated this variety not as a boon (as would later writers and scholars) but as an index of black social and economic stratification—the further disaggregation of black citizens into what George, following Eugene Robinson, termed "the already-haves and the never-will-haves."[117]

Although George himself expressed more concern than enthusiasm about the dawn of post-soul, contemporary theory has generally sidelined his inconvenient critique in favor of the more optimistic accounts advanced by Greg Tate in his 1986 *Village Voice* essay "Cult-Nats Meet Freaky-Deke" and Trey Ellis in his 1989 *Callaloo* article "The New Black Aesthetic"—this despite the fact that neither Tate nor Ellis uses the term *post-soul*.[118] The latter essay, now a canonical text of post-soul theory, began as Ellis's midterm paper for a black studies course at Stanford in 1983. Students had been assigned Addison Gayle's anthology, and Ellis felt that, while some of the essays therein had merit, others "seemed essentialist, defining blackness as some clunky combination of African and not-white."[119] The essay he wrote in response celebrated a new cohort of second-generation college-educated self-styled bohemians with eclectic tastes and a great deal of confidence, both in their ability to navigate white spaces (newspapers like the *Village Voice*, schools like Stanford), and in their potential to found black institutions (the Black Rock Coalition, Def Jam Records) that could formalize and sustain their own cultural ascendance. These friends embodied Ellis's "New Black Aesthetic."

The group's collective enthusiasm about the many ways of being black (or, by then, "African American") had a counterpart within the academy, where literary critics such as Deborah McDowell and Houston Baker were organizing the field of black literary studies around their own responses to the notion of a Black Aesthetic. These scholars were systematizing the insights and provocations of writers like Neal, while also insisting on the complexity of the so-called black experience.[120] Their critiques of essentialism were not merely contributions to poststructuralist trends; they were potentially urgent interventions into public discourse at a time when mass media representations demonized black poverty and glorified black success.[121] These two representational poles suggested either that public assistance for black citizens was no longer necessary, given the heightened visibility of black college students, elected officials, entertainers, and athletes, or that such assistance was undeserved, given the visibility of black "welfare queens" and drug dealers presumably caught in a culture defined by criminality and victimization. To insist on a multiplicity of black experience, in this context, was to try to stem the tide of public divestment from black communities.[122]

But it is one thing to argue for black diversity and nuance in order to challenge policy-shaping mass-mediated images of black people, quite another to distinguish oneself and one's peers from racist representations while leaving the myths themselves intact. Ellis's project is the latter, as his brief allusion to Edmund Perry in "The New Black Aesthetic" makes clear. Perry was a seventeen-year-old black prep-school student who, in the summer of 1985, was shot and killed in Harlem by a white cop named Lee Van Houten who accused Perry of trying to rob him. Ellis writes, "Edmund Perry, bouncing from Harlem to Exeter and on his way to Stanford, might have been shot by that white police officer because the old world, both black and white, was too narrow to embrace a black prep from Harlem."[123] Having roped "both white *and black*" citizens into responsibility for Van Houten's act of murder, Ellis implies that what should have saved Perry was his status as "a black prep from Harlem." Ellis does not critique the conditions under which all black people, whatever their economic privilege or academic standing, are vulnerable to state-sanctioned violence; instead he laments an "old world" understanding that confuses "real" black thieves with innocent intellectuals like himself and his friends. His myopic view is clear when he writes, "We're not saying racism doesn't exist; we're just saying it's not an excuse."[124] We must ask, Not an excuse for what or for whom? since racism could indeed be posited as Perry's "excuse" for not having achieved the kind of potential Ellis ascribes to his cohort, or even for living to see his eighteenth birthday.

The sharpest, most self-reflexive voice cited by Ellis in his essay is that of writer Lisa Jones. The daughter of Hettie Jones and Amiri Baraka (and therefore a literal "soul baby," to invoke Mark Anthony Neal's term), Jones acknowledges the New Black Aestheticians' debt to predecessors, including her own father and Larry Neal (without whom "we wouldn't have the freedom to be so nonchalant"), and she worries that her generation's movement will become "a little elitist, avant-garde thing."[125] In her own 1994 collection of essays, *Bulletproof Diva*, drawn from a column she wrote for the *Village Voice*, Jones frames her work, and that of her black women's performance troupe, Rodeo Caldonia, not as a struggle against architects of the Black Aesthetic but as an attempt to explode the pervasive "assumption that being black and a woman carried with it a responsibility to be dire and remorseful. Or mystical and abandoned. Or issuing proverbs from the rocking chair."[126]

Jones's gender critique is important, as is her position as one of the few women associated with the New Black Aesthetic or, for that matter, with post-soul. Yet Jones's titular figure, the "Bulletproof Diva," inadvertently registers her generation's losses more than its gains. "The Bulletproof Diva is not, I repeat, *not* that tired stereotype, the emasculating black bitch too hard for love or piety," Jones writes. "It's safe to assume that a Bulletproof Diva is whoever you make her—corporate girl, teen mom, or the combination—as long as she has the lip and nerve, and as long as she uses that lip and nerve to raise up herself and the world."[127] The empowering ideology that Jones's parents and their contemporaries might have called *soul* is here individuated into a figure that combines conventional investment in group uplift with a post-Reagan self-help ethos. The bulletproof diva "raise[s] up herself and the world" not by drawing on communal resources but by using her own gifts of "lip and nerve" (mother wit and the courage to speak it). The community's absence is ironically palpable in Jones's declaration that the bulletproof diva "is fine and she knows it. She *has* to know it because who else will?" That question was not rhetorical for theorists of soul like Claude Brown, who had described the soulful woman "walkin' down the street in a way that says, 'This is me, muh-fuh!'" That woman expected an everyday audience who shared her knowledge that she was fine.

The New Black Aesthetic that Jones and others represented was nonetheless a useful concept for managing class alienation while navigating institutions and markets that seemed newly open to but not designed for members of the young black elite. Mark Anthony Neal admits as much when he assesses the powerful potential represented, if not realized, by the NBA artists and their academic counterparts. In his 2002 account of the "post-soul intelligentsia," Neal describes a group of black academics uniquely poised to "critically engage the [civil rights] movement's legacy" and refigure the academy "as a site to influence public policy and critically confront the spectre of race in America."[128] In their critical attunement to the internal diversity that any movement would need to address— differences of gender, class, geography, and sexual orientation among black people—these scholars might help re-form a broad-based movement. They would be "post," then, in their historical situatedness in the wake of a post-movement backlash, "soul" in that their attention to internal divisions might make possible a literal regrouping. You have to acknowledge a gap if you're going to bridge it.

Yet Neal's call for this kind of post-soul critique, like George's critique of post-soul, is obscured by current scholarship that uses the term not as a critical call to arms but as a scholarly object. That approach was codified for African American literary studies in a 2007 special issue of *African American Review* devoted to "Post-Soul Aesthetics." In his introduction to that issue, editor Bertram Ashe claims that post-soul artists break with the "fixed, iron-clad black aesthetic" of the 1960s by representing "blackness [as] constantly in flux."[129] Post-soul artists "trouble blackness . . . worry blackness . . . and hold it up for examination in ways that depart significantly from previous—and necessary—preoccupations with struggling for political freedom, or with an attempt to establish and sustain a coherent black identity."[130] While this exploratory post-soul work is "ultimately done in service to black people," post-soul artists, now freed from the "[struggle] for *political* freedom," can work to expand *cultural* conceptions of how blackness might be lived.[131] Here Ashe establishes a dichotomy between culture and politics that would have been untenable in the soul era, when, as Fred Moten writes, "political insurgency and cultural performance seemed almost interinanimate."[132] Ashe's special issue codified post-soul literature as a body of work that represented "unconventional" aspects of black experience (queerness, mixed ancestry, nerdiness), as if that representation was a good unto itself. To *whom* such internal variety was being announced—and how its announcement constituted a "service to black people"—was unclear. Meanwhile, soul itself was retroactively framed as the reason black diversity had been suppressed. Thus Ellis himself, in an article about Barack Obama published the same year as Ashe's special issue, claimed that black people's questions about Obama's blackness reflected a "Stalinism of Soul."[133]

So pervasive is the caricature of soul advanced by post-soul scholarship that it informs even Francesca Royster's otherwise deeply nuanced work. Royster's 2013 monograph on "post-soul eccentricity" engages several subjects with great rigor, yet takes a typical reductive and unsupported view of soul:

> Soul is often male centered. Soul is informed by the revolutions around it, but it seeks a kind of consistency. Soul is driven by style, deeply invested in its own coolness, and for that reason, it sometimes ignores the lessons of its deepest reaching, when the spirit, the rhythm shakes us, or leaves us confused. Soul privileges the natural over the artificial, the pure over the mixed. As an ideal, it privileges and polices heterosexuality and masculinity, and it reflects a Christian influence at its base (i.e., soul's link to gospel)."[134]

Royster's catalog posits (and personifies) soul as a force of convention and simplicity that serves as a foil to post-soul eccentricity. Since no names are named, we might ask who actually embodies the impulses to which Royster alludes. This is where things get complicated. Even James Brown, for instance, whose 1968 anthem "Say It Loud—I'm Black and I'm Proud" might be heard to exemplify calls for black unity, and whose abuse of women represents the most violent threats of phallocentric leadership, could be said to embody precisely the eccentricity that Royster champions, with his bizarre support of Richard Nixon (which he later withdrew by recording "You Can Have Watergate, Just Gimme Some Bucks and I'll Be Straight" [1973]), his campy sequined jumpsuits, and his aforementioned screams. So, too, could Brown's forerunner, Little Richard.

That is to say, post-soul artists are no more eccentric than their soul forebears. So Royster's theory does not describe a historical break from soul so much as it describes a new *critical* orientation toward it. While Royster suggests that post-soul artists resist soul-era calls for black unity through their performative claims to individualism, that paradigm fails to recognize that calls for unity in the soul era were issued in socioeconomic, not aesthetic, terms. If anything compromised soul artists' blackness, it was not aesthetic strangeness but decisions to hire white managers or to play in segregated clubs. And even these were not fatal blows to black stardom so much as occasions for intraracial debate and artists' possible changes of tack. This was so, again, because blackness, whether performed through problack business decisions or through culturally coded aesthetic practices, was, as it always is, being worked out. What is therefore unique about post-soul artists is not their status as black eccentrics but a critical context that overstates their relative transgressiveness, assuming as it does that these artists are flouting soul-era rules about the "proper" performance of blackness.

Ironically, in strictly musical terms, that soul/post-soul divide can be traced to Nelson George himself, who, as a twenty-four-year-old writer at *Billboard* in 1982, pushed the magazine to rename its "Soul" chart (so titled in 1969) the "Black Music" chart. The new designation, according to the magazine's editorial statement, would "[reflect] the diverse nature of music which that field now encompasses"—a diversity that, by implication, the term *soul* no longer signified. George himself, writing in the issue, emphasized "the eclectic nature of black music today" and noted that, since the 1970s, black people had been "making and buying pop music of greater stylistic variety than the soul sound"—a phenomenon he would, again, link to class stratification six years later.[135] What is remarkable about the *Billboard* renaming is that George's statement about black musical eclecticism repeated the magazine's reason for renaming the "R&B" chart the "Soul" chart in the first place: "The term 'soul,'" the editors wrote in 1969, "more properly embraces the broad range of song and instrumental material which derives from the musical genius of the black American."[136] To compare these two editorial statements from 1969 and 1982 is to see how, Brackett writes, present pop music heterogeneity is often imagined in contrast to the supposed "stylistic homogeneity" of the past—or, as Paul Taylor notes, in his analysis of post-soul theory, "contemporary diversity seems to diverge from a common, unitary root only if we flatten out the diversity that has always existed among African Americans."[137]

That seems incontestable. But the question is, again, to what ends are arguments about black diversity mobilized in particular contexts? I have suggested that arguments for internal black difference could have powerful implications for public policy in the 1980s and 1990s. It was in that spirit that Robin D. G. Kelley, in his 1997 study of black urbanity, framed soul in a way that informs my own sense of it—not as black essence but as a "discourse" through which black Americans reimagined the contours of their community in the late 1960s.[138] Kelley writes, "[T]he concept of soul was an assertion that there are 'black ways' of doing things, even if those ways are contested and the boundaries around what is 'black' are fluid."[139] Post-soul theory not only reduces that complexity; it repeats the neoliberal logic of treating (black) diversity as an end in itself, and black identity as defined by the range of products one buys or makes. This version of post-soul privileges Tate's and Ellis's portraits of black artists unfettered by Black Power strictures and free to "crossbreed aesthetic references."[140] It posits soul itself, meanwhile, as an essentializing program of cultural-political unity that still somehow "polices" inauthentic enactments of blackness. That this threat is colloquially signaled as the "soul patrol" reveals how post-soul discourse displaces the threat of the police state onto soul itself.

That critical mode was not inevitable; it simply won out over the more promising aspects of post-soul's investment in difference—namely, the impulse to "democratize black critical discourse" and, in so doing, to "problematize simple constructions of black identity and black thought" in the interest of collective struggle.[141] My aim in this book is to show that soul itself reflects such efforts. Soul-era commentators, including everyday people, heard important ideas about sociality in the music itself. In foregrounding their insights, I follow the methods established by black feminist scholars—including Barbara Smith, Angela Davis, Hazel Carby, and Ann du Cille—who institutionalized calls for complexity while positing popular culture as a rich site for the theorization thereof. By advancing an expansive yet detailed understanding of soul, I hope to show that there are many ways to enact what I, following Moten, would call a soulful "will to proceed" in a world that, to paraphrase Lucille Clifton, might try to kill you every day.[142]

In a roundtable discussion of soul held at NYU in the late 1990s, the writer Thulani Davis asked, "Do we still have a common language with which to resist? Or has such a language been ceded to and commodified by the 'mainstream'?"[143] I have suggested that the "mainstream" is less to blame than a repressive state, but neither force has entirely stifled the potential or need for the "we" that the language of soul helped call forth. What Steven Drukman writes of Black Power is also true of soul: it persists in the form of an "eternal half-life, an uncontainability."[144] Each of the following chapters moves toward the present to show how soul's energies carry beyond what Baraka described as "the time when we were winning. When revolution was the main trend in the world today!"[145]

It is crucial to hear those energies in the midst and in spite of an interpretive context that elevates personal entrepreneurship and savvy consumerism over civic engagement—a climate in which the word *socialist* is used as a slur and even subversive slogans such as *Not My President* and *#MeToo* are phrased in individual terms. Indeed, ideas about personal and historical progress intersect in the assumption that one's quality of life is determined solely by one's freely enterprising program of self-improvement in accordance with the presumed arc of historical betterment. With regard to race, such progressive accounts at once mask the erosion of civil rights and Black Power gains and idealize the Black Lives Matter movement in contrast with earlier struggles.[146] Challenging the post-soul paradigm that comports with these ideological trends, I contend that soul is less about conformity or invulnerability than it is about mutual aid: collective erotics, intergenerational spirit, and black encouragement. Scholars of African American culture concede too much if we treat these radical forces as passé. The following chapters therefore use the rubric of soul to show what they look and sound like.

2　WE SHALL OVERCOME, SHELTER, AND VEIL

Soul Covers

Having traced soul's emergence in the late 1960s, as a logic that under-scored the redemptive possibilities of black suffering, here I show how soul artists enacted that logic by transforming expressive deprivation into abundance—namely, by crafting ingeniously syncretic, semantically lay-ered cover versions of other artists' songs. From Nina Simone's striking version of George Gershwin's "I Loves You, Porgy," a record that, accord-ing to a 1959 *Ebony* profile, "rocketed the singer-pianist into the star class and transformed her from a little-known performer to the most discussed new jazz singer" of that year, to Aretha's Franklin's great awakening of Otis Redding's "Respect," which propelled her to global stardom in 1967 and earned her the title of "Queen of Soul," cover versions have played a key role in soul artists' efforts to launch new musical and emotional ideas—as well as themselves—into the American pop musical landscape.[1] Indeed, one could tell the story of soul music solely through such recordings: Ray Charles and Margie Hendricks's radical maturation of "You Are My Sun-shine" (1962); Otis Redding's showstopping "Try a Little Tenderness" (1966); Isaac Hayes's operatic expansion of "Walk on By" (1969); Kim Weston's wailing "Eleanor Rigby" (1970); Roberta Flack's poignant "Kill-ing Me Softly" (1973).

Amiri Baraka had a characteristically provocative take on the matter, which he advanced in his essay "The Changing Same (R&B and New Black

Music)" (1967). Discussing a young Stevie Wonder's refashioning of Bob Dylan's "Blowin' in the Wind," Baraka declared:

> Dylan's "Blowin' in the Wind," which is abstract and luxury stuff with him, is immediately transformed when Stevie Wonder sings it because it becomes about something that is actual in the world and is substantiated by the man singing it. That is, with Dylan it seems just an idea. A sentiment. But with Wonder (dig the name! and his life-style and singing is, of course, more emotional, too) you dig that it is life meant. In life.[2]

While Baraka's claim about the force of Wonder's version is debatable (it is, to my mind, one of his least inspired covers), his comments reveal how soul covers shaped the discourse of soul: by moving critics to theorize expressive superiority born of racial oppression, that "*something* that is actual in the world and is substantiated by the man singing it." That emotional effect is produced not merely by the black performing body that Baraka highlights but by the many narratives, both self-styled and imposed, that circulate around soul artists and their work—what Richard Dyer might call their "total star texts."[3] Here I analyze the convergences of biography and aesthetics that together activate soul logic in several recordings: Nina Simone's live 1968 performance of "Life," which brings together two anthems, "Ain't Got No" and "I Got Life," from the rock musical *Hair*; Aretha Franklin's 1971 recording of Simon and Garfunkel's "Bridge over Troubled Water"; Rotary Connection (featuring Minnie Riperton)'s 1969 cover of "Respect"; Donny Hathaway's 1973 recording of "Never My Love"; and Aretha Franklin's 1992 cover of Hathaway's "Someday We'll All Be Free."

In biographical, stylistic, and technical terms, these recordings all enact the soul narrative of turning struggle into stylized survivorship. When Simone's frustrated career in classical music spurs her innovative integration of concert music into her pop repertoire, when Franklin emphasizes her own vocal labor to craft a powerhouse version of a chart-topping hit, when Riperton strains her voice in an otherwise effortless-sounding performance to dramatize her quest for respect, when Hathaway exposes the work it takes to remake a romantic rock song in his image, these artists are all advancing the logic of soul, whereby pain and striving yield expressive depth and virtuosity. What is so innovative about all their covers is how they parlay cultural displacement into a claim to *multiple* musical traditions. Simone translates "Life," a hippie rock musical anthem, into a gospel-funk idiom with a classical flair;[4] Franklin envelops Simon and Garfunkel's clarion folk recording in a gospel-blues setting; Riperton brings her operatic training to a psychedelic version of a soul standard; and Hathaway draws a Beatles-inspired pop-folk tune into an R&B étude. In the process, these artists recast suffering as brilliant survival and extend that transformative potential to listeners.

Within that broad soul hermeneutic, however, are several diverse and layered effects. Sometimes, black artists' covers of white artists' songs sought to reverse the process whereby, as Simone put it, white groups would mimic "the dress, the songs, the style" of black groups, "and the next thing you know they're featured on television. . . . They *sing* the songs and then white kids who don't know any better think they *did* them." "I don't know *how* to put an end to that," Simone continued, "but the young black kids have *got* to get the advantages."[5] Several black covers of white hits sought to redirect the economic "advantages," while also reasserting black artists' participation in generic traditions (folk, rock and roll) to which their contributions had been obscured. (Simone's recording of "I Loves You, Porgy" subtly recovered the black sources of Gershwin's *Porgy and Bess*, just as her cover of Leonard Cohen's "Suzanne" drew out a nonwhite folk genealogy stretching from the rural blues to the recordings of Josh White and Odetta.) Yet black artists' soul covers served other multifaceted functions as well; in that sense, they displayed the degree of complexity in a single era that Keir Keightley, Sean Dineley, and other historians of covers (most of whom focus on rock) emplot across the entire twentieth century.[6] Insofar as all the artists in this chapter display a fundamentally syncretic musical sensibility—a drive and ability to convene a range of sources, from Stravinsky to the blues and the Beatles—it is a mistake to read their covers even of white-authored material as solely oppositional, competitive, or reclamatory. Notwithstanding Baraka's compellingly agonistic reading of Wonder and Dylan, black uses of so-called white music, like black covers of black-authored songs, could be admiringly sincere, strategically market-oriented, *and* combative all at once.

Black artists' covers of each other's songs opened up yet another set of intraracial and gender dynamics. Rather than seeking to usurp or unseat the original, soul artists sometimes asserted independence by altogether refusing comparison with prior (black) versions of a song. Rotary Connection's psychedelic cover of Redding-cum-Franklin's "Respect," for instance, helps demarcate the group's own distinct "artistic and social identity," as Michael Awkward writes of soul covers generally, precisely because it does not try to compete with Franklin's monster hit.[7] Hathaway's version of "Never My Love," originally recorded by the white American group the Association, likewise does not showcase Hathaway's comparative musical excellence so much as it stages a more modest translation of the song to offer a new sense of intimacy. The meaning of *to cover* thus gains depth in the soul context. It signifies not just a remake but also a process of *covering over* or supplanting an original recording, and of creating cover *behind which* to stage subversive, if not unspeakable, conversations about racial influence, recognition, and profit, as well as intraracial struggles for power and love.

Nina Simone's "Life"

Like so many other soul artists, Simone crossed out of the church and carried its training with her. She did not narrate that leave-taking as a loss. Her most traumatic institutional displacement was her rejection from Philadelphia's Curtis Music Institute in 1950, when she was seventeen. That rejection, which she attributed to racism, changed the course of her life. A musical prodigy by any measure, Simone (born Eunice Waymon) began playing piano in her mother's Tryon, North Carolina, Methodist church at age three. With the support of the Eunice Waymon Fund provided by her hopeful neighbors, she studied with a local white piano instructor named Muriel Massinovich, whom she affectionately called Miss Mazzy. But Simone's training was marked by her alienation from the white world that Massinovich and Western classical music represented. In her memoir, she recounts a town hall recital at which her parents, "dressed in their best," were asked to give up their front-row seats to a white family.[8] Young Eunice protested, "standing up in my starched dress and saying if anyone expected to hear me play then they'd better make sure that my family was sitting right there in the front row where I could see them," but the rage and humiliation stayed with her, making her "a little tougher, a little less innocent, and a little more black."[9] Describing such incidents to a reporter in 1967, Simone noted, "Miss Mazzy never knew how tense I was and how scared those white people made me. I had to go across the tracks [to take lessons]. I was split in half. I loved Bach but the music was never a joy, never a pleasure."[10] These formative traumas were also the source of the style-forged-in-struggle that, for Simone, defined soul: "To me, it's a style of living, a way of feeling, of thinking and doing things," she told a reporter in 1969: "This is the Negro I'm talking about, you understand. We've all suffered. We're more open—we have a certain way of living, a certain way of laughing and talking."[11] Rebounding rhetorically from the subject of suffering to that of openness and laughter, Simone's comments prefigure the hard-won synthesis that her feeling of being "split in half," both musically and culturally, would yield.

Simone began playing in nightclubs to support herself, singing only because the gigs required it, before writing her own songs of protest and affirmation, most famously "Mississippi Goddam," "Four Women," and "To Be Young, Gifted and Black." It was her recording of "Four Women" in 1966, critic Hollie West surmised, that consolidated her reputation as the "'high priestess of soul' and musical voice of the black revolution."[12] Although the song was banned by several white and black radio stations (due to the "militant" lyric that describes a black woman's willingness to "kill the first mother I see," and the allegedly "insulting" reference to black women's complexion and hair texture), "Four Women" also proved that Simone was willing to risk herself for the cause of liberatory truth telling.[13]

Yet Simone's politics were manifest not only in her lyrics but also, as Daphne Brooks argues in an important scholarly essay, through her insistence on stylistic versatility.[14] Like other soul icons such as Franklin, Etta James, Ray Charles, and Hathaway, Simone established a degree of multigenre mastery that suggested she could compose and "sing anything." She displayed that range not simply from one album to another or from track to track (her 1967 LP *Silk and Soul* includes blues, jazz, gospel, and softer pop songs) but also within a single recording. Simone's 1958 version of the jazz standard "Love Me or Leave Me," for instance, weaves a contrapuntally complex solo around a Bach fugue, entwining multiple distinct piano lines together.[15] Through this particular performance of sonic heterogeneity, Simone at once insists on going where few black women are expected to go (into the realm of classical music) and reminds her listeners that she isn't there. The fugue is a thwarted dream folded into another form of music. This enfolding grants depth to the speaker's self-description as "independently blue" and makes the song a site of refuge but also of critique.

By the late 1960s, at the height of her fame, Simone had established herself as what Phyl Garland called "an eclectic, one-woman summation of musical confluence." According to Garland, "Though soul is the convenient label under which she is currently classified, there can be detected in her singing, playing and original compositions, the mark of all the major streams that have gone into the making of modern music."[16] "I was and still am influenced by everything I hear that is musical," Simone told Arthur Taylor in 1970, citing Bach, Louis Armstrong, and Marian Anderson as creative guides.[17] That eclecticism, as well as the sheer amount of work required to develop and maintain it, was a key aspect of Simone's self-representation. She told Taylor, "By the time I got into show business, I had studied the piano seriously for fourteen years, practicing for about six hours a day."[18] Ruth Feldstein rightly notes that Simone's emphasis on the work of musicianship served to resist the myth of the black woman as a "natural" entertainer and to regender the image of the woodshedding jazz hero embodied by John Coltrane.[19] But the more profound if paradoxical effect of Simone's musical excellence—the audible labor of her performances, the thought and deliberation one hears in her slow songs ("Four Women," "Wild Is the Wind") as much as in her Bach fugues—was to help her relate to others. Far from alienating Simone from a black community, her virtuosity resonated with black listeners who could see, in her quest for excellence, the very striving on which their own success and survival seemed to depend. That relatability was, in a sense, the meaning of the Eunice Waymon Fund: Simone's talent inspired pride on the part of black listeners, but also recognition, because the pressure to be "twice as good" as their white counterparts was one they shared.

Simone demonstrates both her virtuosic heterogeneity and her ability to create community—both aspects of what Salamishah Tillet calls her "sonic black radicalism"—in a remarkable performance of "Life," recorded live in Paris in 1968.[20] Brooks notes that by "yoking together" the lyrics from both "Ain't Got No" and "I Got Life," "Simone moves with pointed contemplation through one song's tale of desolation, alienation, and disenfranchisement . . . into a different song entirely, one that is a jubilant affirmation of embodied self-possession."[21] But we might also say that Simone yokes these songs more closely together in accordance with soul logic. Her multigeneric virtuosity itself gives the lie to her claim to a "got-nothing" life: Simone turns the lack of a hospitable expressive system into a performative claim to multiple homes, including a home in her own body. In addition to turning expressive deprivation into abundance, then, Simone also performs a soul recovery by reclaiming the black female body as a source of sensual pride.

Before even starting the song, the last one of her set, Simone asserts her power, as "high priestess" of the musical ritual, to create or refuse community. She introduces the song (the musical was then in its first run on Broadway) and praises the crowd: "You've been a beautiful audience!" Particularly in light of Simone's tendency to reprimand her audiences—a tendency that likely originated in her early defense of her parents and which she explained by noting, "If you can get an audience to like you, that's fine.

If you can't, then you must get them to respect you. You cannot let them humiliate you"—the praise she offers this one sounds like a benediction.[22] She also reverses the usual performer-audience power dynamic; here, instead of being subject to the audience's scrutinizing gaze, Simone turns that gaze back on the audience members. She sits in judgment of *their* behavior, albeit approvingly.

In her pointed "motor-running-running" contralto voice,[23] Simone sings a catalog of deprivation: "Ain't got no home, ain't got no shoes, ain't got no money, ain't got no class." Nor does she have family, friends, culture, perfume, food, faith, love, or God. (Indeed, the song's lyrical irony resides in how it turns lack to abundance through this rich catalog of want.) The repetitive, nonteleological lyrical and musical structure would grow tedious in the hands of a less compelling singer. And Simone is relentless, resisting the embellishments that would ease the monotonous pressure as if determined to carry the song off through sheer force of vocal charisma. But her approach does serve a purpose: to elicit relief when the song finally shifts. After all these statements of lack, she finally turns to what she *does* have, which is, simply, herself:

> *What have I got?*
> *Why am I alive anyway?*
> *What have I got nobody can take away?*
> *I got hair, got my head, got my brain, got my heels, got my eyes,*
>   *got my nose, got my mouth, I got my smile . . .*
> *I got my heart, got my soul, got my back, I got my sex.*

After singing several such verses, Simone plays a false ending, a trick cadenza. This is a technique from the gospel playbook, and its effect is to indicate that the rest of the performance is running on reserves of spirit—an effect she will also produce when she sings the last word. She now leads her band in a long instrumental funk jam, after which she re-enters on the vocals. But at this point, which is several minutes later, she suspects that the sound people have turned her microphone off, so she starts to sing, "The mic is off, the mic is off. . . ." Maintaining the rumbling drama of her gospel piano, she improvises a variation on the statement and adds a bluesy melisma to it: "Am I on? Am I on?" The audience calls back, "Yeah, yeah!" Now, "being on" refers not only to the mic but also to being plugged into the music and the audience's energy. In her memoir, Simone uses the metaphor of "electricity hanging in the air" to describe the connection she feels with audiences in the best moments of live performance: "It was as if there was a power source somewhere that we all plugged into."[24] As befits her image as secular priestess, Simone figures this "power source" in spiritual terms. She writes of the thrill of performance, "Whatever it was that happened out there under the lights, it mostly came from God, and I was just a place along the line He was moving on."[25] It was in these moments that she could create what a reviewer for the *New York Times* called "a rather startling exhibition of mass hypnosis."[26]

As she approaches the final chorus, Simone mixes the language of gospel and blues—"Oh Lord . . . why am I alive anyway?"—and plays a rapid-fire fill on the piano that displays her classical chops. She claps her hands and gets ready to answer her own question: "It's alright," she sings, because she's still "got life." Because she takes only a shallow catch-breath before launching into this line, she sounds spent by the end of it. Here is the sound of a voice at its limit. But the band swells up around her to support the line and strikes up another jam to take the song home.

In that "microphone moment," Simone uses the awkward uncertainty of suspected deprivation to create a stylized recovery—one that generates communion with the audience via the call-and-response and showcases Simone's own on-the-spot skills. It's a granular instance of soul logic—the recasting of technical accident as an entertainer's occasion. More generally, as I have suggested, Simone transforms expressive deprivation into sensual survivorship by performing an extravagant, virtuosic seizure of multiple expressive modes. She also lays claim to the pleasures and pains of the black female body—a body that "Life" lyrically fragments in order to lovingly reclaim and reassemble, piece by piece: "I've got my hair, got my head, got my brains, got my ears, got my eyes, got my nose, got my mouth . . . I got my smile." Rather than reflect a fragmentary subject, then, Simone's intergeneric work seeks to consolidate her self and her community. The notion of having soul, after all, only gains meaning in relation to an imagined community of others who share it. As Hollie West noted in 1970, "Miss Simone echoes the sentiment of so many people in this country that it must be said that this is her time and that many of us are her people. She is like a sorceress whose performances are communal acts between herself and her audience. It is almost as if her listeners rededicate themselves during her concerts to the social and cultural revolutions in the cleansing rite of exorcism."[27] That belief in and rededication to one's own transformative potential is what Simone sought to kindle through another classic song from this era, itself a paean to hard-won wholeness: "You are young, gifted and black / Your soul's intact."

Civil rights activist, singer, and archivist Bernice Johnson Reagon once noted, "Simone helped people to survive. When you heard her voice on a record it could get you up in the morning. . . . She could sing anything, it was the sound she created. . . . Simone's sound captured the warrior energy that was present in the people. The fighting people."[28] What I have tried to suggest is that the collective sense that Simone could "sing anything" (blues, gospel, concert music, songs of seduction and protest) was not incidental to her ability to "help people survive." Simone modeled not only basic survival but extravagant survivorship in performance. Like the self-described and equally syncretic "warrior poet" Audre Lorde, Simone's survivorship was "warrior-like" in that it was precisely *about* doing everything, about claiming a home on multiple stages, and in myriad styles.[29] Those claims could move Simone's listeners to a revisionary understanding of themselves and their people—a revision reflected in Reagon's rhetorical movement from "people" to "the fighting people." Ultimately, Simone's spirited work invited witnesses to create soul stories of their own lives—stories that recast struggle as the very source of sensuality and style and that enabled their sense of belonging to the resilient "we" Ralph Ellison describes: "Though we be dismembered daily we shall always rise up again."[30] *Got my hair, got my head, got my eyes, got my nose . . . got my smile . . .*

Aretha Franklin's "Bridge"

Simone's soul work could seem quite distinct from that of Aretha Franklin, who was nine years her junior and less apt to make political statements in her music (though her social commitments were clear in other ways—Franklin was a tireless fundraiser for Martin Luther King, a family friend; in 1970, she offered to post bail for Angela Davis).[31] In a 1968 interview with Val Wilmer, Franklin did list Simone among the contemporary artists she admired (alongside the Beatles, the Rolling Stones, Oscar Peterson, Horace Silver, and others).[32] But Hollie West drew out the two women's differences. Writing in 1970 for the *Washington Post*, West noted that, although both Franklin and Simone "share unrivaled domains in today's world of popular music,"

> [W]here Miss Franklin frequently sings of lost and unrequited love, Miss Simone emphasizes social protest and concern. The former's music is more for dancing than listening. Miss Simone's music may contain danceable

rhythms, but we are impelled to listen. . . . A concert by Miss Franklin is usually a good time affair where all stops are let out while we watch. Miss Simone cajoles, bullies and even dares us to go on a socio-musical trip with her, and we enjoy doing it.[33]

These are real differences. But they mask real continuities. We might consider, for instance, that Franklin elected to cover Simone's "To Be Young, Gifted and Black" for her 1972 album of that name and that Simone allowed her to do so—a remarkably, even uncharacteristically gracious gesture that Tillet reads as a "passing of the torch."[34] Such moments hint at a kinship that is often obscured between Simone and Franklin's musical and social commitments. As I see it, both artists, as master cover artists and technicians, used amalgamative methods to make powerful claims to black selfhood that resisted figurations of soul women as both natural singers and natural victims.

The year Simone recorded "Life" in Paris was the year *Time* magazine published the ponderous cover story on Franklin and soul cited in the previous chapter. On the cover of that issue was a drawing of Franklin, her eyes downcast as if to affirm Atlantic producer Jerry Wexler's famous and utterly reductive description of her as "Our Lady of Mysterious Sorrows."[35] The article told the now familiar tale of Franklin's passage from her father C. L. Franklin's New Bethel Baptist Church in Detroit to her crossover success with Atlantic Records, emphasizing her abusive treatment by then husband Ted White in order to figure her music as the embodiment of soul's "power, lyricism, and ecstatic anguish"—spotlighting domestic dramas as if Franklin's personal-political losses, from Sam Cooke (1964) to Martin Luther King (1968), would not have been sufficient sources of "anguish" by June 1968.[36]

Although the story positioned her as the pinnacle of African American musical history, Franklin deeply resented its characterization of her personal life. In the following years, she "declined many interviews because [she] did not trust certain journalists," she wrote in her memoir.[37] Still, the *Time* story does show how central Franklin's life and music were to the discourse of soul. What's more, in a kind of feedback loop, the article she inspired shaped her own commentary on soul. The one thing Franklin apparently valued about the *Time* piece was Baraka's commentary in it, which she quoted in a 1971 profile for *Jet*. Author James Goodrich noted,

> For all her popularity as a soul artist, . . . Miss Franklin has made it clear that she does not address her music just to Black people. Her rationale: "It's

not cool to be Negro or Jewish or Italian or anything else. It's just cool to be alive, to be around. You don't have to be Black to have soul." However, she hastens to add: "I agree with LeRoi Jones . . . that 'soul music is music coming out of the Black spirit.' A lot of it," she concludes, "is based on suffering and sorrow and I don't know of anyone in this country who has more of those two devils than the Negro."[38]

Carefully skirting the risk of alienating either black or white fans, Franklin indicated that, although one didn't "have to be Black to have soul," one probably should be. Her representation of soul therefore resonated with Simone's description of it as a culturally specific "style of living, a way of feeling, of thinking and doing things."

Neither Franklin nor Simone imagined that black style as narrow or rigid. On the contrary, both suggested, through their music, that it was fundamentally syncretic. Like Simone, Franklin was a singer-pianist-arranger-composer who could "play anything." "Here's how it worked," her brother Cecil explained. "Aretha heard a song once and played it back immediately, note for note. If it was an instrumental, she duplicated it perfectly. If it was a vocal, she duplicated it just as perfectly. She got all the inflections right, voice and keyboard. Her ear was infallible."[39] Whereas Ray Charles and Sam Cooke had paved the way for her secularization of the gospel sound, Franklin combined and exceeded these predecessors' gifts—not least thanks to a remarkable group of family friends and mentors, including James Cleveland, Clara Ward, Mahalia Jackson, B. B. King, Cooke himself, and Art Tatum. Franklin herself matter-of-factly acknowledged her ability to synthesize various influences, noting in her memoir that she, like Ray Charles and Donny Hathaway, was "multi-musical in the way some folks are multilingual."[40]

Far from compromising the imagined blackness of her sound, Franklin's integration of myriad traditions could be heard to represent it. This is not only to say that her sonic versatility helped her connect with diverse segments of the black public—as Clayton Riley put it, "Gangsters, Militants, Bourgeois inheritors of The Dream. All Black Americans can get to Aretha Franklin because she knows so many ways to get to them"[41]—but that her versatility itself suggested a holistic approach to life, an "everything is everything" union of body and soul, that black commentators often associated with a black worldview. In the words of one "longtime fan" who was interviewed outside the Apollo Theater, where Franklin played two shows for thousands of black listeners in June 1971, "'Retha has the genius of combining all forms of black culture into music; the way black people approach the totality rather than an isolated aspect. Her voice and her style have the totality of the experience of black people in this country."[42] Implicitly linking that "totality" to black survival in the way I have suggested Simone's listeners did, the fan continued, "No matter how pained she is in the song, she is never the victim. She can deal with it. That's the way we are. We can deal with it."[43]

Franklin had had her share of things to deal with, as her fans knew well. Her road to stardom was grueling. Despite the spiritual authority and social capital she derived from being C. L. Franklin's daughter, there was nothing inevitable about her coronation, at age twenty-five, as the "Queen of Soul." Franklin spent half a decade recording nine albums of jazz standards and blues with Columbia Records, all of which failed to bring her the fame she wanted or warranted, before signing to Atlantic, where she scored her first big hits. Then she was on her way. Between 1967 and 1970, she released twelve million-selling singles—a feat topped only by Elvis and the Beatles, "who made their marks in a longer span of time and appealed to a larger segment of the public."[44] She "swept every popularity poll in the industry" and dominated the Grammy Award for "Best Female R&B Vocal Performance" (a category invented in 1968, the year she won for "Respect") for seven consecutive years.[45] But Franklin's fame itself proved to be as grueling as the grind required to get there—which is why, by 1967, she was describing herself as an "old woman in disguise . . . 25 goin' on 65."[46] In 1969, she threaded her personal story into a theory of soul. But rather than start with her life, as the *Time* piece had done, Franklin started with soul, and modeled the process of reading her life through that concept: "Soul is all about living and having to get along . . . about trying to grow up and making mistakes and hurting. . . . You try to learn from the mistakes, and when you don't it hurts even more. And I've been hurt—hurt bad."[47] The pain was personal as well as professional. "I think I've paid my dues as a singer," she said in 1969. "I've done the one-night stands and the joints. I've got a big car now, but I still remember the buses. I also remember the restaurants and hotels I couldn't get in."[48] Through such comments, Franklin invited her fans to understand her biography—the story of how she "got over"—through the logic of soul. The soul she had earned through private and public pain was glorious, but it was not transcendent: hers was a vision of success that still remembered, still retained the grief of what it took to get there, and of what it cost to stay.

Her vocal art itself embodied the soul alchemy through which struggle might yield inimitable style. That effect was perhaps clearest when she covered standards and other artists' songs. Craig Werner insightfully notes that Franklin's original compositions such as "Spirit in the Dark" and "Rock Steady" should have secured her place alongside other acclaimed women singer-songwriters of the 1970s (Carole King, Joni Mitchell, Carly Simon).[49] But Franklin's covers—from the jazz standard "Skylark" to Redding's "Respect" and the Beatles' "Let It Be"—displayed her inventive sensibility just as well. Those covers also revealed her competitive edge. "When Aretha records a tune, she *kills* copyright," the saxophonist King Curtis once said, "because once she's worked out the way to do it, you're never going to be able to come up with a better approach. And it's damn sure you're not going to be able to improve on how she's done it her way."[50] Etta James noted of Franklin's version of "Skylark," "That girl pissed all over that song," and other singers agreed: after hearing Franklin's version, Sarah Vaughan told James, "I'm never singing that song again."[51] In 1970, Franklin recorded a bombastic version of Dusty Springfield's "Son of a Preacher Man," a song she had initially passed on recording herself, as if to trample Springfield's version. And she reminded American listeners of the meaning of "diva" by covering several other women's songs, including Adele's "Rolling in the Deep," on an album in 2014—and, of course, by performing "Nessun Dorma" in Luciano Pavarotti's stead in 1998.

Franklin was a shrewd and relentless strategist when it came to choosing which songs to cover. When she played three dates at San Francisco's Fillmore West in March 1971, she sang several love crowd favorites: "Bridge over Troubled Water," "Love the One You're With," "Reach Out and Touch Somebody's Hand." Through these covers, she was partly seeking to win over white hippies at what she called "the Taj Mahal of flower power" and to break into a rock-folk market that was, as Jack Hamilton has shown, increasingly coded as white.[52] But Franklin's covers of white-authored songs also reversed the process by which white artists have appropriated black artists' work and so offered a new take on the dialectic of "love and theft," in Eric Lott's phrase, that has driven American popular music since the era of minstrelsy.[53] Franklin's covers display her own mixture of love and theft, homage and seizure. Take for instance her recording of "Eleanor Rigby," which remakes the Beatles' chamber song into a hard-driving first-person testimony: "I'm Eleanor Rigby!" she declares at the start. Franklin's Eleanor is a figure emerged to tell her own tale, not just from the margins but also (given that she dies in the Beatles' version) from the grave. The ghost story works on two levels: it's about the haunting title character, as well as the haunting of white musical innovation by black overachievement.[54] If Franklin covered your song, it was often because she was coming for you.

That was one message of her most commercially successful cover from this period, her recording of Simon and Garfunkel's 1970 ballad "Bridge over Troubled Water." Shortly after playing the Fillmore West and releasing her studio version of "Bridge," Franklin performed the song at the Grammy Awards in 1971, when it was nominated for Song of the Year. Simon and Garfunkel's sweet, clarion ballad in fact won the prize that year, but Franklin's version of it won Best R&B Female Vocal Performance one year later.[55] Her recording of the song at once augments her crossover appeal and beats Simon and Garfunkel at their own game—"coloniz[ing] American music for the gospel style," in Anthony Heilbut's words, and reclaiming that style for black women artists.[56] The cover also provides a subversive shield for more intimate in-group conversations. So Franklin's recording makes a statement that is just as audacious and multilayered as that which the supposedly more political and controversial Simone had made with her version of "Life."

Franklin covered Simon and Garfunkel's "Bridge" as though it had been tailor-made for her because, in some ways, it had. Paul Simon claimed he had had Franklin in mind while writing it.[57] Simon had also been inspired by the gospel tradition from which Franklin emerged: he drew the title lyric from Claude Jeter and the Swan Silvertones' 1958 version of "Mary, Don't You Weep," in which the group sings, "I'll be your bridge over deep water." (According to Anthony Heilbut, Simon acknowledged his debt to Jeter not only verbally but also by giving him a check for $1,000—a paltry sum, given the profits Simon reaped.)[58] Franklin's recording of "Bridge" recovers its debt to gospel music; she makes black sacred music the song's origin and its destination. She does this, first, by adding a long introductory frame that expands the original version's brief piano introduction and, second, by bringing in backup singers, in contrast to Art Garfunkel's solo performance. In Franklin's version, those vocalists get the first words, which are these vernacular lines:

> Don't trouble the water [Franklin: I won't]
> Leave it alone
> Why don't you, why don't you let it be
> Still water run deep
> Yes it do [Franklin: I know that]
> Oh yeah [Franklin: If you only believe].[59]

This call-and-response opens onto a long solo on electric piano that Franklin plays, accompanied in the studio by Hathaway on organ. Flouting the convention that would set such a solo at the song's midpoint, Franklin right from the start performs a very particular, and very churchy, mode of stretching out and taking her time. That, along with her use of the choir and organ, draws the song into a black church tradition. She thematizes the practice of call-and-response on which that tradition is founded by answering the backing singers after their very first line ("I won't") and arranging a lovely counterpoint between her work on the piano and Hathaway's organ lines. These performative moves bring Garfunkel's solo performance into an overtly response-oriented tradition, one that depends on a network of voices. And because Franklin foregrounds response as a practice, she encourages us to read her recording itself as a response to the original.

The introductory section takes about two minutes, a third of the total recording. While Franklin eventually sings the song's three verses, she follows them with a long shout section in which the backup singers' initial refrain returns as the closing vamp. What this means is that Franklin's arrangement of the song reconstitutes the Simon and Garfunkel original as a relatively small core or island at the center of a gospel production. Franklin effectively *absorbs* "Bridge" into a historically black formation, baptizing the original song in the waters of the gospel sound. This gradual drawing-in is also manifest in her vocals. She deploys the gospel practice of vocal reaching, or squalling, just once in the first verse ("when evening falls *so* hard!") and several times in the last ("I'm *sail*-ing right be-*hind!*"), as if gradually claiming Simon's lyrics for the gospel style. The technique reaches its climax at the end of the song, when, over the vamp of the backing choir, she sings, "I'm gonna be your briiiiiidge!"

Simon and Garfunkel's "Bridge" was not the only gospel-inspired single by a white pop act to reach No. 1 on the Billboard Hot 100 chart in 1970. The other was the Beatles' "Let It Be," a song that Paul McCartney had brought Franklin for her to record just months before the Fab Four released their own version of it. According to chart analyst Chris Molanphy, the Beatles' "Let It Be" "was released virtually simultaneously with [Simon and Garfunkel's] 'Bridge' and followed the latter into the No. 1 spot"; both groups "said goodbye to the 1960s—and their seconds-away-from-breaking-up groups—with twinned gospel-structured smashes."[60] Franklin's backup singers are clearly alluding to the Beatles hit as well as Franklin's own recording of "Let It Be" when they sing, "Why don't you, why don't you / Let it be?" The allusion works not only as a slyly self-promotional reminder of Franklin's own recent recording. It also functions as a subversive indication of her intention to take the Beatles as well as Simon and Garfunkel to church—and in so doing, to reassert the black roots of white pop hits. Such a reading grants new meaning to her singers' admonition to "leave it alone": we can hear the line as a response to white artists, where the "it" they are instructed to "leave alone" is the black gospel sound itself.

That is not the only intended audience or possible meaning, of course. "Still waters run deep," as the singers remind us, and there are several currents and meanings below. Franklin's recording of the song is, yes, a bridge that reaches out to white listeners. It is also a cover behind which to critique white uses of black music. And it is, finally, an enactment of a specifically black musical tradition of offering emotional and spiritual reassurance and sustenance to other members of one's community. The musical architecture Franklin adds serves to situate Simon and Garfunkel's "Bridge" within the gospel sound. But her introductory frame also works to enhance the intimacy of the verses. The introduction establishes one level of address, that is, to a general audience—the kind of moral instruction to a general "you" one often finds in gospel lyrics ("Give yourself to Jesus," "God will take care of you"). The interior of the song, on the other hand, addresses an individual. Here, in this internal space, Franklin shows what it means to do what the frame has called for: to treat someone gently while loving them, taking care not to "trouble the water."

There are gendered dimensions to this care. In some ways, Franklin plays the conservative role of the strong black mother-woman—the same woman who sings, in "Ain't No Way" (an extraordinary song written by her sister Carolyn), "I know that a woman's duty / Is to help and love a man / That's the way it was planned."[61] At the same time, as I have elsewhere suggested of Franklin's version of "Respect," where her backup singers make a smaller-voiced plea for "just a little bit" of the big respect Franklin demands, the black women in "Bridge" perform different sonic versions of black femininity.[62] As the backup singers take center stage for the song's introduction, they suggest a softer, mellower grace that moves with and against Franklin's sound. Still, their role is most striking when they lock into place behind her. Assuring the "silver boy" that his dreams are "on their way," they sing, "See how they shine!" The line bursts forth and shimmers—the singers are shining, are sure—and in that way, they musically materialize the distant horizon, realizing the dream through sound. The singers' full-force harmonization is all the more powerful because it is layered. As Franklin and the other vocalists converge and diverge, they evoke the many positions and tones that characterized the black feminist movement.[63] In that regard, Franklin's music both embodies and invites alternatives to her own aesthetic, such as the one that Minnie Riperton presents, in her cover of "Respect."

Rotary Connection's "Respect"

As I have said, soul covers do not only represent an oppositional seizure of power by artists who have mastered the master's tools as well as their own; they also stage less agonistic departures from dominant aesthetic and emotional modes and enact intimate conversations about black struggle and desire. Franklin's "Bridge" reclaims the gospel sound for black practitioners while orchestrating a deeper exchange between and among black men and women. The same is true of her recording of "Respect," which functioned simultaneously as a call to white America, as a challenge to black men, as a dialogue among black women, and as an assertion of Franklin's own genius. Riperton's early-career recordings with Rotary Connection worked in similarly multivalent ways. A Chicago-born vocal prodigy who studied opera through her teenage years and came to be known for her astonishing range, Riperton deliberately parted ways with Franklin's powerhouse aesthetic when she recast Franklin's signature song as an eerie exploration of interracial love. Thanks to Riperton's vocals and Charles Stepney's arrangement, Rotary Connection so transformed "Respect" as to nearly evade comparison with Franklin's version altogether.

Granted, the band's version was not nearly as popular as Franklin's. But it did signal an important direction for soul music as well as the broader soul narrative of overcoming I have described. Whereas Simone and Franklin seem to work twice as hard as other artists, emphasizing their own labor and quest for excellence, Riperton does not assert her work in the same way. Instead, she develops a quieter mode of performance that accents more intimate forms of love and struggle. In 1969, the same year Simone expressed her sense that the political climate made it hard to sing love songs—"I hope the day comes when I'll be able to sing more *love* songs, when the *need* is not quite so urgent to sing protest songs"[64]— Riperton embraced the love song, in all its complexity, by making "Respect" into a fraught though seductive interracial duet.

Rotary Connection was an experimental project shaped by compositeness on every level. It was a racially mixed, Chicago-based band that wrapped "a little gospel, a little R&B, and a whole lot of rock & roll" into Stepney's soaring orchestral arrangements.[65] The group convened different kinds of artists (some for the studio, others for the stage show) to record a mix of covers and original songs in an effort to target multiple markets. According to the band's singer Sidney Barnes, Chess Records executive Leonard Chess's son Marshall returned from college a "bona fide hippie" obsessed with psychedelic rock; Leonard, although aggrieved by his son's conversion, grasped the commercial potential of his musical taste and let him pursue it through the Chess subsidiary label, Cadet Concept.[66] Cadet signed the group, which Barnes describes as "a wild, fun experiment" by "a young white, well-to-do stoner" who wanted to record music "that would encompass all of the great styles of music that he loved ... jazz, soul, rock, psychedelic, gospel."[67] To realize this vision, Marshall Chess gathered Barnes, a black composer and singer equally influenced by Lennon and McCartney and Sly and the Family Stone; Riperton, a standout singer from the Chess girl group the Gems who was also a receptionist at the label; Stepney, a classically trained, Beethoven-inspired arranger, musician, and composer; and three white players from a local rock group called the Proper Strangers: drummer Kenny Venegas, bassist Mitch Aliotta, and guitarist Bobby Simms. While the black members held steady across the five studio albums the group recorded between 1967 and 1970, the rest of the group was in constant flux. In fact, Stepney, who reportedly loathed rock and roll and lamented the Proper Strangers' lack of polish, had the Strangers play live gigs but enlisted string players from the Chicago Symphony and Chess veterans (including Maurice White on drums, bassist Louis Satterfield, and guitarist Phil Upchurch) for studio recordings.[68]

The result, perhaps best described as psychedelic chamber music, was not simply a "wild, fun experiment" but a project strategically designed to stand out in a market dominated by the British invasion, on the one hand, and by West Coast psychedelic rock, on the other. In an effort to combine the two, Rotary Connection recorded hits by Bob Dylan, the Byrds, the Rolling Stones, and other rock groups, transposing the songs into classical arrangements and deploying what Barnes calls "weird sounds" to evoke "a wild acid trip."[69] The group did not shy away from anything—their self-titled 1967 album included blasphemously reconstructed versions of Dylan's "Like a Rolling Stone" and the Stones' "Ruby Tuesday"—and their audacity was rewarded when the album charted in the Top 40.

But even as their audience expanded from local clubs in Chicago to bigger dates—they opened for such acts as Janis Joplin, Led Zeppelin, the Stones, and Sly and the Family Stone—their fan base remained predominantly white. Barnes notes, "The white kids were able to show us more appreciation because we were a minority among them, and they didn't feel threatened by us. . . . They seemed to really like the fact that the band was integrated. . . . Because many of these kids had never had much close contact with black people before, they were craving that contact, and this was giving them that chance."[70] The label exploited the group's interracial appeal. The cover of the band's 1969 album *Songs* featured Marshall Chess's (white) nine-year-old son and Stepney's (black) eight-year-old daughter standing on a hillside holding hands, as well as a bunch of balloons in which the faces of the group members appear.

With the exception of "This Town," which Stevie Wonder composed for the group, *Songs* consists entirely of covers. The album's high point is the group's languorous, methodical version of "Respect." In 1967, Franklin had remade Redding's song into a multivoiced feminist anthem that featured a funky horn chart, relentless beat, and Franklin's take-no-prisoners approach. Phyl Garland called Franklin's version "the new Negro national anthem," and its import was not lost on Redding himself, who, upon hearing Franklin's recording, allegedly said, "I just lost my song. . . . That girl took it away from me."[71] Other soul singers tended to steer clear of the song after that. But Rotary Connection so admired both Redding's and Franklin's versions that they felt sure they could do the song well: "How could we mess that up?" is how Barnes put it.[72] In a similarly bold spirit, they decided to recast the song as a duet—but not, as one might expect, between Riperton and Barnes, the group's two professional singers and black members, but between Riperton and white bassist Aliotta. According to Barnes, Aliotta "had a great commercial-sounding voice for that song" and deserved a "chance to shine."[73] The resulting male-female duet paid homage to both Redding's and Franklin's voices—here again, the logic of the composite—while imbuing the song with new issues of race, love, sex, and power.

Sex is the dominant mode of this version, which opens with a slow, methodical groove: quiet piano and violin, harp in the middle register, steady tambourine. Simms's electric guitar snakes its way through the haze in advance of Riperton and Aliotta, who softly reharmonize Franklin's first lines: "What do you want? / Baby don't you know I've got it. / What do you need? / Baby baby don't you know I've got it?" Where Franklin's version clarifies and confronts, this one obfuscates and seduces. Privileging elongation in place of Franklin's lyrical breakdown—the staccato snap of "R-E-S-P-E-C-T" that she gamely explained by saying, "I thought I should spell it out"[74]—Riperton and Aliotta repeatedly voice a plea that gets muffled in Stepney's dense instrumentation: "Give me my respect." In the third verse, they make another lyrical change, revising Franklin's revision of Redding's lyric. Where Redding sings,

> Hey little girl, you're sweeter than honey
> and I'm about to give you all my money,

Franklin asserts herself as the soul-talking breadwinner:

> I'm about to give you all my money
> And all I'm askin' in return, honey
> Is to give me my propers
> When you get home.[75]

Riperton and Aliotta sing,

> I am about to give you, ooh, all of my money
> The only thing I'm asking you to do
> Is to recapitulate my lovin', honey.[76]

The turn from "give me my propers" to "recapitulate" might suggest a stark move away from Franklin's Muscle Shoals–styled vernacular toward Stepney's classical pretension—if, that is, the five-syllable word did not introduce such a hip syncopation. Although it was no doubt selected for its rhythmic effect, *recapitulate* works in other ways, too. The more accurate (and less textured) word might have been *reciprocate*, but *recapitulate* suggests a giving back—both in its primary meaning "to summarize" ("recap") and in its secondary meaning "to give new form or expression to."[77] Here, respect is not just a matter of return or reciprocity; it is also about invention—which is a fitting descriptor for the kind of respect that this cover itself gives to Redding and Franklin.

Rotary Connection recapitulates the song's sexual politics as well as its sound. Listeners without access to the LP, which lists the lead singers on this track as "Minnie and Mitch," would likely have assumed that Riperton's vocal partner was Barnes, not Aliotta—that is, that the singers calling for respect were both black. The ambiguity surrounding the singers' identities served to intertwine more public calls for racial respect with more intimate, erotic ones, suggesting the ways that private lovers' quarrels are enmeshed with larger social forces. Aliotta's calls for respect follow Riperton's own, a sequencing that suggests he is shadowing her. The effect hints at how black women's demands for respect have to vie with those of white men who may take the emergence of other voices as a threat to their own power and centrality (*You want respect? Well I do, too!*). There is only one labored moment Riperton performs on this recording, perhaps her only one on the whole album, when she strains to sing, "*I get tired and I keep on trying.*" And that moment both perfomatively and lyrically foregrounds the struggle that yields soul. But by rendering that "struggle" as something more like sexual tension, Riperton also draws the logic of soul into new sonic and emotional territory. Here, blackness, femininity, and sex can all be tiring, and no less worth it.

According to Barnes, Riperton "had no problem singing the song" (and doing so with Aliotta).[78] But if she appeared to take the task of covering Franklin in stride, her stylistic departure from Franklin's sonic concept was quite deliberate. Riperton became increasingly confident about marking that departure as her solo career took off. Chris Charlesworth reported in 1975,

> Not only does Minnie abhor competition, but she also shakes off the mildest suggestion that she has been influenced by any other singers. "The way that society has you is that you're put into categories. Aretha Franklin is the Goddess of black music and that's what you're supposed to sound like, but I'm me. I'm not like anybody else. I could try to sing like Aretha but I don't want to."[79]

In terms of public opinion, Riperton's gamble paid off. In 1976, she was nominated alongside Franklin for "Favorite Soul Female" at the American Music Awards. Franklin won, but an *Ebony* readers' poll of that year—described as a "major upset"—named Riperton "Best Female R&B/Pop Singer," over Franklin and Roberta Flack.[80] If Riperton's version of "Respect" announced her own fearless departure from an industry that had isolated Franklin as the "goddess of black music," it also offered new directions for other soul artists to pursue complex sounds and visions of love. These included Donny Hathaway, friend of both Riperton and Franklin and one of Chicago's favorite sons.

Hathaway and the Association's
"Never My Love"

Hathaway was, like the women artists I have discussed, a musical prodigy and a radical syncretist. He was also what we might call an emotional virtuoso. An extraordinary vocalist as well as a pianist, composer, arranger, and bandleader, Hathaway was born in Chicago in 1945 and raised by his mother and grandmother in St. Louis; in the late 1960s, he attended Howard University, where he studied music and played gigs around DC before being recruited by Curtis Mayfield to work as an arranger at his Chicago-based label, Curtom Records. While there, Hathaway also worked at Chess, where he played with and was mentored by Barnes; he also met Riperton in the years before they both forged careers as solo artists. "We loved Minnie," Hathaway's wife, Eulaulah, recalls. "I call her [pop music's] first coloratura."[81]

Hathaway's commitment to what he called "music in its totality, from the lowest blues to the highest symphony"[82]—from the work of Franklin to the Beatles to Ravel to Debussy—made him one of the most inventive cover artists of the twentieth century. Whether remaking Leon Russell's "A Song for You," Marvin Gaye's "What's Going On," Gladys Knight and the Pips' "Giving Up," or John Lennon's "Jealous Guy," Hathaway's cover recordings were simultaneously acts of homage that drew out the latent beauty and depth of feeling in the original song and acts of ingenious self-assertion by an artist who knew he could improve on hits by his more popular peers—even if his sales could not compete with theirs.[83] Describing Hathaway's ethos in terms that recall Franklin, Simone, and Riperton, his friend the composer Edward Howard noted that, whereas "some artists lay back on covering other people's songs," "Donny was never afraid to do anything": he "would just kill it, then move on."[84] Yet Hathaway also advanced a model of individual creativity that originated in what he himself called the "black pool of genius."[85] According to this model, each artist was not a lone creator but an original part of that vital continuum Baraka called "the changing same."[86]

Hathaway's version of "Giving Up" transforms the simple pop song—composed by Van McCoy and interpreted in a rather gothic, maudlin style by Knight and the Pips in 1964—into an operatic statement of joy and despair.[87] The recording introduces Hathaway's 1971 self-titled album as if to foreground both his heaviness—he stretches the tempo into an impossibly slow build—and his boundless creative spirit. Jerry Wexler notes, "most songs are lucky to have a single climax," yet Hathaway's "Giving Up" has "at least four: Donny's arrangement builds to peak after peak, [with] King Curtis's bone-chilling tenor break [on saxophone] lifting the spirit to ever greater elevations."[88] In a 1972 appearance at the Houston Astrodome as part of the First Annual Astrodome Jazz Festival, Hathaway folded yet more layers into the song, playing a fierce piano solo in place of Curtis's solo, as if to mourn the absence of the saxophonist, who had been murdered the previous summer.[89] Still, he then turned lament into possibility by ending the song with a double-time jam, a choice that signaled the liberatory possibilities of finally "Giving Up" a long-tended flame—and perhaps even of death itself.[90]

The effect of Hathaway's transformative practice was, again, to enact the soul logic of overcoming. But what he overcame was not always a musical predecessor so much as it was a preexisting standard of technical excellence, creative wherewithal, and emotional depth. In plumbing new expressive depths, he extended Riperton's concern with intimate struggle, and enacted the kind of emotional-intellectual awakening that Baraka associated with John Coltrane. In a 2007 interview, Baraka moved fluidly between the language of thought and feeling to describe how Coltrane's music helped listeners realize new depths of feeling, and so sparked their desire to know themselves better:

> Most of us live at the very surface of our feelings.... But [Coltrane's music] provoke[s] the thoughtfulness in us ... make[s] us reflect on things. It's like something that makes you feel, "Whoa, what kind of feeling is that? What does that make me think?" And, well, that's what art does. But [with] Trane particularly, with those fantastic melodies and the way he uses harmonies, you begin to really feel that you want to know more about yourself.[91]

Decades earlier, Simone had similarly defined creativity as the infinite "varieties of depth of feeling [an artist could access] when ... creating a mood."[92] Even Simone's performances of "I Loves You, Porgy," she noted, a song she had been singing since 1953, made her "constantly surprised at how I feel when I sing it."[93] This phenomenon does not point only to an expanded individual subjectivity; it is also about a collective desire for transformation enacted by the music, which itself, as Baraka writes, "wants to change forms."[94] Baraka and Simone remind us that the act of cultivating a capacity for deeper feeling is a political project, especially in a world that denies, represses, and polices feelings of black discontentment, jealousy, rage, and love. "EACH TIME we love each other a little more," to re-cite Askia Touré, "THIS THING QUAKES!"[95]

One of Hathaway's most unique cover versions, an obscure and post-humously released recording of a 1967 hit by the group the Association, "Never My Love," models a new kind of love and noncompetitive musical intimacy. In some ways, his cover of the song exemplifies the best he could give: a beautiful new classical setting that displays his impeccable sense of restraint, the cry in his voice, his killing-you-softly sincerity. But the recording is an uneven experiment. Unlike Hathaway's other covers, this one does not fit like a glove around, as if to seize, the original. Instead, his "Never My Love" is important precisely because it does *not* decimate, compete with, or even (as with Rotary Connection's "Respect") bravely venture to remake an already great recording. Instead, Hathaway's version departs, in its very humility, from his own proclivity to "kill it and move on," as well as from the macho, competitive mythos often associated with soul music. At the same time, his recording reveals the confidence and integrity it takes to be vulnerable, to try something really new.

The Association's recording of "Never My Love," which appeared shortly after the US release of *Sgt. Pepper's Lonely Hearts Club Band*, is an up-tempo ballad in 4/4 that features the dreamy, lithe harmonies and psychedelic sound popularized by the Beatles.[96] The dominant instrument, in addition to the Association's latticework of voices, is the guitar. Hathaway turns the song into a complex piano étude and thus fundamentally alters the timing, but, in so doing, he creates a rather awkward transition from verse to chorus.[97] Still, his version is lovely. He begins with a simple arpeggio and sings low, with a lump-in-the-throat intensity: "You ask me if there'll come a time / When I'll grow tired of you. / Never, my love. / Never, my love." The drums enter on the second verse, where Hathaway's voice gains volume and force. In the third verse, he replaces the delicate keyboard arpeggios with intricate glissandi and sings at close to full volume: "You say you fear I'll change my mind / And lose my desire. / Never, ha! Never never never / My love." At the song's midpoint, he gives a nod to the source beneath his source, the group that had inspired the Association, by playing a four-chord cadence that quotes the Beatles' "Let It Be"—a move that also recalls Franklin's recording of the song.

But what is surprising and uncharacteristic is that Hathaway's cover starts to sound like a cover. When he sings the line, "What makes you think love will end / When you know my whole life / Depends on you?" one can hear him working to make the timing fit with his new structure.

What is also strange, for an artist so adept at sequentially building a song through mounting dynamics, is that Hathaway belts the last verse at full voice but drops the piano to a more muted level. This might have been an experiment in contrast or a case of "marking" the music, which he might have planned to fill in at a later stage. Whatever the case, the exposed seams of this recording reveal that Hathaway did not always, when covering a song, coax out its latent potential and make it his own. In place of that appropriative method, this recording highlights something else: the effort to forge a relationship between oneself and the work of another. The audible labor Hathaway performs in fact befits this particular song, which stages an ongoing effort to relate to another person—in this case, to dispel a lover's doubts. Whereas the Association seeks to cinch the conversation through a trump card–style reference to marriage—"How can you think love will end / When I've asked you to spend your whole life / With me?"—Hathaway keeps things unstable; he omits the lyric about marriage and instead repeats the earlier line about dependence: "What makes you think love will end / When you know my whole life / Depends on you?" Hathaway's refusal to bind the lovers together through a marriage proposal draws out a double meaning in the song title, which functions in his version not only as a promise ("I'll never leave you") but also as an admission that the love might never be his ("never my love"). And that impossibility of total capture is echoed, on a metalevel, in Hathaway's approach to this song. Unable or unwilling to absorb the original into his version, Hathaway creates a loving homage to the song that is not about ownership. Here is a version of love without theft.

In its expression of these new concepts, Hathaway's recording departs not just from his penchant for outdoing others' compositions but from his dominant cultural image as a tortured artist. Like his version of "Giving Up," which turns sorrow, quite surprisingly, to joy, Hathaway's "Never My Love" ultimately makes the lovers' need for each other not a sign of pathology but a source of assurance. He sings this closing ad-lib in affirmative, church-trained style:

> If you need somebody
> Just stick by my side
> Hey baby, you can call on me
> Cause I need you, need you here by me.

Surely the cover's unreleased and perhaps unfinished condition contributes to this impression, but it sounds like Hathaway recorded this song not because he knew he could kill it, but because someone else needed to hear it.

"Someday We'll All Be Free"

Hathaway's "Never My Love" and Rotary Connection's "Respect" represent a form of soul covering that privileges inventive homage over competition. This approach is not entirely new. Instead, these songs reflect one continuum or "changing same" of black approaches to covering other artists' material—one that stretches back to Thelonious Monk's remarkably straight version of Duke Ellington's "Black and Tan Fantasy" and forward to Lianne La Havas's faithful recording of Jill Scott's "You Love Me."[98] This continuum even included Franklin, who, despite her often absorptive model of covering, could also honor an original, when so moved. She was a gracious keeper of musical history, as her version of Hathaway's "Someday We'll All Be Free" attests. Recorded for Spike Lee's 1992 biopic *Malcolm X* (where it plays over the closing credits), Franklin's "Someday" is a cover in the protective sense—a fortification.[99]

Franklin felt deep kinship with Hathaway, who played organ on "Bridge" as well as "Rock Steady" before his death from an apparent suicide in 1979, at age thirty-three. In her memoir, Franklin describes their shared "multimusicality" and states plainly, "Historians should not forget him. And scholars should get it right: Donny Hathaway was one of the great communicators and masters of soul."[100] Hathaway felt the same way about her. He seems to have learned a great deal from Franklin's inventive audacity and penchant for musical beauty. When at one point he told Jerry Wexler he wanted to record standards, he "pointed to [Franklin's album] *Laughing on the Outside*," Wexler says. "He had it memorized. He wanted to do 'For All We Know' in that vein."[101] Wexler suggests Hathaway was channeling Franklin's 1964 version of that song (rather than, say, Dinah Washington's) when he recorded it with Roberta Flack in 1971.

Hathaway's beloved collaborator Arif Mardin, who arranged Franklin's version of "Someday We'll All Be Free," calls her decision to perform the song "a very important event": "To have that song sung by Aretha Franklin I'm sure was one of Donny's dreams."[102] Franklin's version did not only seek to preserve Hathaway's legacy, as she had instructed historians to do; her recording also revived a radical history of black freedom dreams in which she herself had played a key role. "She is ready whenever [black people] are to do something of benefit for black people," *Jet* magazine announced of Franklin in 1972—whether that meant supporting the victims of the Attica uprising, Jesse Jackson's Operation PUSH, Angela Davis, black students at Kent State, or West Africans plagued by famine.[103] Yet in the years between 1972 and Franklin's death in 2018, she was seldom depicted as a warrior for justice. By reviving and extending her own work in this domain, she pushes back against the postrevolutionary regimes of misremembering I have described, and also revives Hathaway's own obscured involvement in radical politics: his fundraising efforts for such groups as Operation PUSH and the Fred Hampton Memorial Fund, as well as his support of the Black Panthers.

As she had done with her cover of "Bridge," Franklin recasts "Someday" in the gospel style.[104] But she takes Hathaway's song to church more dramatically than she had done with Simon and Garfunkel by adding a big, robust gospel choir. Musical archivist that she was, she evokes, through that choir, another deep cut: Wilton Felder's gospel cover of "Someday," released in 1980.[105] (Bobby Womack sang lead vocals on that track, years before rerecording it for his eponymous 1985 EP.)[106] Franklin honors such precedents while also staging a subtle feminist intervention: where Hathaway and other male vocalists assume a male addressee whom they advise to "keep your manly pride," Franklin regenders her audience, singing, "Keep your womanly pride." In the context of a biopic by a charismatic black male filmmaker not known for his deep consideration of women characters or viewers—a film about Malcolm X's equally flawed brand of black charismatic leadership—this lyrical gesture is striking.

Franklin's expression of love in this song includes subtle critique, affirmation, and homage, as well as mourning. The strain in her voice itself registers struggle and loss: imagine how much life the woman who had called herself "25 goin' on 65" had endured by the time she recorded this song, at age fifty. Listening in this way, we might hear Franklin's recording of "Someday" as an archive of the losses she had sustained since the 1960s: political leaders like Malcolm X (1965) and Martin Luther King (1968); musical idols and peers like Dinah Washington (1963), Sam Cooke (1964), Redding (1967), Hathaway, and Marvin Gaye (1984); her father, C. L. Franklin (1984); her sister Carolyn (1988); her brother Cecil (1989). By the time she recorded "Someday," she had very few people left to compete with and very little to prove. So it made sense for her to revise her own practice of obliterating others' songs, at least for the moment, by literally reviving Hathaway's work—re-creating his song as a gospel revival meant to inspire the radical work that Lee's biopic highlights.

That film, released in the wake of the Rodney King beating and amid growing fantasies of postracial multiculturalism, was bound to upset the American mainstream—one audience to which Franklin refused to pander despite her lasting desire for industry domination. Even at a relatively fallow point in her career, before her appearance at Bill Clinton's inauguration set her on the road to yet another comeback, she was not worried about alienating those who feared Malcolm X and his legacy. She never had been. The choir that accompanies her in "Someday," over which she presides like a matriarch: *that* is her primary (perhaps feminized, certainly black) audience, as well as her primary support.

That choir gives new meaning, finally, to Hathaway's closing ad-lib: "Take it from me, take it from me. . . ." In Hathaway's recording of "Someday," the repeated line is both reassurance and plea: on its surface, it guarantees listeners that freedom is imminent; but it can also sound, after a while, like a request that they "take from him" the burden of working and waiting for it. Franklin takes the weight off of Hathaway and distributes the lyric among a chorus of voices. In that way, she extends her authority to others in a performance that no longer seeks respect but assumes it. Here, she implies, is another way to be—freer if not exactly free.

3   RESCRIPTED RELATIONS

Soul Ad-libs

Another way to perform the freedom that "Someday We'll All Be Free" evokes is by ad-libbing your way through and out of a set text or script. In the last chapter, I suggested that soul artists use covers not only to outdo their predecessors but also to advance subversive ideas and plumb what Baraka calls new "depth[s] of feeling." We hear those uncharted depths in Donny Hathaway's heartfelt homage to the Association, in Rotary Connection's sensual quest for respect, in Simone's sacred song of the self. My discussion of those works sought to expand the range of interpersonal soul affects beyond the compulsory heteromasculinism that post-soul theory presumes and critiques. When we listen to what soul artists are actually doing, that is, we can decouple soul from the supposed regimes of gender, racial, and sexual conformity with which it has long been associated.

Here I extend that conviction and method by showing how the ad-libs soul artists perform, in the studio, on stage, in churches, and in clubs, create an exploratory approach to relationships with the self and others. A term drawn from the phrase *ad libitum*, which instructs one to play a musical passage "at one's pleasure" or "as one desires," ad-libs bring to musical performance a sense of unscripted erotic surprise. They loosen up sonic structures so unexpected possibilities can slip in—bringing an erotic charge to a song about friendship, for example, or a sense of domestic tension to a conventional love song. Here I use the term *ad-lib* to describe vocal and instrumental interpolations that sound spontaneous, although they might well be planned, and I show how soul artists' ad-libs can alter the meaning of lyrical as well as social scripts, including the script that tells them their own improvisatory impulses are not to be trusted.

While there is a massive body of scholarship devoted to the history, techniques, and significance of improvisation in jazz, the practice of improvisation in soul has scarcely been theorized. That oversight reflects suppositions about soul's commercial (rather than creative) ambitions, its emotional (rather than intellectual) aims, and its gospel roots (which, as I noted in the introduction, are gendered, classed, and hyper-racialized). What's more, whereas jazz is considered a fundamentally instrumental genre, soul is largely identified with the voice, a bodily source that itself elicits gendered suspicions regarding a lack of intentionality or expertise. But one need only listen to Nina Simone's incantatory calls for "power" at the end of "Sinnerman" (1965) or to Otis Redding's live performances of the originally staid ballad "Try a Little Tenderness" to hear that soul music, like both the gospel tradition from which it emerges and the jazz idiom it engages, is a field of great improvisers.[1] That many of them are also great cover artists should not surprise us, given the inventive sensibility on which both ad-libs and covers depend.

That inventiveness has social implications, which soul's logic of overcoming draws out: in the soul context, ad-libs reflect the need for artists to revise not only preexisting musical scripts but also dominant social scripts—and thus to survive in a world whose social mandates are often designed to negate them. "I can't depend on the world to name me kindly, because it never will," Audre Lorde noted. "If the world defines you, it will define you to your disadvantage. So either I'm going to be defined by myself or not at all."[2] This creative redefinition relies on deep personal resources, which former Sweet Honey in the Rock vocalist Evelyn Harris suggests we can hear in the art of ad-libbing itself. Harris defines vocal improvisation as "the art of self-trust."[3] The singer has to trust her own sensual-musical intelligence, as well as her right to express it. Her self-trust does not develop in a vacuum; it is born of communal engagement. As musicologist Aaron Johnson writes (in a rare scholarly exploration of live soul improvisation), "While musicians are often vague about what they get from a supportive and appreciative audience, speaking in terms of energy, of love, or of the vibe . . . , what they receive is the security to take risks."[4] Their willingness to stretch out, to try more, to fail is nurtured by black musical communities that offer feedback in the moment. Samuel Floyd Jr. writes, "The black music experience is, to a large degree, self-criticizing and self-validating, with criticism taking place as the experience progresses."[5] What Harris calls "the art of self-trust" is therefore affirmed and enhanced by audiences that are trained to listen for and to audibly appreciate variations on familiar material, on shared musical texts. As such, soul ad-libs affirm the need for and the value of creatively (re)defining oneself, in Lorde's terms, and claiming one's own fluid sensual-aesthetic impulses. These claims are always political in a world that denies and degrades them.

In short, ad-libs enact soul logic by embodying a hard-won and collectively meaningful achievement of self-trust that allows people to break with stifling or destructive conventions. Here I highlight the gendered dimensions of this process—and I do so not only to celebrate black women's agency but also to point to its limits, particularly as those limits are revealed in male-female duets. I first examine a song performed by Sly and his sister Rose Stone, and, in conclusion, one by Prince and his collaborator Rosie Gaines. Along the way, I also revisit some of the previous chapter's cover artists to show how Simone's ad-libs complicate the heterosexual union proposed by her 1965 recording of "Be My Husband"; how Franklin's ad-libs in her live 1971 Fillmore West performance of "Dr. Feelgood" invite listeners into a sexual experience from which her opening lyrics seem to have barred them; how Franklin's performance of "Amazing Grace" (1971) brings that erotic charge to church; and how Hathaway's recordings of "You've Got a Friend" (1971) and "The Ghetto" (1969) facilitate erotic and homosocial group affirmation in the club and the studio, respectively. Through their ad-libs, all these artists open up new relationships to themselves, their art, and other people—whether siblings, lovers, friends, audience members, collaborators, and/or rivals. They also offer honest anatomies of patriarchal dynamics, diva expectations, and other challenges to black togetherness. And in all cases, their ad-libs contest the idea that "the given" *is* a given, that what gets handed down to you is natural, fated, or settled. Soul ad-libs shake things up.

Family Affairs: Sly and the Family Stone's "Que Sera, Sera"

We will begin with one of the greatest and strangest of soul duets, which is also a memorable cover: Sly and the Family Stone's recording of the Doris Day hit "Que Sera, Sera." Released on their 1973 LP *Fresh*, the Family Stone's "Que Sera, Sera" is unusual in part because, unlike most male-female soul duets, it does not stage a romantic situation. Instead, Sly Stone impersonates various familial figures who give advice to the song's protagonist, who is played by his sister Rose Stone. The track is also unusual because, What was the very hip Family Stone doing recording a song by the very unhip Doris Day? Day had first sung the song for Alfred Hitchcock's 1956 film *The Man Who Knew Too Much*. By 1973, it was the theme song to her sitcom. The only way the general public could make sense of Sly's decision to cover it was to generate rumors that he was romantically involved with Day (who was twenty years his senior). Indeed, speculation about their phantom affair still overshadows the actual musical relationship Sly performs with Rose, which is my predicable focus. Sly's primary connection to the Day family was in fact through Day's son, his friend Terry Melcher. Melcher played him the song one day and, Sly told one reporter, helped him "to [hear] it a different way than [he] had before."[6] Sly didn't say what exactly he heard in the song, but he produced a recording of it that was as rich and multilayered as the other covers I have discussed.

In *The Fire Next Time* (1963), James Baldwin pits the music of Ray Charles against that of Doris Day, calling Day one of "the most grotesque appeals to innocence the world has ever seen."[7] In one sense, we might hear the Family Stone's version of "Que Sera, Sera" as staging Baldwin's contrast between black and white worldviews: here is an instance of how black soul triumphs over white mediocrity; here is how the Family Stone advances a radical new model of family that refutes Day's treacly white domesticity. But the Family Stone's cover also stages two other, more intimate conversations: one between Sly and Rose, the other between Rose and Day. First, there is the gendered power struggle I hear as Sly encroaches on Rose's space, in a domineering performance that should temper idealized visions of the mixed-race, mixed-gender band as a utopic familial network. But Rose Stone herself, I'll go on to show, revises Day's script and style of white femininity and, in so doing, reveals a power in her own performance as well as a pathos in Day's.

The siblings who would compose about half of the Family Stone—Sly (born Sylvester Stewart), Rose, and Freddie—grew up in Vallejo, California, a working-class city on the north end of the San Francisco Bay that Sly described as being "like a Watts, only with more whites."[8] They honed their prodigious skills at a Church of God in Christ in San Francisco, where they sang with their family gospel quartet, the Stewart Four (the fourth was their sister Vaetta). Sly later worked as a producer and popular local DJ while mastering a dozen instruments and assembling a powerhouse band: Freddie on lead guitar; Rose on keyboards and vocals; local musician Larry Graham on bass; high school friends Cynthia Robinson and Jerry Martini (who was white) on trumpet and saxophone, respectively; and Jerry's white friend Greg Errico on drums. The group played at suburban bars in Hayward and Redwood City before rising to national attention with their 1968 album *Dance to the Music*.

As Rickey Vincent notes, the group moved black pop into the funk era by combining the acid rock of the Haight-Ashbury district with the heavy grooves of James Brown and the vocal stylings of gospel and soul.[9] Displaying both "the musical wildness of the rock band . . . [and] the utter discipline of the soul group," the band exuded, according to Greil Marcus, "all the good feeling of the March on Washington, and the street cachet that the march never had."[10] The group was consequently claimed by both rock and soul fans.[11] "We got to live together!" Sly declared in the 1968 hit "Everyday People"—and the group seemed to embody the charge, not only because of who they were but also because of how they played: everyone contributed their own distinct sound; they all played an instrument and sang in jagged unison.[12]

They recorded *Fresh* just a few years into their delirious ascension to fame. But those few years probably felt, to them, like a decade. The group released *Fresh* after a series of drug charges, canceled shows, concerts that erupted into riots, and an enigmatic record that seemed both to broadcast and drown the crisis: 1971's *There's a Riot Goin' On*. With *Riot*, Sly seemed to reject his prior role as "the joyous, life-affirming black hero" and to presage a wave of albums by black artists that defied "integrationist ([or] crossover) sensibilities."[13] Critic Dave Marsh cleverly called *Riot* "an all-black album [made] with [Sly's] integrated band."[14] But *Fresh* delivered a different sound and sentiment: one suspended between the bright optimism of the *Dance to the Music* years and *Riot's* murky funk.[15] It was an album that made conflict and ambivalence sound great.

The album's deepest conflict was between Sly's gendered authority and the freedom he had previously granted his band. "As opposed to the Temptations or the Jackson 5," Marcus writes, "what you hear in Sly's music are a number of individuals who have banded together because that is the way they can best express themselves *as* individuals."[16] This might be true of the early years, when the group's democratic approach to performance enacted their claim that "Everybody Is a Star," but *Fresh* marks the end of that era. Not only had slap-bass innovator Graham left the group by then, but Sly had begun to work in a "proto-techno mode," with drum machines, overdubs, and tape loops—all of which departed from the model of the live band and gave *Fresh* a "hypnotic electronic gloss."[17] Sly Stone's efforts, groundbreaking though they were, were largely his alone. That individualism was reflected in *Fresh's* cover photograph by Richard Avedon, which captured Sly in a dramatic solo leap. Neither of the group's next two albums (which would be their last) featured cover images of the band. With that in mind, we can hear their recording of "Que Sera, Sera" as both a resigned farewell to their high-stress experience of the music industry and a sonic indication of the tensions that would dissolve the band. What it meant to "live together" was more complicated than it had appeared.

The first change the Family Stone makes to Day's "Que Sera, Sera" is to slow her upbeat track way down. Their version opens with Sly's dreamy, loping organ and Rose's quiet, straight delivery of the verse. Rose's approach on this song is quite distinct from her other work. Gone is the full, throaty tone and stunning power with which she sings the title phrase "Everybody Is a Star" and turns "Hot Fun in the Summertime" toward innuendo by declaring, "I boo boo ba boo boo when I want to!" In fact, Rose's uncharacteristically sedate delivery in "Que Sera, Sera" might seem to parody Day were it not so understated:

> When I was just a little girl, I asked my mother, "What will I be?
> Will I be pretty? Will I be rich?" Here's what she said to me.[18]

Sly, abetted by a quiet group of women singers, delivers the mother's words in his trademark gritty, nasal sound:

> Que sera, sera, whatever will be, will be
> The future's not ours to see, que sera, que sera, que sera.

Ironically, Sly performs that call to resignation—to "whatever will be"—as if his life depended on it. But this is fitting, because the song itself is marked by paradox: the stable intergenerational cycle by which one mother after another tells her child that one can't predict the future. All that is predictable is one's inability to gauge one's prospects, whether in terms of beauty, wealth, or contentment. Still, in the paradox of certain uncertainty, Sly's ad-libs tip the balance toward the unknown. Both his lyrical variations on the song text and his laid-back approach to timing suggest that the cycle might be, if not broken, then stretched out, unwound.

In one sense, Sly's gospelized performance breaches, by rendering dramatically black, the tradition of white domesticity that Day and her recording represent. His use of the gospel idiom moves the song out of the home and into the church. He also queers the family structure by play-ing the role of the mother. He is not a father figure but an androgynous shape-shifter who impersonates several different characters. At the same time, Sly's genderqueer performance is so domineering that it reinforces the woman's inability to imagine herself as the architect of her own fate.

Still, Rose plays some of her own changes on the script. Here is what happens to Day's speaker when she "grew up and fell in love":

> I asked my sweetheart, "What lies ahead?"
> Will we have rainbows, day after day?" Here's what my
>   sweetheart said.

When Rose sings this second verse, she changes "my sweetheart" to the more mature "my lover."[19] She also creates one of the track's most inter-esting ad-libs or mistakes by singing lyrics from the first verse again; the accident only registers when she drops the word *rich* midway ("ri-"). Sly, both encouraging and demanding, instructs her to keep singing, presum-ably so they can finish the take:

> When I grew up and fell in love, I asked my lover, "What will I be?
> Will I be ri[ch?], day after day?" [Sly: Sing, Rose!] Here's how my
>   love would say.

Stephen Davis, who reviewed *Fresh* for *Rolling Stone*, surmised that, al-though "Rosie . . . botches Doris's lines a couple of times, . . . the take is ob-viously so tough that whoever's at the knobs signals her to keep singing."[20] Whatever their reasons for keeping Rose's mistake (strength of the overall track, lack of money or time), the group's decision to go with it is dou-bly meaningful: it introduces an ongoing lyrical concern with economics ("Will I be rich?") that departs from Day's childish, ethereal rainbows, and it also amplifies the theme of uncertainty by introducing the meta-question of what the lyrics even are.

Sly shakes things up further by singing an ad-libbed answer that itself suspends several different forms of a question: "What, wha-whoever will be will be." The ad-lib, which he later repeats as "whatever, what, whoever," disrupts the voice of authority, turning wise words into fragments and dis-mantling the already mysterious "whatever" that "will be." Still, Sly is the one with the power to dismantle the master narrative—or to "break it down," as he instructs the band to do in the post-chorus vamp. His electric organ now proceeds gingerly, with a staccato pulse—he is breaking down the song form—over a wah-wah guitar. Everything seems to be petering out when the song suddenly revives. We might hear in this false ending an enactment of soul resilience—a refusal to die down, a refusal to end. But we can also hear it as fatalistically enacting the song's lyrics: there is a cycle to fulfill; Rose and Sly have to keep singing. In the last verse, the siblings trade lines:

> ROSE: *When I have children of my own*
>
> SLY: *Well?*
>
> ROSE: *They ask their mother, "What will I be? Will I be handsome, will I be rich?" I tell them wait and—*
>
> SLY: *Well, well, well—*
>
> ROSE: *—see.*

Breaking into the verse, as he seems to have been wanting to do all along, Sly begins his last chorus before Rose ends her line. His ad-libs destabilize the song's sanguine response to the vagaries of history and reject the white domestic ideal that Day's version represents. His queer role-playing also reflects a more flexible approach to gender than reductive takes on soul suggest. But Sly's work on this track also reveals how patriarchal logic might outlast and thrive in spite of a compromised heterodomestic structure. Sly's ad-libs reflect hard-won self-trust, but they also expose the harder-won and often conflicting effort to trust others, especially women.

There is a lot to love about this recording: how the band takes a song about resignation and makes it sound like a revival; how the artists narrate a dire life cycle by showing how it might be opened up. As a cover, the recording also hijacks an American classic for the gospel style—and, in that way, it constitutes a racial coup not unlike the one Sly performs by including white guys in his group. More than bohemian togetherness, Errico and Martini's presence has always suggested, to me, white absorption or conscription into a black sound: Sly puts white men to work in the service of his vision. But he puts black women to work too. So we need a more sensitive method than we get from most music critics, with their celebratory, male-oriented accounts. To read "Que Sera, Sera" only as a feat of black male charisma is to miss what is happening with and between women. A black feminist lens reveals more nuanced gendered intraracial tensions. And it asks us to think again about Rose.

To return to the comparison between Rose's sedate delivery and Day's abrasively cheerful tone is to see, first, how matter-of-factly Rose claims the roles of mother and daughter for black women. There is no big declaration here—it is simply her voice in that space. It is with a similar lack of fanfare that Rose creates a more grown-up woman speaker by trading Day's "sweetheart" for a "lover." To see Rose's quiet delivery as its own source of power is to consider that she *lets herself* be overshadowed by Sly—that her refusal to compete with her brother's big sound is not a concession but rather the point. Her subdued aesthetic, in addition to taking black domestic femininity in stride, serves to cast into relief Day's manic approach to the song. Day recorded "Que Sera, Sera" for decades, again and again—perhaps, as Colleen Boggs has suggested, in an attempt to maintain her idealized image despite the scandal of her personal life.[21] Beneath Day's signature song, with its vision of innocent, unscathed white womanhood, was the domestic abuse and violence Day suffered. She suppressed that reality, as the patriarchal entertainment industry demanded she do, with warmth and good humor. But there was a compulsory cheer in her sweetheart role that Rose Stone's own quiet performance can be heard to expose and resist.

Labors of Love: Nina Simone's "Be My Husband"

To suggest an alliance between Rose Stone and Doris Day—one founded on the contrast between their singing styles and what it reveals about the cost of Day's fame—is to show how vocal performance itself might hint at unlikely feminist connections. This is the case even in songs that are about women and men and even in songs that figure other women as threats to monogamous coupling. In the first chapter, I suggested that cheating songs recorded by women artists, even when they seek to defend male-female unions, can create a homosocial community of women whose experiments in self-fashioning are at least as important as their experiments with new male partners. I discerned this dynamic in Gladys Knight and the Pips' "If I Were Your Woman," a song that reimagines the speaker's identity not in relation to her would-be lover but in relation to his current partner: it's not clear what Knight would do if she were his woman, but it is clear that she would avoid the supposed errors of the woman he's with, that imagined shrew who fails to see he's "a diamond" and instead "treats [him] like glass."[22] Knight's "if-then" formulation recalls Aretha Franklin's 1967 hit "Do Right Woman, Do Right Man," which uses a similar conditional grammar to establish the form of reciprocity (and sexual stamina) on which the heterosexual partnership depends: "If you want a do-right, all-day woman / You gotta be a do-right, all-night man."[23]

Such romantic contingencies are expressed not only through song lyrics but also through the way singers perform them. Take, for instance, Nina Simone's 1965 recording of "Be My Husband."[24] First released on Simone's album *Pastel Blues*, the track sounds like a one-sided rendition of a song that should be a duet. Instead of employing a male co-vocalist, Simone enlists drummer Bobby Hamilton as her counterpart: Hamilton's lash-like hits on the hi-hat and snare provide the song's second voice. The stark arrangement accents Simone's ad-libs, which themselves highlight the female labor needed to sustain the heterosexual contract while also seeking to loosen that framework in a way that echoes the Family Stone's "Que Sera, Sera."

Simone's "Be My Husband" is based on the traditional work song "Rosie," in which a group of male convict laborers hails a woman who has promised to wait for the speaker until he returns home:

> *Stick to the promise, gal, that you made me*
> *Won't get married till I go free.*[25]

Simone had likely heard Alan Lomax's 1947 recording of the song, which was performed by inmates at the Mississippi State Penitentiary (Parchman Prison) and released by Tradition Records in 1958.[26] In that recording, credited to "C. B. and Axe Gang," C. B. leads the group in song against hammer hits on the one:

C. B.: *Be my woman, gal, I'll*

AXE GANG: *Be your man*

C. B.: *Be my woman, gal, I'll*

AXE GANG: *Be your man*

C. B.: *Be my woman, gal, I'll*

AXE GANG: *Be your man*

C. B.: *Every Sunday's dollar in your hand*

In a beautiful reading of "Rosie," Marisa Parham suggests that the song does not only highlight "domestic and sexual ruptures" that date back to slavery; it also exposes "the historical overdetermination that has built black womanhood into the locus of black masculinity."[27] "Be my woman, gal, I'll be your man": "If she is not his woman," Parham asks, "is he a man?"[28] The absence of the woman's voice heightens the uncertainty. This is a call-and-response in which men, bereft of women companions, answer each other; the women whose fidelity might shore up their manhood are gone. Simone's recording redresses that absence—she plays the woman come to claim her man—but it also introduces new questions: What does it mean to be claimed?

She transposes "Rosie" into a more conventional marital register, singing "be my husband," not "be my man." But it soon becomes clear that "being my husband" is not the endgame. That's just where the work of this work song begins:

> Be my husband, man, I'll be your wife
> Be my husband, man, I'll be your wife
> Be my husband, man, I'll be your wife
> Love and honor you the rest of your life.

Simone gradually details the terms of this contract, telling the man to "love [her] good" and asking that he stop "treat[ing] [her] so doggone mean" (a disturbing reminder of her abusive treatment by husband Andy Stroud, who is credited with writing the lyrics). Clapping, grunting, and breathing heavily to render audible her bodily effort, Simone sings vocal ad-libs that either dart up an octave or drop below the melodic line. She is stretching the possibilities of this domestic arrangement, straining against its limitations:

> Stick to the promise, man, you made me—dah dah!
> Stick to the promise, man, you made me—yeah yeah yeah
>   yeah yeah
> Stick to the promise, man, you made me, whoa
> That you'd stay away from Rosalee . . .
> If you want me to, I'll cook and sew
> If you want me to, I'll cook and sew—bah dah dah dah!
> If you want me to, I'll cook and sew, yeah
> Outside of you there is no place to go.

Simone's reminder that the man has promised to "stay away from Rosalee" makes for a clever reference to the original song, but it also introduces the chilling possibility that she has already been betrayed: she can tell her lover to stay away from Rosalee, but, insofar as her version is haunted by the original, her man has long been longing for "Rosie." The seeming inevitability of betrayal is one thing that makes Simone's love song so much work. At the same time, her relentlessly inventive vocal practice—the way she embroiders the line "If you want me to, I'll cook and sew" with a high-pitched wordless ad-lib—seeks to expand if not to escape the song's overdetermined, repetitive confines. Even as Simone sings "Outside of you there is no place to go," she darts away from the lyrics via several wordless ad-libs—"bah bah bah!"—as if to forge an escape route.

Farah Jasmine Griffin notes that Simone recorded "Be My Husband" the same year she mourned the deaths of Malcolm X and her dear friend Lorraine Hansberry, while also "serenading the marchers" at Selma: "In this season of mourning and wakefulness," Griffin writes, the song suggested that struggle was foundational to the act of loving "a man, a people, a nation."[29] When we consider that Simone's track was also released two months after the Moynihan Report was leaked to the press, we can also hear how she exposes the gendered labor about which Moynihan was so concerned (and the labor that "Rosie" asks for), where black women hold it down and stay at home.[30] But this labor itself involves the act of seeking other "places to go"—creatively roving within and around the domestic sphere so that it won't feel like a prison. Hence Simone's reorientation of the drumbeat to the offbeat instead of the convicts' plodding beats on the one. This is the inventive labor of trying to make work not feel like work.

Still, the recording enacts and gestures toward companionship. We hear this, first, in Simone's interplay with Hamilton. The drummer creates suspense and propulsion with hits on the upbeat of every measure, whereas Simone sings way behind the beat. That contrast creates tension, but it also displays a kind of synergy, an embodied understanding that allows both Simone and Hamilton to "stick to the promise" of their own rhythm. On a more symbolic level, "Be My Husband," like the cheating songs I have discussed, fashions a self in relation to other women: these women are not just the Rosies and Rosalees who show up uninvited but unknown sisters, potential comrades, and friends. When, in her memoir, Simone describes her own feminist awakening, she imagines that countless black women had to be "thinking the same way" she was: "that along with everything else [in the black struggle], there had to be changes in the way we saw ourselves and in how men saw us."[31] The very contradictions and escape routes she enacts in "Be My Husband" might be heard as offerings to other women, as gifts. Her own feminist consciousness-raising had, after all, been indebted to female collaboration—namely, to Simone's conversations with Hansberry.

"Be My Husband" creates what Richard Iton might have called a "deliberative space" in which to question not only the institution of marriage but also its constitutive categories, woman and man. That's one function of many cheating songs, too, which is why Michael Awkward attests that songs like "Woman to Woman" taught him "to conceive of R&B as an extended debate about how men and women do and should behave, what attitudes were deemed warranted, and which ones were likely to cause harm, deep embarrassment, and a desire for seclusion."[32] Alongside such texts as Toni Cade Bambara's 1970 anthology *The Black Woman* and Toni Morrison's 1973 novel *Sula*, black women's soul performances helped to convene a queer and black feminist dialogue—a conversation that helped to contest, well before the "post-soul era," the conservative gender politics associated with black nationalism. What made these texts and songs scandalous was less that they exposed extramarital affairs than that they articulated a community of black women still in the making and still on the move.

Tough Love: Simone's Dance

Simone literalized such unpredictable movement through her vocal ad-libs but also through the seemingly ad-libbed dances she performed at her live shows. Simone was an intensely physical performer, even when seated at the piano—from which she often rose to enact a series of limber moves drawn in part from West African dance. In so doing, she presented the spectacle of her body confidently *owning* its own labor, *working it*, in the colloquial and economic senses of these terms. Like the vigorous stage stalking of Otis Redding and the frenetic footwork of James Brown, Simone's performances of physical effort enacted the soul alchemy whereby struggle yielded superior technique and style. So compelling was her movement that one critic declared her danced interlude the highlight of a 1964 show; the review was titled, oddly, "Nina Simone Has College Crowd Sizzling with Hot African Dance."[33]

Still, one performance reveals an *anti*social component to Simone's dancing. Toward the end of a late 1960s performance of Billy Taylor's "I Wish I Knew How It Would Feel to Be Free" (which is featured in Joel Gold's 1969 documentary *Nina: A Historical Perspective*), Simone improvises over a vamp sung by her backup singers.[34] In a funny, gracious moment, she makes a joke about her own reputation as a difficult diva. If she knew how it felt to be free, she sings, she might be "a little less mean," "a little less bitter." Salamishah Tillet writes of this performance that Simone's "ad-libs themselves invite the audience to join her, transforming her singular meditation on freedom into a communal desire."[35] Yet Simone soon returns to diva form when one of her backup singers interjects a harmony she doesn't want, or perhaps sings too loudly: "Easy, *easy!*" Simone sings in response. Visibly annoyed, she expresses her frustration through a perfectly pitched complaint—"Get in my way!"—before leaping up from her piano bench and dancing. She feints or jukes, moving slowly in one direction and then quickly in the other. In keeping with a West African movement vocabulary (after a 1961 trip to Lagos, Simone increasingly drew on the region's aesthetics[36]), she generates a contrast between restfulness and urgency, fluid and staccato movements. She starts her solo by casually wiping her brow, then bursts into a spine-snaking, vibratory dance. She grooves back down to the piano bench and finishes the song with a dramatic cadenza. As with the microphone glitch during her performance of "Life," Simone makes experiential accident an occasion for stylized recovery.

In this performance, she recuperates not only the burden of the body but also the burden of other people, as represented by her irksome singers. The song itself, of course, also invites us to hear this social burden in terms of the society that denies Simone freedom. The fact is, the freedom she sings about is most fully realized through the act of performance—it won't be out there waiting for her when she leaves the stage. And that makes the stage a sacred space, not only for Simone but for her listeners. This doesn't mean that other people won't "get in your way" there; it means that, when they do, you can improvise responses to them, drawing on inner resources to ride difficult moments in spectacular style.

Feeling Good: Aretha Franklin at the Fillmore West

While Franklin's songs were sometimes framed, as in the *Washington Post* account cited in the previous chapter, as romantic pop alternatives to Simone's heavy political reckonings, Franklin's live performances were similarly hypnotic explorations of the ties (and chains) between people. Franklin's ad-libs generated affective networks between women, in particular; by fostering female camaraderie, her ad-libs loosened the affects of suspicion and competition that governed her relationships with women singers throughout her career.[37] In light of Franklin's careerism and jealous guarding of her status as the Queen of Soul—she reportedly resented such pop stars as Natalie Cole and Roberta Flack, and she was not above staking her claim to a soundtrack, Curtis Mayfield's *Sparkle*, that Mayfield had first promised to her sister Carolyn—it seems unlikely that Franklin would have performed a song by a woman artist in the mode of modest homage that characterizes her recording of Hathaway's "Someday We'll All Be Free." Yet Franklin's live shows, and the incredible ad-libs she performed there, opened up new spaces of female collaboration. In this regard, her onstage ad-libs served to alter some of her own behind-the-scenes diva scripts.

In 1971, Manny Tinsley described the remarkable gendered effect Franklin had on her fans in live performance:

> It's like she's saying, "Now girls, let's get down and talk some life about these men and the way they're treating us." She starts rapping and the girls start relating to her and saying to themselves, "Damn right. That bastard treats me just like that." They get very emotional and start jumping and screaming. Then Aretha comes right back and whips on 'em something like "Dr. Feelgood" or "You Make Me Feel Like a Natural Woman" and those same girls start saying to themselves, "Yeah, he's a mean so and so, but he sure knows how to take care of business," and then they get very emotional in another sort of way. See, Aretha just sings about everyday people in everyday situations. She doesn't sing about utopias because black people don't have very many utopias. They just have all those problems Aretha sings about.[38]

Franklin's vocal ad-libs, for all their virtuosity, helped produce the effect that she was just "rapping" with her fans about "everyday situations." We hear this in a live performance of "Dr. Feelgood" that she recorded—along with her live version of "Bridge over Troubled Water"—at San Francisco's Fillmore West in March 1971. While Franklin might have been unsure of how the hippie crowd at the venue would respond to her, Atlantic was confident enough in her reception to record a live album during her three-night run. *Live at Fillmore West* records her triumph. She recalls in her memoir, "Soul oozed out of every pore of the Fillmore. All the planets were aligned that night, because when the music came down, it was as real and righteous as any recording I'd ever made."[39] (Billy Preston, who played organ at the shows, concurs: "It wasn't that the hippies just liked her. They went out of their minds. . . . The hippies flipped the fuck out.")[40] While Franklin's covers of hits by Stephen Stills and the Beatles were characteristically great, her most inspired performance was of her self-authored blues "Dr. Feelgood" (1967).

Seated at the piano, where she was always most at home, she introduces the song with a few chords and a call: "Does anybody feel like getting the blues?"[41] The slow build that follows displays Franklin's flair for the dramatic but also her attunement to the erotics of performance. She stretches out the first line, "I don't want nobody," and draws the "s" of the next word through the following measure to almost painful effect: "ssssssssssssssssssittin around me and my man." (Wesley Morris notes that this prolonged "s" "sounds less like a consonant and more like a lit fuse.")[42] She finally releases the tension, checks in: "Ain't that right girls? Ain't it right? Yes, it is." What she's building up to is an epic ad-lib not included on her studio version of the song. Describing how "me and my man get to lovin'," Franklin groans, whoops, sings too fast, and strains so high that her voice cracks. It's an astonishing, calculated loss of control. And it serves to remind listeners, as Simone does in "Be My Husband," that sex is work. ("Dr. Feelgood" is subtitled "Love Is a Serious Business.") But the ad-lib is also scandalously funny—such a surprise from the do-right preacher's daughter. Franklin's simulated orgasm invites her listeners into a scene from which the opening lyrics have blocked them ("I don't want nobody / sitting here looking at me and that man"): here she lets fans in on what happens once the "company" leaves. In another show of intimacy, Franklin concludes by suggesting her listeners try her "good doctor" too:

> And after one visit to Dr. Feelgood
> You'll understand why Feelgood is his name!

This finale refashions Dr. Feelgood, as both subject and song, into a pretext for female homosocial bonding, or what Franklin's gospel idiom encourages us to call communion. The crowd-turned-congregation sings along with the chorus at full voice.

According to Charles Sanders, Franklin could bring "all 16,000 people [in a sports arena] into a kind of spiritual thing with her, sort of like what must have happened on the Day of Pentecost, and those people—all kinds: dudes, sisters in Afros and those in blonde wigs, even church-looking people—would start moving with the music." Before long, "some of them would scream and jump up on their seats, and even men like 50 and 60 years old would run down to the stage and try to touch her, just touch her."[43] Franklin's ad-libs brought everyone higher, not only women. But by arousing a collective energy *in the service of* black women's desire, songs like "Dr. Feelgood" reveal the woman-oriented vision that is a crucial facet of Franklin's music. We hear this orientation in her work with women backup singers, as well as in her live engagements with women fans.

Ann Powers writes, "If Motown was about the possibility of becoming what you wanted to be through a little dreaming and a lot of charm—the teen imperative—Aretha-era soul was about discovering what you were already and finding that beautiful. It was an adult vision, comfortably sexual, aware of the hardships of the world but still willing to try for a little grace."[44] Through her concerts and studio recordings, Franklin made a graciously permissive space for the range of women's voices that Ntozake Shange, four years after Franklin's run at the Fillmore, would formalize in her San Francisco–based choreopoem, *for colored girls who have considered suicide / when the rainbow is enuf* (1975). In Shange's innovative, syncretic work, as in Franklin's music, women's stories of struggle yield sensual survivorship: "i found god in myself / & i loved her / i loved her fiercely," the rainbow women testify at the end.[45] But whereas Shange's women first discover their divinity and then love themselves, Franklin starts with sexual pleasure and self-love, and makes those proof of divine grace.

Erotic Communion: "Amazing Grace"

Franklin creates erotic sociality even when she is not singing *about* love or sex, because her ad-libs themselves often generate a pleasurable tension that her fans experience together. We might call this an erotics of friendship—or, in church parlance, of "fellowship." We hear this dynamic on Franklin's "cross-back-over" album *Amazing Grace*, which was recorded at the New Temple Baptist Missionary Church in Watts, Los Angeles, in January 1972. Franklin's performance of the title hymn displays some of her improvisational techniques for generating tension, suspense, climax, and release. These are fundamentally erotic effects, and Franklin uses them to consolidate spiritual community.

These effects were made possible not only by her vocal skills but by her extraordinary sense of timing. Franklin was well aware of this facet of her art, telling Garland that she owed it to her father: C. L. Franklin had given her "a sense of timing in music, and timing is important in everything," she said.[46] As Clayton Riley noted, Franklin "seems to sense—more completely than any singer I know—exactly where the elaboration of joys and sorrow are bound to take us (closer to ourselves) and just how long she should keep us there (never long enough)."[47] Her use of timing to access and arouse her listeners' feeling is apparent when she sings John Newton's "Amazing Grace," a song whose simplicity gives her ample room to play and whose structural arc helps her turn up the drama. The hymn is composed so that its melodic peak arrives on the word *grace*, which makes the rest of the line a dénouement leading down to the word *home*. Franklin generates erotic expectation by delaying the resolution for as long as possible.

She sings few ad-libs in the first verse but uses an array of delay tactics in the second:

> *Through many dangers, toils, and snares*
> *I have already come*
> *It was grace that brought me safe thus far*
> *And grace will lead me home.*[48]

That is the text of the song, but, as we will see, Franklin sings several additional words in the four minutes it takes her to sing this one verse. She starts with five iterations of the word *through*. As she tarries over the word, working through it, her melismata increase in length and complexity and then taper off after the third time to create a peak at the threshold of a verse about barriers to survival and faith:

> *Through, through, through, through, through many dangers,*
>   *toils and snares*
> *I-I-I—I've been right in the midst of it and have al—*
>   *have already*
> *I have already—Jesus was with me and I've already come.*
>   *Yes, I have . . . .*

These musical peaks and valleys reflect an erotics that privileges process over destination. When Franklin hits a high C on the word *dangers*, she establishes a precedent and generates an expectation that the climax might arrive again. It does—although, like all good things erotic, one has to wait for it. She now teases the audience, singing "it was" six times before arriving at the subject: "grace." That "grace" is pitched a little lower than one might expect, given her earlier high C on "dangers." But she gears up again, singing "it was" another six times to rev back up to the high C—at which point, the documentary of the concert reveals, the choir members seated behind her leap to their feet.[49] Like the love in Simone's "Be My

Husband," Franklin's grace requires erotic, pleasurable, and difficult work. But her pacing also guarantees those gathered at New Temple Baptist that they will eventually get there together.

The political charge of this work becomes clear at the end of the song, when Franklin sings, "It won't be nothing but that same grace—I know that it won't—that's gonna lead me and mine right on." Instead of singing the word *home*, she pauses at the doorstep to stage a last moment of secular-nationalist solidarity, trading the phrase "right on" back and forth with the choir and crowd: "Right on!" "Right on!" Through this call-and-response, Franklin gathers the "me and mine" she has just named, as if to bring them into the house with her. This gathering and nurturing are the point of her performance, which utterly revises the individualist, past-tense structure of the hymn. In its original form, "Amazing Grace" describes a singular, over-and-done-with experience of salvation: "*I* once was blind but now *I* see." Franklin's ad-libs remake the song into a collective testimony to the grace that has continuously led—and is always about to lead—her and her people home. Their ad-libbed "right on" looks forward to, even as it resists, the final resting place that might absorb their revolutionary energy.[50]

"More than any singer in the soul bag, [Franklin] makes . . . salvation seem erotic and the erotic seem like our salvation," Albert Goldman wrote in 1968.[51] Franklin's rendition of "Amazing Grace" bears this out. She uses patriarchal forms of religious worship—the conventional role of the preacher, here crystallized through the influence of her father and the presence of her accompanist and family friend, the Reverend James Cleveland—to ad-lib a woman-led experience of spiritual and erotic conviction. That experience is charged with ideas and feelings about sex, revolution, black excellence, spirituality, and friendship all at once. In the midst of seemingly endless "toils and snares" of state-sanctioned antiblack violence, Franklin's music helped body forth—helped black people to hear—their own powerful sanctified allies. That was her musical ministry.

Erotic Camaraderie:
Donny Hathaway On- and Offstage

At one point in Franklin's church concert, she ingeniously interweaves Thomas Dorsey's gospel classic "Precious Lord" with Carole King's 1971 hit "You've Got a Friend." Franklin might have been thinking of the cover version of King's song released by her label mates Donny Hathaway and Roberta Flack in May 1971. It is unclear whether Franklin knew that Hathaway had also recorded a solo version of "You've Got a Friend" for his album *Donny Hathaway Live* (1972). But both Franklin and Hathaway's live covers of the song proposed an erotics of friendship. Although Hathaway rarely sang about sex, he shared Franklin's attunement to the erotic potential of performance. Even when playing eminently chaste songs like "He Ain't Heavy, He's My Brother," he teased the audience with impossibly slow tempos and delayed climax through rumbling rubatos.[52] Like Franklin, he used such techniques to generate a sense of black togetherness that was sensual, revolutionary, spiritual, and virtuosic—although he did so, I will suggest, not just in the clubs that were the sites of his best-known performances but also in the studio.

First to the club, though. Hathaway recorded "You've Got a Friend" at an intimate Los Angeles venue called the Troubadour in late summer of 1971. Several of those gathered in the room that night apparently knew the version of the song he had recorded with Flack: they cheered upon hearing him play the first four notes on his Wurlitzer.[53] They even sang along with the first chorus. While Hathaway often orchestrated sing-alongs on such songs as "The Ghetto," he does not seem to have initiated this one.[54] Yet he registers and rides the crowd's response immediately by singing harmony for his fans as he had done for Flack. Like his recording of "Never My Love," his rendition of "You've Got a Friend" does not try to outdo the original so much as it extends King's message. Still, the effect of his performance is unique. Whereas King plays the supportive friend to an absent addressee, Hathaway, in performance, ends up enjoying the support of at least a dozen singing women—who, although they might seek to supplant Flack's quasiromantic role in the song, also support, and so befriend, each other. "Would y'all sing 'you've got a friend' for me?" Hathaway asks them toward the end. He doesn't instruct them on how to sing the line, as he did when asking fans to sing in counterpoint along with "The Ghetto," but the crowd, perhaps trained in such impromptu gestures by their own experiences in church, just figures it out. "This might be a record here!" Hathaway affirms, audibly smiling. Ad-libbing their way through the song together, Hathaway and his listeners transform King's one-way expression of friendship into a reciprocal, erotic event.

Well before the sets that produced *Donny Hathaway Live*, however, Hathaway's ethic of audience engagement shaped his studio work. Sometimes he hailed an imagined audience: in "He Ain't Heavy," for instance, he sang church-inspired ad-libs—"you all don't know what I'm talking about!"—that were geared toward live performance. But Hathaway also brought his friends into the studio with him. So whereas I have elsewhere suggested that his studio recordings anticipate a future audience, it seems more accurate to say that his work in the studio undoes the binary between studio and stage altogether by capturing live interactions among friends.

"Sugar Lee," a recording on Hathaway's debut album *Everything Is Everything*, features Hathaway on piano, Marshall Hawkins on bass, Ric Powell on drums, and what Powell calls "the old Howard University gang having a real swinging party."[55] The band jams while the "gang" vocalizes whatever comes to mind. "We're gonna have church tonight!" says one man (maybe Hathaway himself). "Let's get it goin'," says a woman. "Preach, preach!" says someone else. The group claps along with Hathaway's piano work, temporarily coalescing around various ideas including a woman's declaration that she wants "sugar in the morning, sugar in the evening, Sugar Lee!"; one man's spoken phrases in Spanish; and a series of swooping "woo!"'s. If Hathaway ended up thinking that "You've Got a Friend" "might be a record," it is unlikely that he thought the same about the raucous four minutes of "Sugar Lee." But the very fact that he included the track on his debut record reflects his all-encompassing vision for the album, which would record the sound of everyday black camaraderie along with Hathaway's exceptionally deliberate craft: *Everything*.

On Hathaway's first hit song, "The Ghetto" (1969), cowritten with Leroy Hutson, the group of revelers "having a real swinging party" is the band itself.[56] Although we tend to assume that studio recordings are relatively staid and scripted endeavors compared with live performance, "The Ghetto" exemplifies the opposite: a song whose live-in-the-studio recording is messier and more impromptu than the live version, where Hathaway directs the male and female call-and-response I have described. The reason for this inversion is that the members of Hathaway's band, unlike his generally dutiful audiences, don't always heed his instructions. But this friendly insurgency, this messiness, itself makes "The Ghetto" a record of black male camaraderie. Hathaway can therefore be said to produce the effect that Marcus ascribes to Sly Stone, whereby "Sly's musical authority ... gives his singers freedom ..., builds a home where freedom seems worth acting out."[57]

"The Ghetto" evokes communal freedom in the tight space that is home. As such, it improvises on the script of the nefarious "inner city" that dominated national discourse in the wake of urban uprisings. In the aftermath of the 1968 Kerner Commission Report, which advanced the notion of "two societies, one black, one white—separate and unequal," the iconic ghetto was framed by outsiders as a site of unmitigated violence and despair.[58] In contrast, Ric Powell explains in his liner notes to *Everything Is Everything* (which contained an uncut seven-minute version of "The Ghetto"), the song took listeners "not on a tour of desperation and deprivation, but on an exploration of the happy elements, 'the elements of the street that we enjoy,'" as Hathaway said.[59] "[Hathaway] glamorized the ghetto. He made it sexy," radio host Dyana Williams averred.[60]

Like "Sugar Lee" as well as "Voices Inside (Everything Is Everything)" (1970), "The Ghetto" is an instrumental jam; what few lyrics it has are primarily meant to establish its title. Jerry Wexler described "The Ghetto" as a "master tone poem,"[61] which makes sense insofar as the track is not *about* the ghetto so much as it evokes the communal sounds and rhythms of that space (in live performance, Hathaway described the song as representing "the percussion side of town"). In a tongue-in-cheek play on the moralizing discourse surrounding black urban life, a man sings, in an extremely low bass register, "You know you ain't doing what you s'posed to . . . you doin' what you wanna do, but you know you wrong . . . good to be wrong." After this gesture, Hathaway calls on "everybody"—although it isn't clear what he wants them to do. Perhaps they are meant to clap on two and four, as some of them do, or to repeat the phrase "the ghetto," as the deep-voiced singer does. In any case, whatever collective effect Hathaway is hoping for doesn't materialize. He shrugs it off: "That's alright—everything is everything." His ad-lib is crosscut by another, as someone shouts, "Hey, Hoss!" a term of endearment.[62] Voices enter unexpectedly and fail to come when called, but Hathaway seems pleased with the happy disorder. "Good job," he answers the "Hoss" man sardonically, before singing a series of sounds that suggests he is listening, while vamping on the piano, for whatever is yet to come: "Heh? Heh? Heh?" Ad-libs beget ad-libs here, as Hathaway and his friends resist the fixed myth of "The Ghetto" by creating a space filled with life's unpredictable textures. "Everything is everything, y'all," Hathaway repeats. "Pass the joint," someone else says. Hathaway's baby daughter Lalah starts to cry—albeit with an unusual beauty that seems to predict her own future career as a singer.

Hathaway's openness to chance in this recording is rewarded when Earl DeRouen launches into his conga solo. "Yes!" Hathaway says, full of enthusiasm and something akin to relief at this incipient musical "moment." DeRouen's solo gains intensity, and Hathaway goads him on: "Get it!"

Hathaway displays the same kind of camaraderie and pride in his band when, two years later, in his live performance of "Voices Inside," he gives each of his bandmates a solo turn, telling the audience each man's name and hometown.[63]

But DeRouen's solo itself sparks something one doesn't see coming. Nearly six minutes into this unruly recording, the group coalesces and reveals previously inaudible voices, including that of Hathaway's wife, Eulaulah, herself a professional singer. Hathaway sings a full-voiced "ohhhh" to preface a series of unison "hey hey hey"s from his suddenly robust ensemble, as well as a tight soul clap and a backup vocal line: "Talkin' 'bout the ghetto!" If the song is an extended ad-lib on the script of the menacing ghetto, its final moments refute that myth not only by making the ghetto the site of revelry but also by revealing its underlying structure or discipline—the way things come together, in the wake of DeRouen's solo, just as surely as they come apart. Even the crying baby, it turns out, was part of the design. At the appointed moment, Donny and Eulaulah handed Lalah to guitarist Phil Upchurch; Upchurch had a huge Afro that scared her, so they knew she would wail. "That's what [Donny] wanted," Eulaulah noted: "Those were the sounds of the ghetto."[64] What emerges through the play of script and surprise is the song's most striking revelation: the vibrant multivoiced system that Hathaway elsewhere called "voices inside."

Prince's Family Affairs: "Nothing Compares 2 U"

The feminine elements that enter "The Ghetto" through Lalah Hathaway's infant cries and the voice of her mother, Eulaulah, play a bigger role in the work of one of Hathaway's and Sly Stone's heirs. Like both these artists, Prince exuded a restless experimentalism and a keen affective intelligence, though his emotional temperature was pitched somewhere between Hathaway's heart-on-the-sleeve virtuosity and Sly Stone's alpha-male embrace of the carnivalesque. Born in Minneapolis in 1958, Prince Rogers Nelson was the son of musicians and a proud child of funk and soul. According to his first wife Mayte Garcia, "the music that meant the most to him" was the work of James Brown, the Staple Singers, Chaka Khan, and Sly and the Family Stone.[65] If, as one critic claimed, Prince was "the master of eroto-spiritualism,"[66] he was heir, in that way, to Franklin, Simone, Marvin Gaye, and the other funk and soul artists whose legacies he drew into his life and work: by weaving Bill Withers's "Use Me" into live performances; riffing on James Brown in songs like "Housequake" and "Gett Off"; working with George Clinton, Mavis Staples, and Gaye's daughter Nona Gaye; dressing in lamé bolero tops that represented "the eighties version of Sly [Stone]-wear";[67] and forging a deep friendship with former Sly and the Family Stone bassist and fellow Jehovah's Witness Larry Graham. Some compared Prince's Midwestern stable of musical protégés to that of Berry Gordy at Motown, although the obvious difference was that Prince himself was his own brightest star.[68]

But more than any of his male mentors, Prince was candidly indebted to the musical, spiritual, and erotic inspiration of women. From Vanity 6 to Wendy (Melvoin) and Lisa (Coleman), drummer Sheila E, and the all-female band 3RDEYEGIRL, women musicians shaped Prince's work as surely as he shaped theirs. According to singer Susanna Hoffs, whose group the Bangles had a mid-1980s hit with Prince's "Manic Monday," Prince was "in awe of women."[69] That is not to say his relationships with them were untroubled but that his work with them often expressed an erotic and demanding crossgender respect. As a musical leader, Prince combined James Brown's rigorous group direction, Sly Stone's strategic assembly of an interracial male and female ensemble, and Hathaway's love of the band.[70]

He also revealed the *struggle* that gender parity required—perhaps most audibly through his collaborations with New Power Generation vocalist Rosie Gaines. A gifted singer and pianist from Northern California whom Prince himself called "the next Aretha Franklin,"[71] Gaines worked with several funk-soul bands, including one led by former Ray Charles bassist Curtis Ohlson, before joining the New Power Generation (NPG) in 1990.[72] She soon became a key member of the "outfit of Paisley Park love children" through which Prince revived his sound, democratized his stage shows, and recovered from the commercial and critical failure of his film *Graffiti Bridge*.[73] Realizing that Gaines's voice was too powerful for background harmonies alone—"having Rosie Gaines in the band is like having Aretha Franklin on backups," one critic wrote[74]—Prince featured her on the hit 1991 duet "Diamonds and Pearls." Gaines also played keyboards and cowrote two songs, "Money Don't Matter 2 Night" and "Push," for the album *Diamonds and Pearls*, which went double platinum. Prince began to produce a solo album for Gaines, then titled *Concrete Jungle*.[75] And he gave her star turns in live versions of Franklin's "Ain't No Way" and "Dr. Feelgood"[76]—the recordings of which show that Gaines's aptitude for showstopping ad-libbed spectacle matched the Purple One's own.

In late January 1992, the two teamed up for a remarkable performance of the Prince composition "Nothing Compares 2 U," recorded at a show for about two hundred fans at Paisley Park. The track was included on the 1993 compilation *The Hits/The B-Sides* (which Prince released in an effort to fulfill, and so escape, an exploitative contract with Warner Brothers). Initially recorded as a spare yet powerful male-female duet by Prince's side project the Family in 1985, "Nothing Compares" was released as a solo track by Sinead O'Connor in 1990, making it "the biggest hit of [Prince's] career not recorded by [Prince himself]."[77] Prince began performing the song consistently after O'Connor's success.[78] In light of my previous analysis of soul covers, we can see Prince's duet with Gaines as an effort to recover his hit from O'Connor (with whom his relations were strained at best)—to reassert his authorship of the song while restoring its original duet structure and revealing its gospel roots.

In an assessment of Prince's competitive streak, Jody Rosen notes that he "aimed not only to put on a great show but also to show others up" and that "his competitive instincts could overwhelm his gentler, courtlier ones." Rosen cites a 2004 Grammy Awards performance in which Prince joined Beyoncé for a medley of his hits, "ostensibly straining to ... cede the spotlight a bit. But after a few minutes, he appeared to lose patience and cranked up the virtuosity."[79] That dynamic is apparent a decade earlier, in Prince's duet with Gaines. But Gaines, a mercurial scene stealer in her own right, gives Prince a run for his money. Although "Nothing Compares" is clearly a love song, Prince's and Gaines's ad-libs make it one of the greatest nonromantic duets since Sly and Rose Stone's "Que Sera, Sera"—and the site of an even more intense struggle for musical authority. "Nothing compares to you," the lyrics insist ... "except me," the singers' ad-libs imply. Prince and Gaines's professional relationship was marked by such conflict: Gaines left the NPG in the early 1990s, before her solo album was released. It was "the hardest decision I ever made," she told a reporter, "but I had to be true to my sound."[80]

When they sing "Nothing Compares," Prince and Gaines trade verses and come together on the chorus. Prince sings the first verse relatively straight, without lyrical or harmonic embellishment.[81] It is Gaines who first improvises on the rhythm and melody, emphatically double-timing the line "Nothing, nothing can take away these blues." When they link up for the wrenchingly simple chorus—"Nothing compares, nothing compares to you"—Gaines sings harmony as powerfully as Prince sings the lead vocal. At this point, the song, like so many gospel-informed duets, becomes a showcase of the singers' ingenuity. Prince brings a lovely lilt to the melody on "It's been so lonely without you here" and bests himself with a raindrop series of staccato notes: "Nothing can stop this lonely ra-a-a-ain from falling." Not to be outdone, Gaines belts the next verse about seeing the doctor for what turns out to be useless advice—picking up a trope from blues songs like "Dr. Feelgood," where Franklin dismisses her "actual" doctor for ineffectually "fillin' me up with all of those pills." But Prince, like Sly Stone in "Que Sera, Sera," breaks into the woman's narration of her dialogue with someone else. Here, like the shape-shifting Stone, Prince moves from the role of love interest to that of friendly confidant:

> GAINES: *I went to the doctor and guess what he told me—*
>
> PRINCE: *What'd he tell you?*
>
> GAINES: *Guess what he told me—*
>
> PRINCE: *I'm listenin'.*
>
> GAINES: *He said, "Rosie"—*
>
> PRINCE: *What?*
>
> GAINES: *"Try to have fun no matter what you do." Well, he's a fool. / PRINCE: You wanna tell me why?*
>
> TOGETHER: *Nothing compares, nothing compares to you.*

Prince has tried, until now, to keep from impinging on a Rosie Gaines feature, which was no doubt meant to promote her prospective solo album. But now all bets are off. The performance moves from the realm of friendly competition into that of cutting contest. Prince growls about the death of "all the flowers that you planted in the backyard," and Gaines follows up with such force that she fumbles the words: "I know that living with me, baby, is sometimes hard," she sings, "but I'm willing-a, I'm willing to give it one more try!" The lyric should be, "living with *you* is sometimes hard," but Gaines fittingly, through both her lyrics and her vocals, turns the spotlight on herself. So it is all the more remarkable when, after the last two iterations of the chorus, Prince and Gaines come together and ease into the conclusion without fanfare or friction. Having briefly given in to the pleasure of their own competing talents, the singers return the song to the realm of efficient, time-conscientious performance. We now see that the singers' real love object has been not each other but the music, as well as the admiration their performance might draw from the intimate crowd.

That is Prince's focus, anyway. The video of this performance shows that every time he sings, "Nothing compares to you," he points not at Gaines but at the audience.[82] Although Gaines appears ready to address him each time, he doesn't turn to face her. Reading the live footage alone, one might assume Prince's failure to address Gaines reflects his immediate perturbation about her attempts to upstage him. But the video for "Nothing Compares" as a whole, which intersperses shots of Prince and Gaines onstage with images of Prince alone and of his future wife Garcia, suggests a sustained decision to deromanticize his and Gaines's relationship. The video closes with a series of images. First, Garcia, the belly dancer who reportedly inspired Prince's 1994 hit "The Most Beautiful Girl in the World," arches her back, bathed in blue light. Then we see Gaines, shot in sepia-toned black-and-white, seated on a couch with a child on each knee. Then Prince appears in shadowy profile. Sandwiched between Prince and his superlatively beautiful petite lover, the powerhouse Gaines is assigned an asexual, maternal, even grandmotherly role.

Yet it is here that Gaines's challenging, elevating ad-libs with Prince seem to matter most: her powerful, scene-stealing contributions to the song resist her impending visual domestication. Such marginalization was common to black women belters of the MTV era, whose plus-size bodies, as C+C Music Factory's Martha Wash would discover, were sidelined from the R&B hits that their voices made possible.[83] In this context, we might imagine Gaines taking her cues from Simone's vocal ad-libs in "Be My Husband," which insist on the sound if not the sight of Simone's body. Both artists model black women's ways of improvising a way out of oppressive relationships, even and especially when it seems there ain't no way.

4 EMERGENT INTERIORS

Soul Falsettos

The question of where else one might go—both alone and with others—is a question we can hear in one particular vocal practice: singers' flip into the higher register known as the falsetto. Whereas in the last chapter I explored private and social relationships through vocal ad-libs, here I delve more deeply into both interiority and sociality by discussing several singers who made the falsetto a key aspect of their style. Namely, I show how Ann Peebles, Al Green, Isaac Hayes, and Minnie Riperton, all of whom entered the national spotlight between 1969 and 1973, used their higher vocal registers to limn the contours of expressive possibility at key moments of personal, artistic, social, and communal emergence. Emerging out of the church, out of other artists' shadows, out of the traumas of scarcity, riots, and death, these artists enacted soul's recuperative logic by laying claim to an expansive interiority, an irreducible complexity that could not be neatly categorized or fully commodified.

Singers who prioritized the falsetto register offered a quieter alternative to the big-voiced "soul-shouter" sound of the late 1960s. But it would be a mistake to hear their softer aesthetic as a matter of withdrawal. Instead, the soul falsetto signals an expansion of psychic space, the implications of which are profoundly social. What Nathaniel Mackey writes of Miles Davis's muted, spare approach to the traditionally bombastic trumpet is true of the falsetto in soul: it marks an "inward turn, an expansion of ruminative space" that "wrest[s] hard-won . . . black interiority from a social sphere and performance venues invested heavily in assumptions of black outwardness."[1] The falsetto singers I consider here perform dramatic claims to rumination, vindication, mourning, and joy and, in so doing, encourage black people to bring their own complex psyches to bear on the most pressing musical and political issues of the post-King historical moment. The falsetto, as a socially resonant musical technique, allows artists to ask how high it is possible to go, how vulnerable it is permissible to be—how sexy, how extravagant, how cool and effervescent—and to emphasize the importance of cultivating and nourishing one's own interior, especially in times of insurgent transition.

In making this argument, I am breaking with recent theories of black interiority and quiet that associate those concepts with apolitical singularity or anti-spectacular introspection, as well as from dominant theories of the black falsetto that emphasize male vulnerability and bodily pain.[2] The latter tendency is most potently rendered in Nathaniel Mackey's *Bedouin Hornbook* (1984), where Mackey writes that Al Green's falsetto singing "indicts the insidious falseness of the world as we know it" by "alchemizing a legacy of lynchings—as though singing were a rope he comes eternally close to being strangled by."[3] Memorable though it is, it is strange to see Mackey's poetic meditation taken up by scholars as diverse as theorist Fred Moten and musicologist Michael Jarrett as an *explanatory* account of black falsetto singing—strange not least because that uptake limits our sense of the falsetto's affective range.[4] Women falsettists, for instance, can be heard to *refuse* histrionic performances of pain and desire, and thus to reject the kind of sentimentalizing gestures through which Aretha Franklin was framed, in the 1968 *Time* cover story she so resented, as a figure "cloaked in a brooding sadness."[5] When singers like Riperton showcase their falsettos, they are not alchemizing a history of lynching, or what Moten terms "desperate testimony and flight";[6] they are expressing the complex pleasures of (gendered) self-reinvention—which is to say, the complex pleasures of the black interior. The same is true, I would argue, of Green himself.

By distributing across several different artists, times, and spaces the weight of signification that Mackey and Moten would have the falsetto carry, I make the simple point that the meaning of falsetto, like that of any expressive practice, varies according to the situated, gendered bodies of those who deploy it. (Here I will note that some critics have denied the existence of a female falsetto altogether, arguing that women's "naturally" high voices negate the possibility that their higher vocals could be "false" or forced as the term's Latin etymology suggests. But these claims misunderstand how deliberately women singers, like their male counterparts, switch their voices to this register.)[7] Falsetto singing *was* associated with male artists in the soul era, but it was feminized in Riperton's coloratura work, as well as in Peebles's mid-1970s style. These women soul singers made the falsetto available, as a feminized technique, to Solange Knowles, who credited Riperton with inspiring her to "[explore] her falsetto" on her own ruminative, soft-speaking 2016 album *A Seat at the Table*. Solange combines Riperton's determined joy with the buoyant edge of Peebles, Green, and Hayes to craft her own gift for the Black Lives Matter era. One lesson she seemed to inherit from the scene of the velvet-voiced Hayes performing at Wattstax before a hundred thousand mostly black fans in the summer of 1972 is that you don't have to raise your voice to call an army.[8]

Ann Peebles's Reflections

Although critics tend to associate soul music with the cathartic, gospel-inspired shouts of James Brown, Otis Redding, Wilson Pickett, and Mavis Staples, in the late 1960s and early 1970s, singers such as Peebles, Green, and Hayes changed the sound of Southern soul by developing a more re-strained, introspective approach—one that in some ways recuperated and restylized the eerie falsetto sounds of Delta blues innovators Son House and his protégé Robert Johnson.[9] Peebles is not generally credited with fa-cilitating this change, but her 1974 hit "I Can't Stand the Rain" is an exem-plary model of it. The song came together one stormy August night when Peebles and her partner Don Bryant were scheduled to do a gig with B. B. King in Memphis. A local DJ named Bernard Miller came to pick them up, but it was raining so hard they had to stay home, and Peebles com-plained that she hated the rain. The statement sounded like a song—one that would refute recent R&B odes to stormy weather like the Dramat-ics' "In the Rain" and Love Unlimited's "Walking in the Rain."[10] Peebles, Miller, and Bryant composed it in fifteen minutes; it was "the fastest song [they] ever wrote."[11]

If Stax was Motown's scrappy, less polished Southern counterpart, Pee-bles's label, Hi Records, was Stax's poorer Memphis cousin. Peebles, a na-tive of St. Louis, didn't have a star's name, glamour, crossover hits, or even ambition. But her decision to sign with Hi in 1968 kick-started the label's transition from country-rock to soul. Before Al Green joined Hi and critics began to refer to Peebles as his female "equivalent," it was she who helped to establish the label's moodier, more humid aesthetic, as distinct from Stax's high-octane mid-1960s sound.[12] Peebles released the strange and wonderful "I Can't Stand the Rain" on her 1974 album of the same name. The song was nominated for a Grammy, it sold nearly a million copies, it reached the R&B Top 10, and also did well on the pop chart. It therefore marked a moment of emergence when it seemed that Peebles might slip out from under Green's shadow into crossover stardom. As it was, though, the song turned out to be her commercial peak.[13]

The recording starts with a blippy electric timbale that drops eight notes in the first bar and six in the next before Peebles sings:

> *I can't stand the rain against my window*
> *Bringing back sweet memories.*[14]

The timbale was a new gadget for Hi Records at the time, and on this recording it's not quite in tune with (or perhaps even tunable to) Peebles's voice. The producers emphasized the discrepancy between voice and timbale by withdrawing an organ track that would have sutured the distance between them—a clever move that makes Peebles's voice as alienated from the timbale as her character is from the rain she resents. The band soon enters to provide Peebles with an array of sonic witnesses—drums, piano, horns, and, most sympathetically, an electric organ that delivers periodic shrugs on the offbeat—but she continues to address the window pane as her sole accomplice: "Hey window pane, do you remember how sweet it used to be?" This is an inside thing, a memory thing, and it is related to something Peebles is doing with her vocals, and which the truly odd sound production serves to enhance: she flips her voice to an eerily high-pitched falsetto every time she sings "rain."

> *When we was together*
> *Everything was so grand*
> *Now that we've parted*
> *There's just one sound that I just can't stand*
> *I can't stand the rain.*

When Tina Turner recorded the song a decade later, she smoothed out the intervallic jump between "stand" and "rain" by belting out both words. (She also massaged the grammar, singing, "When we were together.") Peebles could have sung "rain" at full voice, like Turner, if she had wanted to. Her earlier albums showcase the belting skills she had honed by singing with the family choir at her father's Baptist church, trying to emulate her idols Mahalia Jackson and Aretha Franklin.[15] The second track of *I Can't Stand the Rain* itself reveals Peebles's range. There, she sings the line "I can't stand the rain" at full voice, before reprising it in her falsetto: "Like I said in my last song, 'I can't stand the rain.'" She therefore marks the trapdoor vocal change as deliberate, as the result of what she described as "experiment[ing] with different vocal techniques."[16]

In general, the album *I Can't Stand* features more muted, veiled vocals than Peebles's previous efforts. Her vocals are set back in the mix, amid punchy horns and a piercing organ that underscore her refusal to shout. Phyl Garland, for one, perceived the aesthetic shift, noting that Peebles's decision not to "shout or engage in vocal pyrotechnics" helped to create what she called Peebles's sound of "cool grace"[17]—or what I would term a cool interiority. Fittingly composed on a night when Peebles stayed home instead of going out to perform, the title track sets its speaker inside the domestic space and inside her own head; it also enacts a sonic withdrawal as Peebles slips the word "rain" back into her throat. But that withdrawal from the social is inextricable from it—a pane of glass is all that separates the speaker from the rain outside—and it has important implications for the world beyond Peebles's door.

Al Green's Flights

Peebles's label mate, Green, became Hi's biggest star thanks in large part to his almost spookily supple and versatile voice. But Green's falsetto, although central to his vocal art, was, like Peebles's, the result of careful cultivation. Green developed his falsetto through painstaking collaboration with his manager and soul mate Willie Mitchell. Together, they forged a sound that was instrumental to both Green's emergence and 1970s Southern soul.

In his 2000 memoir (coauthored with Davin Seay), Green describes his family's migration from rural poverty in Arkansas to industrial exploitation in Michigan, and he recounts a period of destitution in 1968, when he broke from his group the Creations and toured for nine months as a solo act, singing night after night for small groups of people who "just barely remembered" the Creations' 1967 hit "Back Up Train."[18] It was during this abject tour that Green met Mitchell, the producer, musician, and ideas man from Memphis who helped him rebuild his style from the ground up. By setting Green's "jazz vocal style with those mellow chords and progressions . . . over a sandpaper-and-grits R&B rhythm section," Mitchell and Green developed a new aesthetic: "silky on top . . . rough on the bottom."[19]

They woodshedded for months before recording Green's solo debut, *Green Is Blues*. Released in 1969, when Green was twenty-three, the album is, in all ways, a statement of emergence. Its title alone highlights Green's decision to drop the last "e" from his surname (where Sam Cooke had added one to his)—a move designed to differentiate his past self, that "poor farm boy from Arkansas," from his new image as "a star. A man on his way to somewhere."[20] The songs were chosen to emphasize what the liner notes described as Green's difference from "the usual 'belt it out full blast technique' of today."[21] But these recordings, most of them covers, performed both the self-declarative as well as the more subversive function of other covers I have discussed. The complex meanings of Green's work on his breakout album are especially audible in his recording of "Summertime."

Green humbly notes in his memoir that he, Mitchell, and the band "even managed to breathe some new life into that old *Porgy and Bess* chestnut, 'Summertime,' the hands-down, watch-me-do-my-stuff showboater of all time."[22] His performance of the song is remarkable, on one level, simply for *how much* Green manages to do within the confines of the four-minute recording: swooping, soaring, halting; ascending to falsetto and then combing a word back down though his throat.[23] Green's versatile style conveys multiple personas—he is by turns mournful, sexy, protective, even maternal, insofar as he (like Sly Stone in "Que Sera, Sera") surrogates the mother who sings the song in *Porgy and Bess*. Other black male artists who had charted with "Summertime"—the doo-wop group the Marcels (1961), Billy Stewart (1966)—had recast the lullaby as a love song. One exception to this rule was Green's idol, Sam Cooke, who recorded the song in 1957 with guitar, drums, and ethereal backing vocals by women singers. Green followed Cooke's affective template, but he sang the song in a much higher register. By enfolding into his own performance the higher voices that hovered above Cooke, Green was restoring some of the range Cooke had ironed out of his own recordings when crossing over from gospel to pop.

Green's first training ground, as I have said, was the church. He sang with his family quartet, the Greene Brothers, before forming the Creations. Music critic Anthony Heilbut, who has explored the gender politics of falsetto singing in the gospel tradition, notes that male falsetto singers are seldom heard as queer or effeminate; rather, they have often been viewed as ladies' men renowned for their sex appeal. (As another of Green's idols, gospel star Claude Jeter, put it, "Nobody ever said I sing like a lady. They say I sing like a cat.")[24] By bringing gospel's more liberal performances of gender and sexuality into soul, Green expanded the sound of male (hetero)sexual soul seduction, beyond the gruff, strident vocals of Otis Redding and James Brown. Precisely by sounding introspective and sexy, he was making a social statement—making available to others alternative modes of expressing black male desire. Marvin Gaye, for instance, although nearly a decade into his tenure at Motown at the time of Green's debut, was no doubt inspired by the singer to embrace and exploit his own falsetto, in the 1970s, in the service of sensual soul.

Green's approach to the lyrics of "Summertime" gestures both inward and outward. On one hand, his second-person address functions as an address to the self: an announcement of his own flight from his past, his family, poverty, and the performances of black masculinity he associated with Southern soul. He ends the phrase "and the cotton is high" with a series of jerky notes that evoke deep situatedness in, and the effort it takes to emerge from, one's own history and landscape. But his recording can also be heard to evoke a broader movement. When Green introduces the song's central image of flight, he changes the pronoun from "you" to "we"; in so doing, he changes the meaning of uprising, of what it means to "rise up." Buoyed by the Memphis Horns, especially tenor saxophonist Andrew Love, who plays in counterpoint to Green with increasing, even militant, force, Green raises his voice and shouts:

> *One of these mornings!*
> *We're gonna rise up singing*
> *We'll spread our wings, and we'll take to the sky, wooooo!*
>
> *But there ain't nothing! Nowhere, no no*
> *There ain't nothing gonna harm you, touch you, baby, yeah yeah*
> *You know why? Cause your daddy and your mommy be*
> *Is gonna be standing by . . .*

Green and his bandmates make "Summertime" the simmering site of potential rebellion. "Woooo!" Green sings as though the vision were becoming clear to him, or as if sending his followers off through the fields, Nat Turner–style. That promise (or threat) is soon muted, as Green returns to the quieter, albeit complex, mode in which he begins: part seducer ("nothing's gonna harm you, touch you, baby") and part parent ("daddy and mommy be . . . standing by"). But the prior event lingers like an ongoing possibility that has merely been re-veiled. Green's call for a "new world" on this same album lifts the veil again.[25]

Notwithstanding that call, Green's subjects, like Aretha Franklin's, were seldom overtly political. "At a time when message songs seem to be the thing, Green sticks resolutely to songs dealing with the variables of romantic love," according to a 1973 profile in *Ebony*.[26] Still, Green's voice itself, in its determined mutability, registered both the fierceness and the vulnerability of black people in transition. His music therefore recalls the social function of the blues, as theorized by that other alienated and ambitious son of the South, Richard Wright. In 1960, Wright described the blues as a record of black people's "confused wanderings over the American southland and . . . intrusion into the northern American industrial cities."[27]

Green's music resembled the blues not only in function but also in form, insofar as the lyrics he composed could, like blues verses, seem to be collated at random. As such, Green's lyrics implicitly asked—and this was another aspect of his emergent experimentalism—how much confusion and ambivalence it was possible for contemporary love songs to express.[28] The success of Green's incoherent love songs indicates that the answer was, quite a bit—if, that is, the lyrics were delivered with a striking amount of skill and charisma. "Love and Happiness" opens with a verse in which "Something's going wrong / Someone's on the phone / It's three o'clock in the morning." What does that call have to do with the song's title concept? What is happening in "Here I Am (Come and Take Me)," where Green initially celebrates the love "burning deep down inside" him but then laments that his lover has broken his heart again, although he's glad he "can always call [her] for a helping hand," wants her to know that she "can't always trust everybody," and yearns for her to "teach [him]" an unidentified lesson? Green's exploration of the interior, if it could yield inchoate lyrics, performed the sound of thought and feeling so convincingly that no one seemed to mind.

While his charisma on record helped to obviate the need for cohesive storylines, his live performances made it clear which lyrics mattered most. In a 1972 performance of "Love and Happiness" on *Soul!* Green slowly gets the spirit and jump-dances around in a circle singing, "I think I got the power!"[29] The performance displays the same theatrical impulse that would soon have him handing out roses to women at shows—as well as his superior and hard-won vocal chops. By 1973, according to Peter Bailey,

Green had acquired a fan base that ranged from "teenagers to grandmothers, from cultural nationalists to debutantes"; six of his singles and two of his albums had gone gold, with "Let's Stay Together" selling more than two million copies; he was the first male singer to be voted "Top Male Vocalist" by *Cashbox, Record World,* and *Billboard*; and August 31, 1972, was declared "Al Green Day" in Memphis.[30] What Green understood, or learned along the way, was that the complexities of any love story didn't have to add up if the performance of interiority was sufficiently virtuosic and bold. What is "the power" we are to understand Green has gotten by the end of that performance? Religious, social, sexual, vocal? The question can't be answered simply, which is the point.

Isaac Hayes's Expansions

Like Green, Isaac Hayes presented himself with all the bravado but at half the volume of other soul men, while fashioning himself as a sensitive, enigmatic figure—a restless creative whose composition process, in Hayes's case, involved gazing through his third eye.[31] But whereas Green tended to fit every aspect of his vocal art (falsetto feats, off-topic ad-libs, gospel moans) into three-minute songs, Hayes stretched his hushed, unhurried vocals over a much broader musical canvas. (His laconic 1969 cover of Green's "One Woman" is a case study in that contrast.) Hayes ranged farther as a vocalist too. Whereas Green shaved the bass from his lower tones and compressed his sound into a narrower and higher vocal margin, Hayes mainly sang in his baritone register but could also ascend to a dry, vibrato-less falsetto. With his velvet voice, opulent orchestrations, and flamboyant clothes, he emphasized the quiet and time needed to mull a thing over, while taking up vocal, musical, and physical time and space as if at home with himself and in the world.

This was a lifelong act of soul-style recovery. A self-described "poor, black, nappy-headed" child whose mother died in a mental institution and whose father abandoned him, Hayes was raised by his grandparents, who moved the family from Covington, Tennessee, to Memphis; they nearly froze in the winters and starved all year long.[32] While in and out of school as a teenager, Hayes sang with several groups, including a gospel quartet, a doo-wop group, a blues band, and a jazz combo. His vocal idol was Nat King Cole. Sufficiently skilled as a pianist to fill in for Booker T. Jones at Stax when Jones was away at college, Hayes soon proved himself to be especially gifted as a songwriter. Along with David Porter, he wrote some of the label's most iconic hits, including Sam and Dave's "Soul Man" and "Hold On, I'm Coming."[33] He wanted to cut a solo record, but as he later explained, Stax co-founder Jim Stewart thought his voice was "too pretty": "At that time we were living in a James Brown era," Hayes noted. "Rough singing. Nat Cole was long gone, [but] I was a soft singer. . . . So Jim put me off."[34] But producer Al Bell encouraged him, so in 1967 Hayes recorded *Presenting Isaac Hayes*; its sales were unimpressive.

Music historians often suggest that the pivotal moment, for both Hayes and Stax, was Hayes's 1969 release of *Hot Buttered Soul*. Certainly, the forty-five-minute concept album, consisting of just four extended psychedelic-orchestral tracks, was one of the most extravagantly beautiful musical manifestos of the modern era. But, as Mark Anthony Neal has noted, Hayes was moved to make the album, and Stax was willing to entertain its experimentation in the first place, because of a series of losses: the death of Stax star Otis Redding in a freak plane accident in 1965; the label's loss of its back catalog to Atlantic in 1968; and the assassination of Martin Luther King in Memphis that year.[35] For Hayes, the loss of King, who was his friend, was especially traumatic. After King's death, the singer "flipped," in his words, and became more "rebellious" and "militant."[36] For a time, he also went quiet. "I could not create properly," he said. "I was so bitter and so angry. I thought, 'What can I do? Well, I can't do a thing about it so let me become successful and powerful enough where I can have a voice and make a difference.' So I went back to work and started writing again."[37] Hayes recorded *Hot Buttered Soul* as part of Stax's "Soul Explosion," a release of twenty-seven albums designed to help Stax recover from the loss of Redding and the disastrous distribution deal with Atlantic. But Hayes's ambitions were less commercial than creative: "I didn't give a damn if *Hot Buttered Soul* didn't sell," he said, "because there were 26 other LPs to carry the load. I just wanted to do something artistic, with total freedom."[38] That freedom meant, in part, "stretch[ing] [the songs] out and milk[ing] them for everything they were worth."[39] Combining what drummer Terry Johnson called "that laid-back, barely-make-it-to-the-next-measure bluesy soul feel" with string arrangements by Detroit artists Johnny Allen and Dale Warren, *Hot Buttered Soul* featured more expansive, and expensive, productions than anything recorded at Stax.[40] (In fact, it wasn't technically recorded there; Hayes cut it at Ardent Studios across town.)[41]

Insofar as the album rejected the kinds of radio singles that Hayes and Porter had a made a career out of writing at Stax, *Hot Buttered Soul* was an act of self-reinvention.[42] Hayes took songs he loved and reconstructed them to "[target] the black listening audience."[43] So it came to pass that one of the nation's leading composers of three-minute soul hits recorded an album filled with ten-plus-minute covers of his favorite white pop tunes. Despite being what Garland described as "probably the strangest record hit of the year"—indifferent to Top 40 radio play and a radical departure from mainstream R&B—*Hot Buttered Soul* sold an average of twenty-five thousand copies per week, becoming the first Stax LP to go gold.[44] Those album sales put Stax in league with competitors Motown and Atlantic, and outdid them by selling a million records to black fans alone. In quintessential soul style, Hayes had internalized King's death, the era's preeminent sign of black vulnerability, and reemerged as a giant.

Before he released his 18.5-minute cover of Jimmy Webb's "By the Time I Get to Phoenix," which had been a hit for country singer Glen Campbell, Hayes had practiced it at a local black nightclub. He enfolds that setting into his studio recording: like a cross between a lounge singer and a preacher, Hayes tells his listeners he will bring "Phoenix" "down to Soulsville" (the nickname for Stax), and he invites them to "travel with [him]" as he tells of a lovelorn man who leaves his wife after he catches her cheating on him eight times. The song lyrics imagine the wife's movements through the day while the speaker drives away. So there are several levels of interior transport here: into Soulsville; into a club where one might hear this kind of introduction; and into the story, which itself describes both geographic and imaginative journeys. Still, Hayes enacts his most intense turn toward the interior in a final section of ad-libs, where he tries to convince himself (although rhetorically addressing the woman) that he needs to leave: "You were sweet to me, yes you were / But on the other hand, you were real cold / You just kept me, oh, you kept me hanging on, yes you did." This outro lasts for seven minutes; the opening monologue stretches over eight. This means that Hayes devotes exactly three minutes to covering the original song, effectively absorbing it—as Franklin would later do when covering "Bridge over Troubled Water"—into his version. What it means to "take a song to Soulsville," then, is not to give it a funky horn chart or a shout section but to subsume it into the contemplative black interior.

On *Hot Buttered Soul*, Hayes stakes out plenty of room for black interiority through epic orchestration, long songs, and ponderous lyrics. He furthers that expansionary project on *Black Moses*, two years later, through his use of falsetto. His 1971 cover of "Going in Circles" ends with a dreamy ascent into the falsetto range as Hayes sings of being "strung out over you, over you, over you," higher and higher. Whereas Green's thinner, lighter tone seems designed to reach such heights, the ascent of Hayes's husky voice can seem uncanny, as if a large adult were hoisted into the air by a child. But these moments constitute a dramatic expansion of vocal space and thus an important dimension of Hayes's experiments with size and scale, as well as with gender performance. His admission, in "Going in Circles," that he has "lost his head" over love verges on self-feminization; however, that effect is tempered by the women backup singers who sing stratospherically high adornments in the song's outro. These singers limn the outer limits of falsetto singing in Hayes's work; however high he goes, he will not reach the near hysteria they represent.

In "Part Time Love," a blues made famous by Little Johnny Taylor in 1963 and covered by Peebles the year before Hayes released it on *Black Moses*, women backup singers deliver the pathos that, by contrast, enables Hayes's serene sound. The song opens with a funky wah-wah guitar riff before escalating into an unfunny carnival: spires of strings, acoustic piano, bombastic horn. Psychedelic opera meets Southern gothic at the bridge, where Hayes and his backup singers tragicomically invoke the dead: "People in the cemetery, they don't live all alone / Some turn to dust, some to bone / I'd rather be buried six feet in my grave / Than to be so lonely each and every day." The highest falsetto lines are performed by the ghostly women singers, who repeat a single question: "Can't you see I'm working on it? / Can't you see I'm working on it?" Like exasperated, put-upon cupids tasked with securing Hayes's part-time love, they keep "working" for him and the song, singing this physically demanding line for two minutes after Hayes drops out. Again, he can stay cool because they get so worked up.

Hayes was, like so many activists past and present, less progressive on gender than on race—but he was more progressive on race than were most in the industry. According to *Ebony* reporter B. J. Mason, he "raised hell at Stax Records in a successful effort to achieve racial equity in employment."[45] He helped register black voters in the South and cofounded a group called the Black Knights to protest police brutality and housing discrimination in Memphis. When interviewed for a 1973 spread in *Penthouse*, he took the opportunity to publicize not only his obsession with sex but also his disdain for "white businessmen with fat stomachs and big cigars" and his commitment to black economic empowerment.[46]

Hayes's gold chains, zebra cloak, luscious furs, trend-setting bald head, and gold-plated Cadillac were the visual counterparts to his sonic largesse. Here was a template for hip-hop before hip-hop: an audacious claim to space and selfhood expressed in part through innovative fashion and what a later generation would call "bling." But even in his own era, Hayes's musical and sartorial self-fashioning were political. At a moment when black people were being made to feel acutely unwelcome in the public sphere—patrolled by police in their own neighborhoods, maimed and killed for being "in the wrong place at the wrong time"—Hayes took up time and space as if it were owed him, crafting a persona that embodied at-home opulence and ease. As a musician, performer, and businessman, he also enacted the questions of size and scale that drove black-owned record companies in the age of Berry Gordy's Motown and Al Bell's emergence at the helm of Stax: Is it ever time to downsize? How much bigger, how much blacker, could you be?

Even by his standards, Hayes's headlining performance at Wattstax on August 20, 1972, his thirtieth birthday, asked these questions in a big way. Stax flew several of its artists out to LA for the concert, which tapped into an annual festival designed to help the Watts community recover from the riots of 1965. Those riots, sparked by police harassment, unjust housing policies, and racist employment practices—and immediately occasioned by reports that police had assaulted a black male driver, his mother, and a woman who was thought to be pregnant—resulted in thirty-four deaths, one thousand injuries, and four thousand arrests.[47] The Watts Summer Festival was established the following year. William Earl Berry used soul logic to describe it: "Every year since 1965, the citizens of Watts have channeled the energy, fervor, and emotion that was used to 'burn, baby, burn' into the Watts Summer Festival, celebrating black culture instead of burning down their own community."[48] Wattstax drew about 100,000 people to the Los Angeles Coliseum (they each paid one dollar for admission or else were given free tickets), making it "the largest gathering of blacks since the March on Washington."[49]

"In an era when popular music concerts were increasingly held in large municipal stadiums," Neal writes, "Stax/Volt dared to present such a concert as a gift to urban black America."[50] Given that LA's black population largely comprised African Americans from Texas and Louisiana, the concert was even more specifically a gift issued from a black Southern company to uprooted black Southerners at a time of transition for both.[51] Wattstax helped to consolidate Stax's new image as a black-owned company led by Al Bell—one that would invest materially and emotionally in the black community white America had abandoned (literally, in many cases, via white flight). By donating concert proceeds to local organizations such as the Sickle Cell Anemia Foundation, the Martin Luther King Hospital, and the Watts Summer Festival itself, Stax not only made an extravagant claim to black public space; it also expressed concern with the *quality* of spaces in which black people lived.[52] Hayes, whose continued ability to "relate to the dudes on the block" was a key aspect of his persona, told a reporter that he hoped his music would inspire Watts residents and that he identified with their sense of precarity and frustration.[53] Of course, beyond his own desperate childhood, he might have noted a more recent point of connection with Watts: his own hometown had been the site of riots four years earlier, triggered by the assassination that had sent Hayes himself underground.

Without naming any of those losses, Hayes memorialized them onstage at Wattstax through his epic rendition of Bill Withers's hit single "Ain't No Sunshine when She's Gone" (1971), which he combined into a medley with the Doc Pomus song "Lonely Avenue" (1956). After performing "Sunshine" for over three minutes, Hayes launched into a spoken ad-lib describing a crisis set in "the streets":

> You're walking the streets, you're looking for her, you can't find her, and you might stand up on the corner and you say, "Baby . . . baby . . . oh babe! Oh babe! Oh babe! Oh babe! Whoa babe! Lord, come back home to me, come on, come on, back home to me."

Hayes refuses to shout to bring his lover home. Instead, he reconceptualizes the notion of raising one's voice by raising pitch instead of volume. He sings a very high-pitched "baby" to try to lure his lover home. But then, in a passage that blooms from the absurd to the sublime, he raises the pitch yet higher as he repeats the phrase. He plays piano fills to give himself time to catch his breath and shifts from "oh babe" to "whoa babe," leveraging the consonant to heave the sound up. What begins as a crowd-pleasing church trick gradually comes to sound a bit hysterical, the sort of moment people might have witnessed with both awe and mirth. It is extreme.

Hayes's use of extreme falsetto resonates with Federico García Lorca's theory of duende, which Mackey theorizes as an intense, self-surpassing mode of performance that expresses an artist's cultivation of or possession by another voice—"a voice that [appears] other than that proposed by one's intentions, tangential to [them], angular, oblique."[54] Through Hayes's falsetto rise, which is all the more striking because rare for him, he cultivates this other voice, generating a sense that he is, in Robert Duncan's terms, "speaking more than one knew what."[55] We can therefore hear his "Sunshine" ad-lib in at least two registers: as a lament for lost love and a lament for the losses produced by the riots that Wattstax was meant to commemorate. Mackey writes of duende, "It's a conversation with the dead, intimacy with death and with the dead."[56] By performing a song of lost love and solitude for seventeen minutes, Hayes enacts a reaching away from singular or static meanings and out of a world marked by violence. His use of falsetto in particular makes his medley a love song, a lament, and a prayer—a repetitive incantation meant to show lost loved ones how to take to the sky.

Sometimes, however, as I have said, Hayes's intense performances of duende are made possible by the voices of others, especially women. Whether these women are singing the title word "Shaft" or otherwise enhancing the emotional force of his music, Hayes's backup singers are central to his aesthetic. Their falsetto work often frames and supports Hayes's experiments with size, space, and pathos. That point attunes us, moreover, to the material ways that his elaborate orchestrations sometimes came at others' expense. At Stax, as at any label, resources were limited, and singers such as Carla Thomas, who was rarely given material equal to her talent, remained in the shadow of Hayes's largesse. Granted, Hayes had pioneered the company's rebranding as a musically adventurous, socially conscious, and problack label, and he was, in every way, "the biggest artist Stax ever produced."[57] But Thomas was one worthy artist who languished in the wake of his ascent. She was still singing her first hit "Gee Whiz" (1960) at Wattstax when Hayes was playing new covers and originals. His headlining set lasted an hour, while most other musicians got three minutes, and as the show went on, some were withdrawn from the roster altogether due to time constraints.

Minnie Riperton's Adventures in Paradise

While Hayes's backup singers are subordinate to him—performing the expressive labor that allows him, even when singing in falsetto, to play it relatively cool—Minnie Riperton brings the female falsetto sound to center stage. Indeed, her coloratura soprano range and iconic whistle register made Riperton the most dramatic pop falsettist of her era. As a former backup singer herself, as well as a preternaturally gifted vocalist with operatic training, Riperton could use her falsetto in myriad ways: to generate atmospheric effects and adornment (a function akin to that of Hayes's singers); to create dialogue with instruments as various as a string section ("Les Fleur"), electric guitar ("Reasons"), and harmonica ("Our Lives"); to bring a seductive or aspirational longing to her lyrics; and to amplify or liquidate words. In all cases, her falsetto marked a refusal to shout and an embrace of an expansive, often buoyant interior life for which Riperton sought both musical and social space. Her quest was especially resonant in an era of black feminist emergence, which, as scholar Maureen Mahon notes, included first books by Alice Walker, Toni Morrison, Toni Cade Bambara, and many other women writers, as well as the founding of *Essence* magazine, the presidential run of Shirley Chisholm, and the organization of the Combahee River Collective.[58] Through her falsetto, as well as her often self-composed lyrics, Riperton contributed to these feminist efforts to make more space for black women's interiority, both its pleasures and demands.

In chapter 2, I described the innovative soul aesthetic that Riperton advances, in a powerful yet nonagonistic way, through her Rotary Connection cover of Franklin's cover of Redding's "Respect." Rotary Connection, an experimental group characterized by Riperton's transcendent vocals and Charles Stepney's ornate arrangements, forged a new spiritual-ethereal pathway for soul—one most famously pursued by Riperton's Chess label mate Maurice White, with his group Earth, Wind & Fire. Riperton's solo work also extended this route, away from conventional sounds and worlds and into new ones. As Farah Jasmine Griffin writes, "The enormity of [Riperton's] gift, the discipline of her operatic training, and her grounding in black music traditions all contributed to a hybrid, emergent aesthetic sensibility."[59] Although one contemporary journalist described her as "a throwback to San Francisco and 1967"[60]—a very different California from the one Isaac Hayes engaged at Wattstax—in fact Riperton advanced a vocal, musical, and personal aesthetic that was future-oriented and optimistically geared toward what she called, on a 1975 album, "Adventures in Paradise." In the refrain to that song—"step this way for another adventure in paradise"—Riperton moves from a growling tone up through a tier of higher notes into her whistle register, making more and more sonic space for adventure and for faith in an encompassing paradise, perhaps on the other side of this world.

Born in 1947 in the Bronzeville district of Chicago, Riperton was the youngest of eight children and the daughter of a homemaker and a Pullman porter. As I have noted, she studied opera for years. Although she knew well that opportunities for black classical singers were extremely limited, she did not, like Nina Simone, narrate her detour from concert music as a racial trauma. This might have been a matter of temperament or a strategic omission. Or it might have been due to the fact that Riperton had always had another place to land: she had grown up near Chess Records, the crucible of Chicago soul. While in high school, she was recruited for the Gems, a girl group that made their own records and sang backup for other Chess acts. And, of course, in the late 1960s, Riperton joined Rotary Connection, the band most widely known for opening for Led Zeppelin, Sly and the Family Stone, and the Rolling Stones.

In 1970, shortly after Chess cut the uncategorizable and thus largely unprofitable Rotary Connection from their roster, Riperton recorded her first solo album, *Come to My Garden*. With ornate arrangements by Stepney that built on Hayes's concept album format and a cover shot of a gloriously Afro'ed Riperton seated amid flowers, the album presented an otherworldly space and an image of what Griffin calls "black bohemian femininity."[61] The title track, which links inside and outside through the image of the private outdoor garden, is at once personal and epic. Riperton moves into and out of the dense atmosphere of orchestral interludes, ascending to her falsetto on the chorus and singing the verses in quiet, low tones. Although she aims to seduce the listener away, the lyrics keep an eye on what she wants to escape. "Come to my garden, no more dreams filled with cries," Riperton promises—and, one verse later, "I'll take your hand and lead you from these bad times."

Like Riperton's work with Rotary Connection, *Garden*'s blend of R&B, opera, rock, pop, and gospel was at once innovative and hard to sell. But Riperton embraced the diversity of her skills and interests, telling one reporter, "My life is filled with so many things and not just exposure to one kind of music. I've been exposed to every kind of music you can imagine; Japanese, Chinese, Balinese, African, South American, East Indian, the lot, and it's made me an individual."[62] She also defied category by declaring she did not have the gospel background generally associated with soul, as well as by singing songs of encouragement, a choice she described as a break with raced and gendered expectations: "Because I'm a Black woman, everyone thinks I should sing the Blues. But I have nothing to be blue about.... I'm a happy person."[63]

Such declarations masked an edge that sometimes struck through Riperton's image as soul's princess of pleasure. Especially when speaking with UK journalists with whom Riperton might have felt freer to speak her mind than she did with her fan base at home, she told the truth about racial categorization and black dehumanization. In a 1975 interview with British writer Penny Valentine, she explained that the solo work she had recorded in the 1960s before joining Rotary Connection "wasn't what you'd call black music so therefore nobody knew what to do with it. I mean, in the record industry if you were black you were black and you couldn't be anything else. At that time you were Negroes, you weren't even human beings. That's the way it was then, that's the way it is now."[64] Riperton told Chris Charlesworth of *Melody Maker* that during a trip out West, she found that the people who had wanted to sign her when they heard her music changed their minds once they saw her: "They freaked out because I was black. They didn't know what to do, because [my] name didn't sound black. It's not like Jones, is it?"[65]

In the early 1970s, partly in response to such indignities, Riperton and her husband, Richard Rudolph, her cowriter and accompanist, "retired," as she jokingly put it, to Gainesville, Florida (they were still in their twenties). The interracial couple had their second child (the actor and comedian Maya Rudolph) and continued to write songs. A few years later, Riperton agreed to sign with Epic Records, the one label that took her seriously as a writer. The family moved to Los Angeles, where Riperton's friend and admirer Stevie Wonder produced her album *Perfect Angel*. That album's third single release, "Lovin' You," hit No. 1 on both pop and R&B charts and at last brought Riperton and her five-and-a-half-octave range to national attention.[66]

An aesthetically lighter but no less profound production than *Come to My Garden*, *Perfect Angel* features pared-down arrangements that foreground Riperton's voice. As Al Green described Willie Mitchell doing for him, Wonder sets Riperton's voice "right in the middle of a song..., giving it room to stretch and breathe and feel its own power."[67] Riperton exudes this power by integrating her falsetto more directly into these songs; instead of saving the skill for set-off instrumental sections, she ascends several octaves right in the middle of a verse. Just as significant as her vocal performance and Wonder's production is Riperton's coauthorship (with Rudolph) of nearly every song. Whereas *Come to My Garden* occasionally betrayed Stepney's male authorship—on the opening track, "Les Fleurs," Riperton sings, "Inside every man lives the seed of a flower / If he looks within, he finds beauty and power"—*Perfect Angel* allowed Riperton to explore female interiority. (In this she was aided by Rudolph, her compositional and personal soul mate.) As she stated of her later LP, *Stay in Love*, her decision to write love songs from a woman's perspective marked a feminist intervention: "I wrote the album as a story—from a woman's point of view. Usually all the love stories you hear are written the way a guy sees it. Even when women sing them, it's a man's attitude. But women definitely have their own ideas about how they want to say things to men and how they feel about things."[68] That these things are not all serious is one message of *Perfect Angel*'s cover image: Riperton smiles at the camera as if amused; she wears overalls but no shirt, and eats a melting ice cream cone.

The album is no less intellectually rich for being playful. In fact, its up-tempo opening track, "Reasons," serves as a treatise on singing; as such, it offers a theory of Riperton's practice that can guide our understanding of the album as a whole. The song's first lyrics suggest a movement from outside to inside—"The reasons for my life are in a million faces / Like aching promises I feel them in my bones"—that the next lines reverse: "Slipping through my fingers to dance along the road / The reasons for my life are more than I can hold." Moving from her chest voice to her falsetto and back again while keeping pace with Marlo Henderson's stunning work on guitar, Riperton insists on taking up a great deal of sonic space and exceeding her own boundaries just as the reasons do, "slipping through my fingers to dance upon the road." Both lyrically and sonically, then, Riperton conjures an expansive interior life that overflows the boundaries of the individual psyche and body to radiate outward. The "inner light" that singing sparks might be hers, or it might be the listener's:

> *But oh the sweet delight to sing with all my might*
> *To spark the inner light of wonder burning bright*
> *You're not alone. You're not alone!*

Riperton leaps to her whistle register on the last "alone." She takes time to explore the stratosphere, darting up and down and mimicking Henderson's guitar riffs with her voice. The song is a showcase of both her nimble vocal technique and her gift for expressing joy through performance. Yet just as "Come to My Garden" evokes both the possibility of escape and the world that needs escaping, "Reasons" shows that her self-validation is not only joyful but *necessary* in a world that denies her worth. As she sings, "The reasons for my life are more than I was told."

Perhaps not since Simone's recording of "Life" had a soul singer issued such a vibrant yet serious claim to life and presence. Riperton gives voice to this complex interior life across the course of the album: even the seemingly simple last track, "Our Lives," expresses both optimism and the imagination needed to sustain it. Cowritten by Riperton and Rudolph, the song is a lovely, modest ballad framed by Wonder's work on harmonica and Rocki Dzidzornu's conga lines. It conjures idyllic images—apple trees, sleep during rain, "the light of children's laugher," "the glow of lovers' souls"—and its world-making project is explicit: "Side by side in the sun, we will build the world we're after." But closer attention to the song's framing lyrics reveals that its dreams are prospective:

> Any day now can't you see
> You'll be coming back to me
> Coming back to where you want to be.

Riperton is describing what she *hopes* will happen, not what already is. So her coloratura in this song can be heard as an alluring sound, as in "Come to My Garden," but also as a mode of keening. The song might lure her lover back—and one might hear, in the wordless duet Riperton sings along with Wonder's harmonica, a bridging of two distinct personalities that signals a lover's reunion—but there are no guarantees. Just as "Reasons" acknowledges by challenging those who have devalued the speaker's life, the last track acknowledges the complexities that underwrite its scene of "perfect" love. *Perfect Angel* celebrates profound love and great sex, but it additionally stages soul's intimate struggles—the work it takes to bridge the distance between lovers and to create a confident sense of oneself.[69]

Such complexity could be harder to come by in Riperton's public statements, since positive thinking and gratitude were central tenets of her star persona. She told one reporter the year after *Perfect Angel*'s release, "I am very happy. I have a beautiful husband and two adorable children. I know I am lucky."[70] When, a year later, at age twenty-seven, she was diagnosed with terminal breast cancer, she only amplified her message: "Every time I sit down to eat, when I get up in the morning, when I see my children . . . I always thank God . . . for permitting me to be alive."[71] She died four years later. If Riperton's brief life can be narrated as a series of emergences—out of the role of backup singer and into the spotlight as a solo artist; out of "retirement" in Florida and into the studio in Los Angeles; from local renown to national fame—no move was as dramatic as her emergence from cancer treatment. In 1976, she had a partial mastectomy and was given a prognosis of six months to live; yet, when she made the news public, she discussed the surgery as if it had cured her. Months before her death, she touted the healing powers of green magma, discussed an upcoming European tour, and hinted at a new fashion line. Not that there was any rush. As she told

Ebony's Bob Lucas, "I know that I'm going to be around for a long time."[72] While she fretted privately to her sister that she did not want to leave her children, she continued to perform the optimism that had shaped her career; as she had sung, before her diagnosis, in "Adventures in Paradise," "I believe any dream that I want to."[73] Her decision to sustain that disposition was strategic. According to Rudolph, "There was no way she could live as fully and freely if everyone knew her real condition." One journalist noted, "She didn't want anyone to mourn her death before she died or to buy her records out of pity or sorrow."[74]

Riperton's public response to her illness followed the soul logic of enfolding pain into a narrative of survival. But she brought that logic, in an act of great service, to a specific subcommunity of women with cancer. In 1978, she was appointed the education chairwoman for the American Cancer Society. She was the youngest woman and the first African American to hold the position—no small feat in the years before Audre Lorde's *Cancer Journals* (1980) and related efforts to break the silence around breast cancer. "I had to be vocal and let these people know they were not alone, that this is not something you have to hide from," she said.[75] In her work as an advocate, she translated the spectacular reassurance of "Reasons" to other women: "You're not alone!" Still, Riperton's positive thinking does highlight the limited options for black women in the public eye, where one could choose among, but not combine, the roles of strong, sassy diva; professional mourner; or perfect angel. Consequently, her optimism did not accommodate the prospect of *not* surviving. Neither did that of Stevie Wonder, who wrote a song for her, titled "Minnie, Get Well Soon," to which she listened on her deathbed: "Like a bird singing earthly songs of love / We need your love around / Minnie, get better."[76]

As usual, Riperton's own recordings told a more complicated story than her public comments did—especially when her music embraced the lamentation she had negatively associated with the blues. In "Memory Lane," a ruminative song of the interior released two months before her death, she mourns the end of a love affair. At the end of the phrase, "The way you held me / No one could tell me / That love would die," she leaps up to her whistle range. (Even though her body was failing, her voice remained remarkably strong.) While Riperton avoids articulating the word *die*, her performance evokes death as a world beyond, a spiritual realm that her falsetto had perhaps always intimated. What her ethereal, playful, and jubilant music conveys, at least in retrospect, is a soul unbound by the living body. As Rudolph noted in the wake of her death, "She always said she had been here a lot before," in previously incarnated form.[77] Riperton's falsetto marked a claim to an interior, transcendent spirit that had been around before this lifetime, and might well be back—not least, in the form of inspiration for other artists.

Solange's Welcome Table

Nearly forty years after Riperton's last recordings, Solange looked to the singer's world-making music to stage her own emergence. As Solange explained to Daphne Brooks in a 2017 conversation, she had become accustomed to bending herself to fit particular industry spaces—black contexts where her work was labeled "urban," white indie cultures where her blackness seemed unwelcome.[78] But as she worked on *A Seat at the Table*, she realized, "I have to actually create from the ground up the space that I want to exist in."[79] Echoing Audre Lorde's realization that she had to name herself without "depend[ing] on the world to name [her] kindly, because it never will," Solange saw that she would only fully belong in "the space that I create for myself."[80] That space became *A Seat at the Table*, her critically acclaimed 2016 album that "[felt] architectural," according to critic Doreen St. Félix, in its meticulous composition and arrangement, and whose central domestic-social metaphor itself evoked an expansive interior space.[81]

While Solange's vision on the album is highly individual—she produced, arranged, and wrote it herself—it is also deeply curatorial. She features running commentary by rapper-producer Master P, as well as guest spots by artists Sampha, Lil Wayne, and Kelela and recorded conversations with her parents about integration and problack politics. These other figures help Solange expand the boundaries of permissible racial discourse in the Black Lives Matter era, showing how it is possible to conduct "inside" conversations about black life in the mixed company of the public sphere. That experiment also shapes Solange's videos, which set black people (many of them her friends) in indoor-outdoor environments such as gazebos and patios—acknowledging without demurring to what Brooks has called the panopticonic culture of cybersurveillance.[82] Emerging from restrictive social and musical cultures (and indeed from her sister Beyoncé's shadow), Solange comes into her own, on *A Seat at the Table*, by finding her people. The album therefore extends not only the soul era's investment in black community—the ethos she evokes in "F.U.B.U. [For Us By Us]"—but also its understanding of black interiority and solidarity as mutually enforcing rather than conflicting energies.

Still, it is Solange's voice, by turns wisp-thin and heavy, that provides the album's emotional center. In an interview published shortly after the release of *A Seat at the Table*, Beyoncé asked Solange about her vocal choices on the album: "The tone of your voice, the vulnerability in your voice . . . the sweetness and the honesty and purity. . . . What inspired you to sing in that tone?"[83] Solange replied, "It was very intentional that I sang as a woman who was very in control, a woman who could have this conversation [about race and American culture] without yelling and screaming, because I still often feel that when black women try to have these conversations we are not portrayed as in control, emotionally intact women."[84] In her dialogue with Brooks, however, Solange explained her use of falsetto rather differently: as enacting the traumatic "out-of-body" experience she felt when bombarded by images of black death.[85] These divergent descriptions reflect the tension between control and lack thereof that animates *A Seat at the Table*. If Solange's falsetto at times communicates emotional restraint, it also signals a feeling of being unmoored that she describes in the song "Weary": "You're leaving not a trace in the world / But you're facing the world." The album does not decide whether such trauma can be relieved, but Solange's work with other artists does offer the kind of reprieve that she cannot, and should not have to, provide for herself.

Her vocals are weightless on "Weary," where she breaks line endings up like lace and serenades the listener as a disembodied voice: "I'm gonna look for my body, yeah / I'll be back real soon." On this line, her voice arcs up and back down to where she started as if performing the promised return. But the lyric is uncanny, suggesting as it does not only a person alienated from her body but a ghost cast out into the world at which she levels a quiet critique: In a world that so devalues black women, if she were to go missing, who else would go find her? She goes to look for herself. Solange's voice gains heft and height on "Cranes in the Sky," which she begins in a feathery falsetto before moving into her chest voice. After narrating her efforts to "drink," "dance," "read," "write," and "cry" away an unnamable pain, in the refrain, she simply repeats "away," moving higher and higher into her falsetto. The passage recalls Riperton's use of coloratura, as well as its complex meanings: Solange's movement from earthy to ethereal vocals implies that music might help her forge a way *through*, if not away from, pain. Her voice stays light—but whether to express the "out-of-body" weightlessness she described to Brooks or the dignified refusal to raise her voice that she described to Beyoncé, it is hard to tell.

If the music itself refuses to reconcile that tension, Solange's videos more assuredly represent the potential to turn pain into power. Directed by Solange and her husband, Alan Ferguson, and shot by legendary cinematographer Arthur Jafa, the videos feature the singer and other black men and women in muted hues and mixed landscapes—a sunroom with trees, mountains with rock walls. The figures strike positions of repose, sometimes confronting the viewer, but more often being quiet and still with each other, evoking Rainer Maria Rilke's description of music as the "breathing of statues."[86]

The statuesque figures come to life especially when guest artist Sampha enters the picture. The famously introspective singer-pianist accompanies Solange on "Don't Touch My Hair," a song whose mixture of declarative rhetoric and pensive tone exemplifies Solange's public claim to black interiority. She and Sampha sing, "What you say to me?" over and over, repeating the line until the answer doesn't matter. The video shows them looking jubilant beneath a bright blue sky. Sampha turns his head to the sun, while Solange breaks from her careful choreography by dancing in a way that looks fun and spontaneous. This might be the only time, in any of her videos for the album, when she smiles. By using Sampha's deeper tone to bear some of the song's sonic—and, the video indicates, emotional—weight, Solange reverses the gender dynamic whereby Hayes's backup singers allow him to stay cool. "Don't Touch My Hair" stages a uniquely affirming use of falsetto because Solange's voice does not labor alone.

In a profile of Solange written by Salamishah Tillet for *Elle* magazine, Griffin tells Tillet that Solange's "speak-softly approach" recalls artists such as Riperton and Deniece Williams—singers who, by "quieting things down, call for a kind of introspection on the part of the artist and the listener."[87] Particularly in the midst of a "traumatizing" moment when black people are "bombard[ed] by images of violence," Griffin notes, Solange's "aesthetic reminds us that we are people who have an interior self that needs to be tended to."[88] I have suggested that Solange's use of falsetto itself bespeaks the pain of that live and mediated assault and that her album tends to the interior not only by honestly expressing that pain but also by gathering others around the proverbial table to help share the weight of it. As Solange interviews her parents and enlists her friends to appear in music videos that she directs with her husband, she aims to establish her place at the table but also to convene the right people around it.

Departing from Riperton's discourse of positive thinking, Solange revealed to Brooks that she often wondered, while working on the album, "How much responsibility do I have to express optimism and resolution?" "I didn't always feel that," she said. "But I also wanted black people to feel elevated. So I am grateful to my mother and Master P for bringing that optimism [when I didn't feel it]."[89] *A Seat at the Table* admits how hard it is to transform black women's pain into strength, the ideal of soul logic. But if Solange does not represent her own pain as a resource, she does represent other black people as such. Her mother comments, in one interlude, "It's so much beauty in being black. . . . I've always known that. . . . I've never wanted to be anything else." On another track, Master P defines "glory" as one's ability to live and create in a way "where you can go to sleep at night"; he concludes, "The glory is in you." As it was for Solange's soul-era forebears, the work of seeking and protecting that inner glory is a collective project: "For Us By Us." Through falsetto vocals and guest features that both unsettle and recenter the self, Solange performs a socially meaningful quest through the interior. So it is fitting that she links internal language with communal recovery when expressing her hope for the album: that it would serve as "a mantra to help us get to the other side."[90]

5 NEVER CATCH ME

False Endings from Soul to Post-soul

> Aretha, perhaps more than anything else, reflects a specific
> level of the Black female survivor's spirituality. A kind of
> endlessness. For this music and its people are movers and
> bound, I do believe, to endure. A kind of just going on some-
> where else. Changing. CLAYTON RILEY, 1973

How does one get to the other side without even knowing if another side
exists? The arrival of that place, which might get to us before we get to it,
that new start that turns out to be just what we needed—this is the gift
of the false ending, the musical practice to which I turn here. Technically
speaking, the phrase refers to the act of bringing a song to a close and then
striking it back up again. Some artists in this chapter use false endings in
this way—as when Mahalia Jackson and Otis Redding tack surprise choruses onto their songs in live performance and Aretha Franklin extends
"Dr. Feelgood" into an unexpected sermonette. But other artists I discuss
here perform different modes of declension and revival—as when James
Brown physically collapses and staggers back to his feet when performing
his famous "cape trick" and when Marvin Gaye subtly reprises musical
elements across the course of *What's Going On* (1971).

Each of these false endings structurally enacts—and, thanks to its
roots in gospel practice, helps to sacralize—soul's message of black group
resilience. Each offers a glimpse of the "kind of endlessness" Riley hears

in Franklin's music—this is what it looks and sounds like to suddenly bounce back. This spiritual survivorship is predicated on change: for Riley, it signals "a kind of just going on somewhere else. Changing." Indeed, we might say that the false ending signals the endurance one needs to keep changing—not only oneself but also the world. When Baraka writes, in the passage from "The Changing Same" I have now quoted twice, that the New Black Music "wants to change forms," I take him to mean both that the music wants to change its own form and that it seeks to alter the social conventions or forms of the world that it enters.[1] In what follows, I trace both impulses, showing how the false ending formally mutates over time and, in so doing, enacts different kinds of social critique.

We can see the false ending as a mode of critique by comparing it with the encore. Whereas the encore displays an artist's gracious willingness to extend the parameters of a given performance in response to a crowd, the false ending expresses the artist's more oppositional insistence on excess and refusal of containment. "You're involved and you don't want to quit," James Brown said of his cape trick: "That's the definition of soul, you know. Being involved and they try to stop you and you just don't want to stop."[2] The false ending, then, no less than the ad-lib, is performed "at one's pleasure": it is a self-determined overcoming of boundaries, including social expectations around gender and race. This oppositional charge is, moreover, what distinguishes the false endings I trace here from other forms of musical resilience shrewdly theorized by Robin James. In *Resilience and Melancholy* (2015), James convincingly argues that contemporary pop music's fade-and-soar structure models a form of compulsory resilience that emphasizes individual responsibility over systemic reform.[3] But the performances I discuss here—by Jackson, Brown, Redding, Franklin, and Gaye—do not model the self-restarting capacity of the good neoliberal subject; instead, they issue resilient *critiques* and posit alternative spaces. The false endings Jackson, Brown, and Redding perform in the late 1950s and 1960s can be heard to issue veiled critiques of US hedonism, compulsory labor, and antiblack violence, respectively; in the early 1970s, Franklin and Gaye reshape the practice to express black female authority and black rage. Although it might seem counterintuitive, Franklin and Gaye make more legible social statements through subtler false endings. By turning the showman's trick into a more ruminative dialogue among themselves, their audience, and the divine, Franklin and Gaye enlist the spiritual power signaled by the false ending to create freeing, or at least truth-telling, spaces. Still, I hear Gaye as turning away from Franklin's affirmative ethos toward a disenchanted cyclicality; in so doing, he prefigures contemporary black artists' more haunted false endings, as I suggest through a reading of the electronic artist Flying Lotus.

Without Stopping:
Mahalia Jackson at Newport

At age sixteen, Mahalia Jackson left her hometown of New Orleans for Chicago, where she lived with two aunts (her mother had died years earlier) and did what she could to make money. She worked as a maid, a hairdresser, and a vocalist with a gospel quintet before gaining international acclaim as the "Queen of Gospel." It was a genre that Jackson helped to popularize but also to develop; working with bluesman-turned-composer Thomas Dorsey, she set blues stylings of spiritual lyrics to a rocking Baptist beat. In 1947, her solo recording of Dorsey's "Move On Up a Little Higher" sold eight million copies and made her a star. Several gold records and a European tour later, Jackson performed at the Newport Jazz Festival in the summers of 1957 and 1958. These were the first years gospel singers were included on the festival program, alongside such luminaries as Miles Davis, Thelonious Monk, Dinah Washington, Louis Armstrong, and Duke Ellington. Jackson, while appreciative of the exposure, was apprehensive about performing for the mostly white, secular Newport crowd. Indeed, in later years she would refuse to sing at Newport altogether, feeling it had "become more of a beer festival" than a music event.[4] But in 1957, she defended her appearance there, explaining to clergymen and fans that the setting would not desecrate her music and that she would sing as part of Newport's Sunday gospel program. "Please tell everybody that Mahalia isn't ready to desert the church that made Mahalia," she told one reporter.[5] Jackson returned to Newport in 1958, but now on the condition that she would sing on Saturday at midnight (Sunday morning). That night, in the midst of a rain shower, Jackson and her trio—Tom Bryant on bass, Lilton Mitchell on organ, and her longtime pianist Mildred Falls—played a traditional song that Jackson had first recorded in 1954, "Didn't It Rain." Their performance exemplifies the kind of false ending soul singers would deploy in the coming decades, as well as the tactic's capacity to signify resilient critique.

Two minutes and two verses into the song, Jackson sings a characteristically dramatic, decisive cadenza—"Didn't it rain, rain, rain, rain, rain?"

The audience cheers.[6] But moments later, Falls revives the song and Jackson continues:

> Rained forty days and forty nights without stopping
> Noah was glad when the rain stopped dropping
> Knock at the window, a knock at the door
> Crying, "Brother Noah, can't you take on more?"
> Noah cried, "No! You're full of sin!
> God got the key, you can't get in."
>
> Listen how it's rainin'
> Will you listen how it's how it's rainin'
> Just listen how it's rainin'
> Just listen how it's rainin' . . . .

Although it takes them a moment to recover their rhythm on the other side of the false ending, Falls and Jackson appear to have planned this revival in advance. Regardless of how premeditated it might actually have been, their "sudden" continuation of the song implies that Jackson isn't done getting the spirit—or, rather, that the spirit isn't finished with her. She and Falls thus carry onto the Newport stage the more elastic sense of timing allowed by a black worship context and a gospel performance tradition where the music is composed of what musicologist Mellonee Burnim calls "expandable units of time."[7] "I'm used to singing in church," Jackson once noted, "where they don't stop me until the Lord comes."[8] She was speaking of the challenge of fitting her music into a recording session, but the need to stop was also intrinsic to secular concert settings. She strains against it here.

In so doing, Jackson enacts both the promise and the portent of the song—which, despite its upbeat tempo and cheerful tone, is a rather harrowing account of the flood, described in Genesis, which God sends to purify the earth of evil. Insofar as the world can be said to outlast those forty days of rain, the flood itself is a false ending. In the most optimistic reading, Jackson's continuation of "Didn't It Rain" embodies the hope of life in its wake. We might therefore hear her performing the kind of encouragement that also shaped her work offstage, as a public figure. In 1959, Jackson published a long essay in the *Saturday Evening Post* (later reprinted in her 1966 memoir) that concluded with a testimony to how she "got over." Longing to impress upon "young people"—especially, "young colored people"—the power of God, she wrote, "I say to them, 'The Lord took me, and I was nothing, and He put me up. It can happen to you too. If the Lord can bring me this far—take me out of the washtubs and off my knees scrubbing other people's floors—then He can do as much and more for others.'"⁹

We might hear Jackson's false ending at Newport as similarly inspirational in its aims. But like the multifaceted covers discussed in chapter 2, the practice also invites a wholly other reading: it not only evokes postdiluvian possibility but also reinforces the song's central critique. In the song, it "rains forty days and forty nights without stopping," and Jackson likewise refuses to stop. Her incessant singing, in that sense, doubles down on the song's depiction of *consequences*, siding not with those who frantically knock on the ark, but with Noah, who reprimands them: "No! You're full of sin! God got the key and you can't get in."

This reading is particularly available to viewers of Bert Stern's documentary of the festival, *Jazz on a Summer's Day* (1960), which devotes equal screen time to Jackson's performance and to the laughing, dancing interracial crowd whose giddy reception of her music seems to justify Jackson's sense of Newport as a "beer fest." While Jackson appears to be enjoying herself, she might also be launching a covert condemnation of white American hedonism right in the belly of the beast, in the face of the blissfully ignorant crowd. We might see her operating in the mode of the trickster grandfather in Ralph Ellison's *Invisible Man* (1952), who "live[s] with his head in the lion's mouth" of his enemies, "overcomes 'em with yeses, undermine[s] 'em with grins, agree[s] 'em to death and destruction," and advises his grandson to do the same.¹⁰ Rather than make do with the given as it is, Jackson's false ending suggests that any "conclusion" can be undone and redone. Every flood, every battle, that seems like it is over might have only just begun. This is either an assurance or a threat, depending on which side you're on.

Going on Forever: James Brown's Cape Act

Jackson's fans in the late 1950s might have described her as "soulful," but they probably would not have said that she *had* soul. As I noted in the introduction, it was not until the 1960s that the word *soul* swung from modifier to noun and came to denote black resilience. James Brown was a central figure in this developing drama—an artist whose story, sound, and performance style made him a one-man manifestation of soul's narrative of overcoming. The self-designated "Godfather of Soul" and "Soul Brother No. 1" had picked cotton, shined shoes, and danced for spare change as a kid growing up in Augusta, Georgia. By the late 1960s, the *Amsterdam News* would report that he owned "500–1,000 suits, 300 pairs of shoes," several impressive cars, a "Victorian Castle in Queens, New York," an eighty-five-person production company, and two radio stations—one of which, WRDW in Augusta, he had once shined shoes in front of.[11] A self-taught organist, drummer, and bassist who had trained himself to become a "human dynamo" in performance, Brown's sense of having overcome had shaped him from birth.[12] He often said he'd been "born dead." He entered the world still and silent, until the desperate resuscitations of his aunt Minnie brought him to life. "One good thing about believing you were born dead," quips Brown's biographer R. J. Smith, "is you come to feel nothing can kill you."[13]

Brown's commitment to overcoming—defeating death, destitution, bodily limitation, and all his haters—was manifest in his infamous work ethic. "I don't mean to brag," he noted of the James Brown Revue in 1966, "but we're the only act that can and does work seven days a week, 365 days a year."[14] That's what he meant when he called himself "the hardest-working man in show business." Instead of performing mastery as the illusion of ease, as Philip Gourevitch notes, Brown "[made] the display of effort one of the most striking features of his art."[15] Just because he had overcome didn't mean he could rest.

Brown staged his own work and resilience most dramatically through his cape trick, a device he developed around 1961 but first presented to the nation during his set at the televised TAMI (Teenage Awards Music International) Show in 1964.[16] The year before, Brown's *Live at the Apollo* LP had enhanced his star power among black fans, but his crossover potential was still untested when he joined the impressive lineup of artists (the Beach Boys, Marvin Gaye, the Supremes) playing for a studio audience of screaming white teens. Still, Brown was confident enough to insist that his group perform last.[17] Instead, they were followed by show closers the Rolling Stones, in what Mick Jagger would later describe as the biggest mistake of his life.

Toward the end of their set, Brown and the Famous Flames—Bobby Bennett, Bobby Byrd, and Baby Lloyd Stallworth—do "Please, Please, Please," a song that Brown wrote and arranged. Brown drops to his knees five times in the course of this performance. After every fall, his announcer Danny Ray or one of the Flames drapes a cape over his shoulders and escorts him to the side of the stage, patting and fretting over him while Brown shakes his head in a manner both submissive and defiant. "They are distressed for his well-being," Smith writes, "and though in retrospect a cape is a weird way to express your concern, at the moment it seems like the only possible thing to do."[18] Brown allows himself to be managed for a moment before flinging his cape off and returning to center stage to resume his screaming, struggling, and pleading:

Please, please, please don't go
I love you so!

Brown repeats this fall-rise-cape-return routine with variations. After the second time, he strips off his jacket to reveal a tightly tailored vest. Upon his fourth return to the mic, he collapses before he even gets there but then rises and sings "please" thirty-seven times while jogging in place before falling again. What is consistent, Smith notes, is that Brown always falls to the ground and throws off his cape on the downbeat of a given measure: from within his frenzy, he keeps conducting the band.[19]

Incredibly, even when "Please, Please, Please" finally ends, Brown's set at the TAMI Show does not. He bids the audience farewell, but this is just another kind of false ending because, from here, he proceeds to perform "Night Train" for several minutes. In the midst of this song, he spins, drops into a split, exits; returns to dance again; *sits down* on the stage as if spent—"For a second I didn't really know where I was," he later admitted—then starts dancing again.[20] The televised routine was a representative, if abbreviated, glimpse into Brown's sets in those days, where "Please, Please, Please" could last twenty minutes, due to what Rolling Stones bassist Bill Wyman, with more biographical accuracy than he knew, called Brown's "heart-failure bit."[21] The group would follow that up with "Night Train," with its dance-off, dance-back-on ending. All this to close an hour-long set during which Brown never paused long enough to introduce a song.

Brown, like so many soul singers, was a gospel devotee whose musical education had begun in the church, and he described the cape trick as having "a Holiness feeling—like a Baptist thing."[22] The cape was at once a sartorial nod to black preachers like King Louis Narcisse and Brother Joe May (and to the flamboyantly cloaked white wrestler Gorgeous George) and a theological citation of the Holiness belief in spirit possession.[23] Smith is right to say that the "profound and wondrous force" by which Brown is possessed is "James Brown-ness, the intensity of being *him*."[24]

But Smith is perhaps less justified in *celebrating* this condition, because what was central to "James Brown-ness," at least in the 1960s, was Brown's determination to outdo the competition and kill it every time—even when that meant almost killing himself.[25] He often danced so hard that he needed to be replenished with an IV once offstage. During a weeklong run at the Apollo Theater in 1966, he collapsed twice due to overwork ("Many thought it part of his act," one reporter noted).[26] Brown's knees, which he showed writer Gerri Hirshey, were "scarred, furrowed, and discolored" from years of collapsing.[27] The show had to go on, whenever and as hard as it could. In that sense, Brown was not only performing resilience. He was also exposing the perpetual *need* for black resilience as a crisis.

The dream and the crisis were not his alone. Behind Brown's own labor was that of his employees. On the most basic level, Brown's bloody knees posed "a persistent laundry problem" for his wardrobe attendant, Gertrude Sanders.[28] Sanders was one member of Brown's forty-person entourage—a group of stagehands, personal assistants, women singers, and a twenty-person orchestra that Brown ran "like an infantry platoon," levying fines for such offenses as lateness ($100), drinking on the job ($50), and failing to shine one's shoes ($25).[29] In this way and others, Brown exerted an extraordinary degree of control over his own musical practice and product. The racial politics of that power grab were undeniable: "People of my origin hadn't been allowed to get into the *business* end of show business before," he notes in his 1986 memoir, "just the *show* part."[30] Still, it could seem, in the words of a 1965 *Ebony* profile, that Brown's "passion to succeed almost borders on pathological."[31]

Brown's performance at the TAMI Show—presented to the nation at a moment when his star was still ascending but when, at age thirty-one, he could not be called a very young man—testifies to the payoff of his work ethic and also to its costs. "I danced so hard [that night] my manager cried," he said. "But I really had to. . . . I was up against . . . pop artists—I was R&B. I had to show 'em the difference, and believe me, it was hard."[32] In the fifty years since his iconic performance, critics have uniformly applauded the virtuosity and stamina he displays. But one might see, in Brown's process of rising and falling, not only an exemplary model of black endurance but also a metacommentary on the excessive work required to "make it" in an industry built on black labor. Before long, Brown would innovate the form of his own music by making a single vamp the basis of an entire song. In songs like "Out of Sight," one could improvise on the vamp ad infinitum.[33] This practice, so foundational to funk, was the musical extension of

Brown's staged false endings: both suggested he could theoretically keep going forever.[34] But again, the question he was begging, while he begged his lover "please, please, please" not to go, was: At what cost? Other soul artists would raise the question in their own ways.[35]

Otis Redding: Trying Again

Born eight years after Brown and raised, like him, in poverty in rural Georgia, Otis Redding was a multi-instrumentalist and songwriter who shared Brown's bewildering charisma, stamina, and, to some extent, his valorization of self-sacrifice. While he wasn't one to hurl himself down on stage, Redding's no-holds-barred vocal style did require him to have throat surgery (a fate that Brown amazingly avoided) five years into his career. Redding was, also like Brown, an electrifying performer. "Even his best recordings give only a hint of his total impact on stage," wrote a *New York Times* reviewer who was clearly unprepared for, though appreciative of, Redding's "gyrating, strutting, . . . pelvis-shaking" act and his power as a "singer, showman and sex symbol."[36] What the reviewer was seeing was not, as many assumed, Redding's expression of his "natural" self—it was instead the result of retraining, of practice. As his biographer Jonathan Gould explains, Redding started out as a rather inert singer of ballads and worked to develop his dynamic style. "Marching in place to keep pace with the beat, pumping his fists in the air, striding across stages with a long-legged gait that parodied his 'down home' origins," Gould writes, Redding developed a "confident yet unaffected eroticism" and "a raw physicality that earned him comparisons to athletes like the football star Jim Brown."[37]

I have noted that such performance styles, as deployed by Brown, Redding, and Franklin, enacted soul logic by turning embodied labor into ascendant style. That singers like Hayes, Al Green, and Riperton would develop less physically taxing approaches to performance at the turn of the 1970s didn't undermine the radical charge of their predecessors' claims to space. Redding was born in 1941, the same year as Emmett Till; as Gould notes, he had been "raised in a world where any 'suggestive' behavior by a black male in the presence of whites was potentially suicidal."[38] In this context, soul men like Redding and Brown modeled a powerful form of sexual license. If their effect on black fans could be liberating, their impact on some white fans was mythic. As Grateful Dead founder Bob Weir noted of Redding's set at the 1967 Monterey Pop Festival, "I was pretty sure I'd seen God onstage."[39]

Redding helped to develop and came to represent a soul aesthetic known as the Memphis sound. That sound, which combined aspects of country, blues, and gospel—an easy pulse, minimal overdubbing, and simple lyrical statements—allowed more room than did Brown's for reflection and critique.[40] Take, for instance, Redding's address to his audience at Hollywood's Whisky A Go-Go in 1966. Pausing between songs in the midst of a typically demanding set, he announced, "We can do it all night *long*. I don't know whether you can make it or not! Sure was a groove that time."[41] And then, as if both proud but also resentful of the (sexualized) work his group had to perform: "Man, see how hard we have to work to eat? Man, we have to work *hard*." Through these brief comments, Redding makes explicit both the self-regard and the critique of labor conditions implied by Brown's cape trick. But Redding also, in this moment, presages the request he would make to Brown himself. In the mid-1960s, Redding asked Brown to help him form a union of all black entertainers. He explained his vision simply: "No more getting messed over by the white promoters and managers and people in the record business."[42] Brown declined to support the plan, he explains in his memoir, because he felt that a black musicians' union would replicate the segregated unions that already made black workers "second-class citizens"; such "separatism" would be "going backwards."[43] It was their last conversation before Redding's death.

Redding's epic performances of "Try a Little Tenderness" can be heard to issue a different sort of social critique. Popularized by Bing Crosby in 1933, the paternalistic ballad about the power of male affection to revive female morale had been covered by Franklin and Sam Cooke in the years preceding Redding's version. But both Franklin and Cooke had maintained its basic ballad structure, whereas Redding transformed it into a raucous emotional manifesto. His version became his signature song because it epitomized his gift for synthesizing the sentimental crooning of Cooke and Nat King Cole, the sanctified fervor of his early training in the Baptist church, and the bombastic flair of Macon's other hometown hero, Little Richard. Redding and the Stax band's 1966 studio version opens with a nod to the maudlin mode of earlier versions of the song. Interweaving horn lines arranged by Isaac Hayes set the scene as if drawing a stage curtain.[44] But when Al Jackson Jr. strikes up rim shots on the drum like a metronome, the band starts to build the kind of suspense the song's lyrics describe:

You know she's waiting, just anticipating
For things that she'll never, never, never, never possess, yeah yeah
But while she's there waiting, without them
Try a little tenderness

Gradually, like a group of friends adding their voices to a single appeal for kindness, the rhythm section fills in the space between the spare drumbeat and Redding's vocals: here comes the churchy organ, crossed with an acoustic piano, both soon joined by a chicken-scratch guitar, blaring horns, and hard-driving drums. At this point, Redding bends the lyrics toward the wordless intonations of the band: "*Got to try—ma nah nah—try—try a little tenderness!*"

"Tenderness" soon became the bring-down-the-house closing song of Redding's live sets. The musicians would rush through the curtain-drawing introduction like a formality, picking up speed until Redding was shouting, jumping, and stalking around the stage like a stiff-limbed preacher while demolishing the lyrics: "*ga-ga-ga-ga-ga-ga-gotta-tenderness!*" The group often played several false endings, drawing the song to a close and striking it back up again as Jackson and Falls had done—but here the point was less to evoke Redding's possession by the spirit than to show him in thrall to his own momentum. The song was an obvious choice to close out the sets of the Stax/Volt Revue, a European tour that brought Redding together with label mates such as Booker T and the MGs, Carla Thomas, and Sam and Dave. In fact, the tour marked the first time Redding shared the stage with the Stax house band (he had played shows with touring bands)—and, despite the musicians' irritation at Redding's tendency to speed his songs up when playing them live, the collaboration was stunning.[45] By the time they reached Oslo, Norway, on the last leg of their tour, they were performing at their peak.[46]

A Norwegian television documentary shows how, after playing "Tenderness" for about three minutes, Redding and the band seem to end the song, and the show as a whole. Redding hands his microphone to the Norwegian MC and exits through the curtain at the back of the stage, while the man waves and salutes "Mr. Otis Redding!" But within ten seconds, Redding reappears, retrieves the mic, and sings another two choruses: "You gotta hold her, hold her, tell her, gotta try a little tenderness, a little tenderness, a little tenderness, got to got to you got to you got to hold her, squeeze her, never leave her . . . *ga-ga-ga-ga-ga-ga-ga-ga-ga!*" The announcer, amused but unsure where to stand now that Redding has retaken the stage, seems not to have expected this. Neither does he anticipate Redding's second reappearance. By the time Redding has reemerged from backstage a third time (this instance is surprising in the way Brown's fifth rise-and-fall is: because it beggars belief that he could or would want to do it again), the MC has procured his own mic so he can stay out of Redding's way while still announcing the show: "Here he comes again!" Now, when Redding has sung his piece, the man is too far out of range to hand the mic back to, so Redding looks around, drops his mic on the floor, and waves a real goodbye this time to the stage-storming crowd.

The song, with its ad-libs, rapid tempo, and false endings, was a tour de force. Still, it must be said that there was something bizarre about Redding's version of "Tenderness"—about his decision to call for tenderness in a way that was so *un*tender. Singing (then shouting) about women but not to them, Redding would seem to replicate the very aggression he sought to remedy. But we can make sense of this irony if we consider a way in which Redding's performance of "Tenderness" was not about a woman at all. We might instead hear it—particularly in light of the fact that he had just added his voice to the civil rights cause by recording Sam Cooke's protest anthem "A Change Is Gonna Come" (1965)—as a veiled demand for proper treatment of black people. In this reading, black America itself would be the "she" who is "waiting, just anticipating" the change that Redding and his band want to effect. If one imagines Redding singing on behalf of those citizens subjected to gradualist approaches to integration and brutal antiprotest measures including dogs, water hoses, and death, it starts to seem not odd but wholly appropriate for Redding to shake the song's addressee by the collar and insist that he try—for god's sake—a little tenderness.

This is not to suggest that Redding himself intended the song as a political allegory, any more than Jackson meant for the crowd at Newport to see themselves as Noah's unlucky petitioners. But Redding's performances of the song did make a space for an otherwise verboten display of black male agitation. At a moment when even the most peaceful bids for racial equality could be viewed as attacks on white Southern mores—when simply sitting at a segregated lunch counter or entering an integrated school could be seen as a violent provocation—the show of *actual* black aggression could, of course, be a death sentence. This may partly explain the cathartic force of Redding's performances for his black fans, as well as for an expanding white fan base that might have sensed the power and rage that black citizens were often compelled to restrain.

The same could be said of James Brown's decision to extend songs like "Please, Please, Please" despite those who "try to stop you [when] you just don't want to stop."[47] But to hear Redding's "Tenderness" as a plea for inter-personal love and interracial civility is to locate, in his use of the false ending, a more precise political charge. The technique was a matter of showman-ship, to be sure. But it was also an enactment of critical resilience—a reminder that the struggle wasn't over when it seemed to be, that a band of compatriots could keep pushing, together, toward a change that some-times seemed like it would never come.

When Redding and his band played "Tenderness" to close their legend-ary set at the Monterey Pop Festival in June 1967, Redding clearly wanted to go on reprising it, but their allotted time was up: "I have to go, I don't want to go," he waved to the crowd as he left the stage.[48] His parting la-ment is haunting in light of the fact that he died six months later. On De-cember 10 of that year, the private plane carrying Redding and his touring band the Bar-Kays crashed into the frigid waters of Lake Monona in Wis-consin, killing nearly everyone on board. (His funeral, held just outside Macon, was attended by soul stars like Brown, Franklin, Wilson Pickett, Carla Thomas, and a young singer then known as Little Stevie Wonder.) Even the godlike icon couldn't keep pushing as long as he wanted to. But Redding's work, and in particular his unstoppable performances of "Try a Little Tenderness," served as a reminder that one still had to try.

Still Feeling Good: Aretha

I have suggested that Redding's 1966 recording of "Tenderness" was partly indebted to Franklin's lesser-known version of the song—a turn that Franklin repaid in full the following year when she revolutionized Redding's "Respect." In a similar dance between King and Queen, Frank-lin followed Redding in courting what he had called "the love crowd"—performing at the Fillmore West in 1971 as he had played at Monterey. I have shown how, in one performance of "Dr. Feelgood" at the theater, Franklin uses vocal ad-libs to draw the audience into a woman-centered experience. But I have not shown how she deploys the false ending in order to preach. At her March 6 performance, Franklin extends the song into a particularly poignant reprise.[49] The band draws the song to a close, but Franklin isn't ready to stop, so she keeps singing "yeah," ad-libbing a call-

and-response with the crowd: "People, if you understand some of what I say, can I hear you say 'yeah'?" "Yeah!" This goes on for about a minute while Franklin devises her next moves, which amount to perhaps the most beautiful and unexpected sermonic passages in American popular music:

> Sometimes, sometimes I get a little worried, yes I do
> Sometimes, every night I think, I get a little fearful about different
>   things, yes I do
> But ohhhhh! Just as sure as the sun rises in the morning
> I know that everything—I don't know if you know what I
>   know—but you need to know that
> If you don't never do nothing about it, everything's gonna be all
>   right
> Yeah, yeah, Lord, yes I said yeah . . .
>
> Some people, some people worry about whether they gonna wake up
>   in the morning
> Well, why don't you close your eyes and see? Uh-huh
> Some people worry about, if we're gonna get over this bridge or that
>   one
> And haven't even got to the bridge yet to see if we can walk across,
>   oh yeah . . .
> Some people will worry, talking about, "I don't know what I'm
>   gonna do if something happens to my child"
> Well, ain't nothing happened to your child yet! Wait and see. Will
>   you be able? Wait and see. Will you be able?
> Don't put worry on you before worry gets to you
> I said that! Yes I did
>
> And sometimes it makes me just wanna say, yes, Lord . . .
> Oh, you gotta keep your arms around us. You gotta do that for us,
>   Lord. Yeah, you gotta keep your arms of mercy all around us,
>   you gotta do that
> Go on and take us on home . . .
> Don't get worried before worry gets there. And everything—oh you'd
>   be surprised what big bridges you can meet when you get there
> Ain't it so? Yes it is . . . .

The sermonette (or what, in a black religious context, might be called a passage of "tuning up") extravagantly justifies Franklin's perennial claim that she never really left the church.[50] But the very structure of this performance, from erotic blues to prayer, makes an additional case: that a woman's sexual authority need not compromise her spiritual leadership but might actually fuel it. Herein lies a primary difference between Franklin and Jackson, her mentor and family friend. Both women used gospel techniques to bring sacred energy to nonreligious settings. But whereas Jackson's religious authority relied in part on her asexual, maternal self-presentation, Franklin's sexual agency was foundational to her spiritual clout. In that sense, her false ending advances a theory of the erotic life akin to that of Audre Lorde, who, in 1978, described the erotic as a crucial source of information and power.[51]

"Dr. Feelgood" establishes Franklin as an advocate of women's erotic fulfillment. But her sermonette displays other forms of authority too—what Clayton Riley called "the stunning quality of Franklin's emotional intelligence." "And by that I mean simply," Riley explained, "that she knows more than we do about so many, many sectors of emotional experience."[52] Franklin admits, in the passage, that she gets "a little worried" and "a little fearful" like anyone else. But she knows that "everything's gonna be all right." "Don't put worry on you before worry gets to you": she repeats the injunction twice, so that what begins as an admonition becomes an assurance of divine clemency, of a force that might take you beyond where you thought you could go—"You'd be surprised what big bridges you can meet when you get there." I have discussed Franklin's social commitments—her support of Angela Davis, her contribution to Spike Lee's *Malcolm X*. Those investments, while they were rarely explicit in her music, always add depth to it. They allow us to hear, in Franklin's reference to bridges, such tortured, bold crossings as that of the Edmund Pettus Bridge by civil rights activists marching to Montgomery, Alabama. They allow us to hear, in her reference to fear for one's children, a moment when black youth were on the front lines: integrating schools, joining freedom rides, or simply navigating hostile hometowns.

Franklin's sermonic continuation of "Dr. Feelgood" critiques those systemic forces that nurture fear and self-doubt. As Franklin's Detroit compatriot Marvin Gaye noted in 1974, "From childhood until now, I've been surviving in a state and society constructed to nurture fear and oppression for reasons that are obvious to all."[53] But Franklin's false ending also creates an alternative space of black women's erotic, emotional, and spiritual knowledge and faith.[54] Her false ending is therefore less oppositional and more generative than the others I have discussed: it goes beyond Jackson's tricksterism, Brown's metacommentary, Redding's defiance, and, as I will show, Gaye's critical lament because it stakes out a free black space. What such moments in Franklin's life and career reveal—and this is what made her the Queen, not only of soul music but of soul as a concept—is that her great subject was the exceeding of limits. Her willingness to extend her own vocal technique, to venture beyond herself, to strain to implausible heights, and revive songs that seemed to be over—all these strategies could look and sound like grace.

Going On: Marvin Gaye

In light of my claim that Franklin's sermonette creates a new space, distinct from "Dr. Feelgood" proper, we might ask what makes her move from blues to prayer a false ending instead of a new start. Her sermonette could, after all, be said to break with the song form instead of extend it. The answer comes down to postproduction formatting: the album *Live at Fillmore West* names both parts of the song "Dr. Feelgood"—not, say, "Dr. Feelgood" and "Interlude." (The version of the song I have discussed is not the one included on the album, although in both performances Franklin moves from blues to prayer.) The power of naming to segregate or suture musical units similarly shapes Gaye's *What's Going On*, an album released the same year as Franklin's live album and arranged as a suite of nine distinct tracks.

Gaye's album allows us to consider the false ending as a technique not only of live performance but also of studio recording. By reprising musical elements to create the effect of an album-length suite, Gaye and his collaborators developed a musical version of what critic Brent Edwards calls "serial poetics"—work that recursively returns to certain subjects and so refuses closure, rejecting the idea that one can ever have the last word.[55] Gaye's serial musical poetics highlight the provisional nature of any ending, the fact that what seemed to be over might always start up again. But, as with Jackson's performance of "Didn't It Rain," that potentiality is not always a good thing: the serial poetics of *What's Going On* reflect the seriality of hope but also of trouble. It's that negative possibility that Gaye would later capture in his persona of "Trouble Man"—the sense of witnessing what's going on now, what's *been* going on, and what might well persist.[56]

The album, in its very complexity, signals a moment of emergence for Gaye akin to those described in the previous chapter. Inspired equally by the jazz music Gaye loved and the hymns he had sung as a child, *What's Going On* was an act of creative and personal revival through which Gaye declared his artistic independence from Berry Gordy's Motown regime and made a kind of peace with his religious roots.[57] Gaye, another child of his father's church, grew up in Washington, DC, and sang with the doo-wop group the Moonglows before signing to Motown in 1961. He recorded a series of self-composed hits that helped to establish the label's sound, including vibrant duets with his soul mate Tami Terrell. But at the end of the 1960s, Gaye entered a period of depression compounded by his failing marriage to Gordy's sister Anna Gordy and his grief over Terrell's death from cancer. At this point, he revamped both his image and his sound. Later explaining his decision to stop wearing ties and grow a beard, he told biographer David Ritz, "Black men weren't supposed to look overtly masculine. I'd spent my entire career looking harmless, and the look no longer fit. I wasn't harmless. I was pissed at America."[58] Just as Isaac Hayes had done two years earlier with *Hot Buttered Soul*—a self-redefining concept album fostered by Hayes's own grief—Gaye rejected his hit-making formula to self-produce an album that, against all odds, became a commercial and critical success. Despite Gordy's resistance to the project (he especially hated the album's title track), Gaye managed to create what he described as a divinely inspired work driven by social rage.[59]

For the first time in his career, he addressed a series of current issues: the war in Vietnam ("What's Happening, Brother"), drug addiction ("Flyin' High [in the Friendly Sky]"), global warming ("Mercy Mercy Me [The Ecology]"), the economic injustice of urban poverty ("Inner City Blues [Make Me Wanna Holler]"). Burnim's principle of "expandable units" might therefore describe not only Gaye's principle of musical continuity on the album but also his multiplication of topical concerns: the sense of an artist who, having at last begun to speak the truth, might continue to address new subjects ad infinitum. The sheer range of the album's social ambition might have been overwhelming if the music itself had not radiated such care and restraint. Gaye and David Van De Pitte meticulously arranged strings, conga, bass, and vocal self-harmonizations, and Gaye adopted a quieter approach to suit his laconic lyrics. Perhaps inspired by Hayes and Green, Gaye kept his vocals smooth, and he sketched scenes of desperation with an economy rooted in the blues: "Inflation, no chance / To increase finance / Bills pile up sky high / Send that boy off to die."[60] Only at the end of that song, "Inner City Blues (Make Me Wanna Holler)," the last on the album, did he act out his desire to shout.

The album opens in impeccable style, drawing us into a house party where several friends—played by Gaye's musicians as well as members of the Detroit Lions—greet each other amidst the saxophone's main theme. (The banter recalls Hathaway's use of soul talk on "The Ghetto" and "Sugar Lee," a debt one speaker seems to acknowledge by saying, "Everything is everything.") That in-medias-res opening hints at the sonic flow that is so important to this album, which the composers create by staging little false endings, or re-soundings, over the course of the LP.[61] For instance, at the end of the last song, "Inner City Blues," Gaye reprises a line from the first track, "What's Going On": "Mother, mother, everybody thinks we're wrong / Who are they to judge us, simply because we wear our hair long?" He also crafts more immediate echoes by transposing the background harmony from "What's Going On" into the foreground melody of the following track, "What's Happening Brother." That false ending has not only aesthetic but also social implications, in that it suggests the bringing to light, on "What's Happening Brother," of an obscured interiority: the experience of Vietnam vets such as Gaye's brother Frankie, whose letters and conversations inspired the song. Here, Gaye and his collaborators' compositional practices, as much as the falsetto vocal work at which Gaye also excelled, enact the process I traced through chapter 4, of drawing black (male) interiority into public consciousness.[62]

Gaye's serial poetics on the album express the need to keep bringing into public discourse those realities and possibilities that were being suppressed by state-sanctioned reports ("Are things really getting better like the newspapers said?" he asks on "What's Happening Brother") and repressed by the music industry itself, through Svengali-style managers like Gordy.[63] In fact, we have Gordy to thank for the album's most defiant false ending. Gaye, while listening to the final mix of "What's Going On," allegedly grabbed the fader and pushed the volume back up for a few seconds before letting the song fade out. In light of Gordy's distaste for this particular track, engineer Steve Smith surmises that Gaye's decision to re-up it was the artist's "way of saying 'fuck you' to the company, and . . . more so to Berry Gordy. You think this song you hate is over? Surprise!"[64]

In order to pull off his makeover from romantic Motown hit maker to serious, spiritual artist, Gaye apparently felt he needed to mute one subject that was dear to his heart: sex. "We kept all the love and attraction out of it," Gaye's friend and colleague Elgie Stover notes: "There was no talk of men and women anywhere [on the album]."[65] *What's Going On* does not, in that sense, achieve the holistic vision of sexual and spiritual healing that Franklin creates. In place of Franklin's erotic group climaxes on such songs as "Amazing Grace," Gaye produces, on *What's Going On*, a kind of anticlimactic cyclicality that is at once heartening and demoralizing.

At the center of the album is "God Is Love." The song works as an answer to the questions raised in the previous track—"Who really cares? / Who's willing to try / To save a world / That is destined to die?" (The answer is God.) It also issues a new directive: "All He asks of us / Is we give each other love."[66] When Gaye repeats that line, he cuts it short and ends the song with these words: "All He asks of us, I know." But the music keeps going, segueing into "Mercy Mercy Me," so that the effect is to suggest a colon after "All He asks of us" and to imply that God himself is voicing the following lament and asking these questions "of us":

> *Whoa, mercy mercy me*
> *Oh, things ain't what they used to be, no no*
> *Where did all the blues skies go?*
> *Poison is the wind that blows from the north and south and east . . .*
> *What about this overcrowded land?*
> *How much more abuse from man can she stand?*[67]

The musical extension or false ending of "God Is Love" allows us to hear, in "Mercy Mercy Me," the voice of God himself fretting over his damaged creation.

But if we hear the song as a divine intervention in the way I have suggested, as a moment when Gaye draws God's own voice into the center of his album, we will nonetheless have to admit that God's entrance is anticlimactic. This is not a major epiphany but divine intervention as lament, where Jesus weeps but doesn't help. Then again, the divine voice that comes and goes might reflect the cyclical process by which one "gets" the spirit, or renews one's soul, time and again. Ultimately, *What's Going On* is best understood as both a spur toward insurgency—an album where the previously unspoken keeps surging back into song—and a lament for a world in which such struggle is a constant necessity. In a final gesture that tempers hope with despair, the album ends not with Gaye's appeal to God's unifying love in "Wholy Holy" but with his turn toward the "Inner City Blues."

It is fitting that Gaye's innovations to the false ending should take shape not onstage but through an album-length suite, because his relationship to live performance was vexed. He had always been a subtler performer than Brown, Redding, or Franklin. In his early years at Motown, he cultivated a refined bourgeois aesthetic that was often praised for its "class." But Gaye also suffered from debilitating stage fright and, later, from bouts of paranoia that kept him from the stage for years at a time.[68] Although he, like other soul stars, could move crowds to a state of "ecstatic captivity," he was unique in his willingness to admit his own frailty and rebuff his fans' expectations of him: "To stand out there and entertain people [night after night] gets to be so mechanical, so unreal," he told a reporter for *Jet* in 1973: "Put on the grin, tell the 'jokes' and do the little dance steps."[69] This was a far cry from the self-sacrificing ethos of James Brown. While Gaye, like every other artist in this chapter, worked himself to the point of exhaustion and hospitalization, he also prioritized his own needs. "I care about the people and the fans," he told another interviewer in 1981, "but I don't owe them a hundred percent of my time; I owe them my mind and my creativity and my purpose . . . , but I can't dedicate my entire being to [them]."[70] Here was the dance between self-exposure and withdrawal that defined Gaye's career—as well as, eventually, his politics.

In a stirring essay on Gaye's artistic and social commitments, Mark Anthony Neal contends that the trilogy of albums Gaye released in the early 1970s—*What's Going On, Trouble Man* (1972), and *Let's Get It On* (1973)—symbolized the gradual "demise of the black protest movement" in general and Gaye's "conscious retreat" from radical politics in particular.[71] After *What's Going On*, Neal writes, Gaye's response to "militarized and capitalistic patriarchy" was "to reconstruct himself as a sexualized patriarch in the guise of the black superstud."[72] Neal compares this move to the cultural work of Blaxploitation films such as *Shaft* (1971), which sought to suppress the reality of black men's socioeconomic disempowerment by broadcasting fantasies of their sexual prowess.[73]

But to compare Gaye's false endings with Franklin's is to see the seeds of this retreat or fatigue even earlier, in *What's Going On*. There, Gaye transforms sounds and lyrics in a way that suggests mutation and cyclicality, not the progressive, aspirational energy of Franklin's bridge-crossing creation of an alternative space in "Dr. Feelgood" or her dramatic advancement toward a new collective "home" in "Amazing Grace." Even as the divine enters *What's Going On*, as if to revive Gaye's efforts, the ongoing need for that intervention signifies soul weariness as much as what critic Ben Edmonds calls an unflagging "faith in the life of the spirit."[74] What does it mean to try to "save a world that is destined to die," as Gaye sings on "Save the Children"? What does it mean to keep anticipating a change that, in the fraught years following Cooke's protest song as well as Redding's and Franklin's versions of it, could seem to recede beyond reach?

Leaving: Flying Lotus's "Never Catch Me"

The specific brand of protest politics and revolutionary activity associated with soul did wane in the mid-1970s in response to the militaristic repression and capitalist incentives that Neal enumerates. That era initiated a shift, as I have noted, away from soul's logic of group encouragement and toward a valorization of personal economic fitness. That shift changed the meaning of resilience. The term now tends to signify one's ability to withstand the hardships of a world without public assistance, in a neoliberal context that privatizes success and failure as the result of good and bad decisions. What, if anything, can resilience mean for black artists in this context?

To explore this question, we might look to the work of Los Angeles–based electronic musician, rapper, and DJ Flying Lotus. In 2014, the artist, whose given name is Steven Ellison, released an extraordinary video for his song "Never Catch Me" (which features Kendrick Lamar). The video depicts a funeral for, and the resurrection of, two black children. In that way, it stages death itself as a false ending. But if the video dramatizes James Brown's ideal of perpetual rising, it also resists the positivity or self-satisfaction of neoliberal narratives of resilience. Instead, "Never Catch Me" brings youth, death, and play together in a way that suggests a haunting prescience in Gaye's back-cover image of *What's Going On*. There, Gaye stands on an empty playground in a black suit and tie, looking "as if he were attending a funeral."[75] In "Never Catch Me," the children have not been "saved" as Gaye had hoped, and the worst fears of Franklin's listeners, about which she sought to reassure them ("ain't nothing happened to your child yet"), have come to pass.

For the video, Ellison enlisted a team of West Coast artists: Tokyo-born director Hiro Murai (later known for directing the show *Atlanta*); Filipino American husband-and-wife choreographers Keone and Mari; and young African American dancers Will Simmons and Angel Gibbs. The video opens by panning through a dimly lit church that is sparsely attended by mourners. Photographs of a boy and girl are lovingly arranged alongside the coffins where they now lie, the boy dressed in a dark suit and the girl in a sky blue pinafore. But soon, as if channeling and refining the spirit of Screamin' Jay Hawkins (the singer who staged his own resurrection when performing his 1956 hit, "I Put a Spell on You"), the kids rise from their coffins and jump to the floor. They dance down the aisles, performing a sequence of movements that itself yokes generations—the flat-footed bounce of the 1920s Lindy hop and West Coast popping and locking. The two are invisible to everyone but each other until they exit the church and dance into a parking lot where other kids are playing. When Simmons and Gibbs drive away in a hearse, these kids trail the car down the street.

No one watching "Never Catch Me" in 2014 would have missed its relevance to the state-sanctioned murders of black people and the images of grieving friends and parents that helped to instigate the Black Lives Matter movement. (Everyone in the video is black.) At the same time, the video's locality—it was shot at a funeral parlor in Inglewood and a church in Koreatown—also highlighted those chronically underfunded spaces that had long been sites of death and neglect, whether or not the rest of the world was watching. In this local and national context, the resurrection that the video stages is also an insurrection—it's an exit from this world that also critiques the need to leave it, asking why the afterlife is so much better than life here. "One of these mornings," as Al Green sang, "we're gonna rise up singing." Or dancing, or running away.

This is not about transcendence. When "Never Catch Me" ends, the people in the church are still mourning, and the kids who had been playing are following the hearse. The closing shot of the children trailing the car could imply that they are likewise destined for premature death. Or maybe they just want to be where the action is, as close as possible to the point where the others ride away. Another, uncannier possibility: that the kids outside were dead all along, just waiting, holding vigil, to see the next ones off. Kendrick Lamar's verse on the song registers this uncertainty—he shuttles between curiosity, anxiety, and an embrace of death.[76] With characteristic ambiguity around his mode of address—Lamar might be speaking to himself, someone else, or an alter ego—rap's poet laureate of grief and grievance describes an "out-of-body experience" in which "you been died, you are dead." Like Lamar's verse, the video doesn't decide what kind of false ending death is. But it does reveal the painful, dangerous, and energizing proximity of the dead to the living—the sense in which "every goodbye ain't gone," and the departed aren't over, or other.

"Never Catch Me" is the centerpiece track of Flying Lotus's fifth album, *You're Dead!*, which was inspired by Ellison's reckoning with his own mortality as well as the deaths of his parents, his grandmother, and his great-aunt, who is the harpist and pianist Alice Coltrane. The album explores death and persistence through the serial poetics of flow. As reviewer Nate Patrin notes, "The fleeting cross-sections of chopped-to-bits fusion jazz strung together over the first five minutes [of *You're Dead!*] . . . flow from buzz-cluttered headspaces to spacious serenity so unexpectedly yet naturally that the seams never show."[77] This continuity, as on *What's Going On*, is both satisfying and anticlimactic. One track, called "Turkey Dog Coma," segues into a song called "Stirring," but while that sequence suggests a coming back to life, it's just another stage on the way to "Descent into Madness" and "Your Potential/The Beyond." In one sense, "the beyond" signals death: on "Dead Man's Tetris," Ellison and guest rapper Snoop Dogg imagine joining J Dilla, Freddie Mercury, and Austin Peralta in the afterlife. But it also signals Ellison's own principle of self-extension: having made his name by mixing "scattergun break-beats with abstract noise, using electronica, hip-hop and jungle," Ellison stretched out even further on *You're Dead!* to engage psychedelic soul and free jazz; he collaborated with pianist Herbie Hancock, saxophonist Kamasi Washington, and bassist Thundercat.[78] Finally, "the beyond" denotes Ellison's additive logic: "Never Catch Me" begins with a simple piano line that turns into chords that start to radiate reverb like late afternoon heat. On his last track, titled "The Protest," Ellison discloses the political stakes of his interest in legacy, extension, and persistence. That song consists of one repeated lyric, sung by Laura Darlington and Kimbra: "We will live on forever and ever." The implication is that, for black people, the mere act of surviving, or "living on," *is* a protest. But the song also hints at the insurgent strength in numbers one feels when the ancestors are counted among the living—all of them present "forever and ever."

Still, the organization of sound on this album generates just as much tension and ambivalence as the video for "Never Catch Me." Ellison's sonic permutations provoke hard questions about the "endlessness" that Riley once celebrated with regard to Franklin. Namely, where does the radical will to proceed—the persistence I theorized in the work of Redding, the defiance I read into Brown—become a sheer inability to stop? When does persistence reflect a *compulsion* to protest that is spiritually draining despite one's understanding that, as Angela Davis reminds us, "freedom is a constant struggle"?[79] These are the questions of a postrevolutionary era, and they point to the difference between false endings of the soul moment—which tend to valorize the continued capacity for critique—and those of the recent past, which additionally lament the ongoing need for resistance to violent oppression.

The difference might, however, be one of affect more than strategy. One last glance at the video for "Never Catch Me," with its false ending, concern with black community, and representation of the church as the space in which the soul is formally cherished but from which it might dance away, shows Flying Lotus and his collaborators extending ideas about black expressive culture that were popularized during the soul era. The art of that era continues to haunt, refuses to die, because it continues to offer models for translating black loss into virtuosic affirmation. Through such techniques as the false ending, black artists continue, albeit with varying degrees of fatigue, to indict the white supremacist system that makes black persistence a feat in the first place, while also insisting that, in the words of Alice Walker, "We are not over / when we think we are."[80] Picture a ledge to which you have come or been driven where suddenly there appears a bridge.

CONCLUSION "I'M TIRED OF MARVIN ASKING ME WHAT'S GOING ON"

Soul Legacies and the Work
of Afropresentism

If soul as a musical genre declined in the mid-1970s due to industry consolidation and corporate investment in the crossover market for black
music—phenomena that, for Nelson George, spelled *The Death of Rhythm
and Blues* (1989)—soul as an artifact is everywhere these days.[1] As of this
writing, each week brings news of another soul-related event or product:
a US stamp honoring Marvin Gaye; documentaries about Teddy Pendergrass, Sam Cooke, and Ellis Haizlip; Grammy Lifetime Achievement
Awards for Donny Hathaway and Sam and Dave; a Broadway musical
about the Temptations; the long-awaited film of Aretha Franklin's recording of *Amazing Grace*.[2] These are recent manifestations of what I have
called the twenty-first-century soul boom. Why are they emerging now?

The most cynical, psychosocial take would see these cultural products
as, in part, a means through which nonblack people might telegraph racial
sympathy. It's so easy to like the new Temps musical, to root for the group
on the come-up. For some, these soul productions might serve a function
similar to that of having voted for Barack Obama or of having enjoyed the
2019 Oscar-winning film *Green Book* and other interracial "buddy films"
that cater to the white desire for racial redemption by purveying the fan-

tasy that to love a single black person is to eradicate the sins of one's ancestors and the smear of ongoing privilege. Nostalgic soul-period pieces of the Trump era might also serve to imaginatively turn back the clock to an America made great again by black striving and the benevolent white citizenry who, in the wake of Jim Crow but before black music rose to global predominance, gave black people a shot without ceding them the whole show.

Less cynically, and more empirically, at this point in the twenty-first century, we are witnessing the deaths and fiftieth anniversaries of several key soul figures and albums, all of which provides occasion for in-depth reflection on soul artists and their work. New documentaries and interview-based histories like Aaron Cohen's *Move On Up* (2019) are teaching us a great deal not only about the music but also about soul artists' often suppressed political careers—the powerful and subversive work that icons like Cooke and Franklin did in support of black liberation.[3] Above all, insofar as soul artists working in the 1960s and 1970s were navigating a sociopolitical landscape that resembles our own—in its spectacular anti-black violence as well as its radical mobilization—the soul revival reflects an effort to reclaim soul artists as models of expressing black resistance, joy, and togetherness through the medium of popular song. Clearly, this is where I hope my own work on soul fits in.

When, as rarely, we have credited soul artists with playing a meaningful role in national politics, we have assumed that they did so by recording message songs—Cooke's "A Change Is Gonna Come," Nina Simone's "Mississippi Goddam," James Brown's "Say It Loud—I'm Black and I'm Proud." Those songs certainly helped foster black empowerment and pride. But the current soul boom invites a deeper examination of what soul is and how it works. The revisionist history I have advanced highlights black women, conceptual complexity, and musical craft; it therefore challenges popular and scholarly accounts of the concept that mystify soul artistry, simplify soul-era politics, and undermine black women's role in and leadership of this tradition.

I have defined soul as a logic of resilience that developed in the late 1960s and was enacted through a range of musical practices. That logic, no less than soul music in its various modes of revival, pervades black expressive culture today. In fact, the habit of thought that turns debilitation to advantage is so common as to be hidden in plain sight. Soul therefore persists in the way GerShun Avilez, following Wahneema Lubiano, describes black nationalism's persistence: as a "cultural logic" that outlives its radical origins to become a "general way of thinking among African Americans . . . , a 'common sense' that informs Black self-consciousness, intimate relationships, and cultural productions."[4] For instance, soul logic informs Toni Cade Bambara's 1980 account of the "championship tradition" that continues despite what Bambara called "the impulse to pronounce the Movement dead."[5] Defining that tradition with reference to Muhammad Ali, Bambara described how one "takes the telling blow on the chin and hits the canvas hard, can't possibly rally . . . can't possibly get up. So you do. And you keep getting up."[6] We have seen how soul artists like James Brown literalized that capability in performance—in Brown's case, through his practice of falling and rising. But hip-hop artists have kept it alive. We are hearing soul logic every time a rapper invokes hardship and hustle as the catalyst for his or her superior expressive skill. Soul logic animates popular shorthands like the phrase "and still we rise." And it shapes black feminist theories of pain, such as Akasha Gloria Hull's belief that black women, aided by "the universal divine," can turn traumatic experiences into "beauty and power"—an understanding that is also a premise of Oprah Winfrey's self-empowerment empire.[7]

In the decades since the 1960s, soul logic has likewise been central to scholarship in black studies. This should come as no surprise in light of the fact that several of the field's key figures came of age in the 1960s and channeled their radical energy into the task of institutionalizing black studies as a field.[8] Nathaniel Mackey, for instance, although he is mainly associated with the poetics of jazz, can be seen to advance soul logic when, in 1993, he describes how certain black aesthetic practices convey "impairment's power" and "enabling defeat."[9] That same year, Mackey's contemporary, the British scholar Paul Gilroy, explained how, in black Atlantic expressive cultures, "what was initially felt to be a curse—the curse of homelessness or the curse of enforced exile—gets repossessed. It becomes affirmed and is reconstructed as the basis of a privileged standpoint from which certain useful and critical perceptions about the modern world become more likely."[10] In his 2010 study, Darieck Scott reads a series of literary texts to show how black male rape and other forms of "historical subjugation" might "[endow their] inheritors with a form of counterintuitive *power*."[11] Six year later, in another important book, Christina Sharpe claims that black people's condition of being "in the wake"—"with no state or nation to protect us, with no citizenship bound to be respected"—might nevertheless "[avail] us particular ways of re/seeing, re/inhabiting, and re/imagining the world."[12] Each of these scholars espouses soul logic by locating an unlikely power in the state of dispossession.

Soul is also with us in the oddly intimate and impersonal space of social media. For one exemplary instance, we might turn to the critic Greg Tate. Although he is an icon of post-soul culture, Tate's writing—in books, essays, and, indeed, on Facebook—often embodies soul logic. In a 2016 Facebook post, Tate described visiting the then new National Museum of African American History and Culture (NMAAHC) in Washington, DC. Observing that several museumgoers marveled at black people's ability to survive the horrors on display, Tate wondered

> how any Non Black person could view even half that litany and liturgy of ongoing horrors and not wonder why we hadn't burned this place to the ground a long time ago. And truth is, Well, not for lack of trying: After all, we did attempt that course of action in about 100 American cities on April 4, 1968. But being fundamentally a race of epic poets, romantic beboppers, aerodynamic lindyhoppers and acrobatic abstract expressionists, we've apparently decided that LITERALLY lighting this AmeriKKKA thing up was too gauche and got back to burning down the stage as our preferred mode for going incendiary on these fools (Ferguson and Baltimore's recent '68 redux flambés notwithstanding). All the same, the epiphanal upshot of strolling through the NMAAHC's . . . 500 year deep maze/ emotional rollercoaster of radical transfiguration of That Bullschitte, was this: Never in the history of the world have one bountiful generous and way-too-forgiving people expended so much concerted time and energy beautifying their small corner of hell while trying to convince a rotten house full of homicidal lunatics, barbarians and zombies that white supremacy was a fiction doomed to failure—especially given the ingenuity, indomitability and utter Negrocity of Mama Afrika's most badass, superfly self-loving and Blackety-blue-black-rocking freedom swangin' Soul-testifyin' stolen progeny.[13]

Tate's rhetorical performance is indebted to the soul discourse that, as Portia Maultsby explained, was literally devised while the fires of the 1960s that Tate describes were burning.[14] Channeling soul's self-reflexive fabulousness ("superfly self-loving") and its way of turning existential horror into creative gold ("radical transfiguration of That Bullschitte"), Tate builds, in the manner of a gospel-trained soul artist, to his extravagantly recuperative claim that "never in the history of the world have one bountiful generous and way-too-forgiving people expended so much concerted time and energy beautifying their small corner of hell"—a line whose syntax itself enacts soul logic by rebounding from the "rotten house full of homicidal lunatics, barbarians and zombies" toward "the ingenuity, indomitability and utter Negrocity of Mama Afrika's . . . freedom swangin' Soul-testifyin' stolen progeny." If one were to accuse Tate of essentialism, of implying that some ahistorical essence fuels black people's survival and style, one would also have to acknowledge that his claims, and the way he presents them, are themselves rooted in a history: in an intellectual tradition of encouragement and critique, which music plays a key role in advancing and which I have called soul.

All this is not to suggest that soul has continued to signify the same thing for the past fifty years. Tate himself, in creating a paradoxically vibrant portrait of the US zombie madhouse—he devotes nearly as much rhetorical energy to describing white supremacist horrors as he does to detailing black ingenuity—defies the national tendency to bracket those evils as over-and-done-with relics housed in a museum. As we have seen in the work of Solange and Flying Lotus, resilience means something different in a post-soul age, when people's relative worth and dispensability are determined by their ability to recover from crisis, as if survival were solely the result of personal effort, cleverness, and will. The post-1970s musical performances I have considered claim community and critique the need for resilience in ways that challenge conservative tendencies to blame and abandon those who can't "get over." This is the kind of modulation through which the "changing same" of soul stays changing.

So if the term *post-soul* means anything to this study, it describes performance strategies that evoke what Baraka called "the time when we were winning" while also reminding us that the battle is not won.[15] These dual gestures shape what I call *Afropresentist* art.[16] As I have suggested, Afropresentists figure the present as the yet unfulfilled future of a radical past. I theorize this paradigm as an alternative to Afrofuturism, the concept first coined by Mark Dery in 1994 to describe African American art that "appropriates images of technology and a prosthetically enhanced future."[17] Whereas Afrofuturists often use mythic iconography (Sun Ra's ark, Parliament's Mothership) to conjure fictional elsewheres, Afropresentists use the past (in the works I discuss, "the past" means citations of soul music) as a resource for rethinking this world.

Rather than critique Afrofuturism as a framework, I mean to challenge its hegemony within black cultural studies. Afrofuturism is too often the go-to paradigm for talking about new world orders, as if radical change were necessarily an otherworldly project best situated on Sun Ra's "Other Side of Time" or in Janelle Monáe's futuristic Metropolis. The works I highlight, in contrast—by Beyoncé, Erykah Badu, and Monáe herself—seek to provoke change in the present. Turning back to the music each artist produced at an earlier stage of her career (an approach that itself resists the teleological tendency to privilege pop artists' most recent output), I outline the Afropresentist logic of Beyoncé's black Southern domestic and national drama *Lemonade* (2016); Erykah Badu's 2008 sonic gauntlet for the George Bush years, *New AmErykah Part One*; and Janelle Monáe's exploration of an outdated future on her 2013 album *Electric Lady*.

Although I focus on black women, I do not see Afropresentism as solely a woman's project. To give one example: D'Angelo and the Vanguard's 2014 album *Black Messiah*, which owes a great deal to Badu's *New AmErykah Part One*, is a work of Afropresentist art. The album takes its title partly from a sermon by Khalid Abdul Muhammad, which D'Angelo samples at the start of his song "1000 Deaths." In the sermon, Muhammad paints Jesus not as "some blue-eyed, blond-haired cracker Christ" but as a "black revolutionary Messiah."[18] Because Muhammad is a less recognizable cultural figure than, say, Malcolm X, he can't be as readily bracketed into the past; rather, this harder-to-identify, harder-to-place voice might be that of a leader organizing the next rally in a city near you. This is one example of how *Black Messiah* uses an archive of the past to critique and complicate the present.

To cite two examples more directly related to soul: in the 1990s, both Dr. Dre and the Wu-Tang Clan sampled Donny Hathaway's "Little Ghetto Boy" to issue dire prognoses of the present.[19] In the original song, Hathaway plays the role of an elder, instructing the "little ghetto boy" to get himself on track and assuring him that, if he does, "everything has got to get better." In Dr. Dre's "Lil' Ghetto Boy" (1992), which samples Hathaway's hook, Dre and guest rapper Snoop Dogg play the role of the boy; they chronicle life in the streets but omit Hathaway's statement of hope. So, too, does the Wu-Tang Clan, whose "Little Ghetto Boys" (1997) resumes Hathaway's moralizing stance by telling "fake" rapper-competitors to "grow up and take responsibility" but doesn't suggest that anything will "get better" if they do. These Afropresentist samples of Hathaway's work expose the absence, in rappers' own eras, of the black optimism and encouragement associated with soul.

There are many such examples of male Afropresentists. But women might lead Afropresentist innovation because they are less taken with "the future" in the abstract. What, after all, is *on* "the other side of time"? Where is the Mothership going? These have traditionally been women's questions—not, of course, due to women's failure of imagination or nerve but because of gendered historical conditions that have permitted and driven men beyond the pragmatic, immediate concerns of the home.[20] Afropresentists think beyond the here and now—but they do so by reckoning with "beyonds" that have come before, turning back to earlier freedom dreams to see what was lost and what might be regained.[21]

Beyoncé's Other Women

Whether declaring, with Destiny's Child, that she was a "survivor" whose hardships only spurred her to work harder, alluding to Sam Cooke's "What a Wonderful World" on her ballad "1 + 1," or playing a young Etta James in the Chess Records biopic *Cadillac Records*, Beyoncé has engaged with soul icons and logic throughout her career.[22] In 2016, the hardest-working woman in pop music also revived soul-era politics by storming the field at the Super Bowl Halftime Show with black women dancers dressed in Black Panther gear. On *Lemonade*, the visual album Beyoncé released shortly thereafter, she revived soul icons through visual references and musical samples. Her video for the song "Sandcastles" opens with a shot of Nina Simone's *Silk and Soul* LP, while a song from that album, "The Look of Love," plays in the background of the scene.[23] But Beyoncé's most compelling engagement with soul on *Lemonade* is her sample of Isaac Hayes's "Walk on By" on the song "6 Inch." Beyoncé's use of Hayes reveals that her album did not only speak to the racial politics of 2016 but also to the way that soul itself was being remembered at the time—namely, in works such as James McBride's James Brown biography *Kill 'Em and Leave* and Cynthia Mort's biopic *Nina*, which either wrote black women out of American popular music or portrayed them as secondary characters in their own stories.[24] This is to say that Beyoncé, who is a musical archivist in the spirit of Franklin, engages with the soul tradition to pay tribute to its icons and to write herself into their lineage, but also to challenge the gender politics of soul historiography.

"6 Inch" is an alternately sultry and skittish song that evokes Donna Summer's 1983 hit "She Works Hard for the Money" to describe a sex worker who "walked in the club" and "murdered everyone" with her style.[25] The track, as I have said, samples Hayes's 1969 recording of "Walk on By," the epic opener of *Hot Buttered Soul*. The song was composed by Burt Bacharach and Hal David and originally recorded by Dionne Warwick in 1964. I have discussed how *Hot Buttered Soul* transformed the sound of Southern soul by staging Hayes's defiant reemergence and space-taking in the wake of Martin Luther King's death. The reference to Hayes's album makes sense in part because *Lemonade* marks a similar moment of self-fashioning for Beyoncé—one in which she becomes an album artist, in contrast to a purveyor of hit singles (a redefinition that began with her 2013 album *BEYONCÉ*), and also emerges as an activist, in the context of the killings that sparked the Black Lives Matter movement.

Beyoncé samples Hayes's fierce network of ascending strings and in so doing harnesses Hayes's grand orchestral treatment to a woman's story. But she also samples the line sung by Hayes's three female backup singers: "Walk on."[26] Those singers are Pat and Diane Lewis and Rose Williams, a group that Hayes amusingly yet narcissistically named Hot Buttered and Soul and who sang the backing vocals for several of his hits on Stax. By looping these women's vocals, Beyoncé amplifies the women's voices within Hayes's work. She might even be heard to hint at other black women "behind" it—Dionne Warwick, but also Carla Thomas, who, as I have noted, was overshadowed by Hayes, although her hits helped to establish Stax as a Southern soul label in the first place. There is one other way in which *Lemonade* revives the muses or ghosts of the soul tradition: by inviting us to read the album as a chronicle of her marriage to Jay-Z, Beyoncé creates the most radical airing of a couple's dirty laundry since Marvin Gaye's 1978 breakup album for Anna Gordy, *Here, My Dear*. Beyoncé, in telling her story from a woman's perspective, invites us to imagine Gordy—whom Gaye had left for the much younger Janis Gaye—writing back.

By reviving these women as spirits or shadows within *Lemonade*, Beyoncé forges a sisterhood of rebels. I have suggested that soul music, like the blues, is filled with "other women" (and men) that threaten monogamous coupledom. On the surface, *Lemonade* extends this tradition: its central crisis is the cheating man, often read as Jay-Z himself, whose infidelity motivates the album's Afrodiasporic journey from injury to healing. But *Lemonade*, no less than the earlier love triangle songs I have discussed, also draws women into relationship with one another. Whereas Hayes bemoaned the confusing pull between "One Woman" and another and Nina

Simone imagined both being and competing with "The Other Woman," Beyoncé takes the other women who should be her competitors and makes them kin.

The *other* "other women" of *Lemonade* appear in a section of the film called "Resurrection," which features the mothers of several black boys and men killed by white vigilantes and police. Trayvon Martin's mother Sybrina Fulton, Eric Garner's mother Gwen Carr, Michael Brown's mother Lezley McSpadden, and others are seated in a darkened room holding pictures of their sons. Here, the album's theme of personal betrayal opens onto the issue of state brutality. The resurrected memory of the sons' deaths and the mother's unspeakable pain spurs rebellion in the form of the film's Southern gothic women's uprising. At the end of the video for "6 Inch," Beyoncé stands before a burning plantation house at night. The camera slowly pans out to reveal several other black women behind her. The shot literalizes and collectivizes the lyric about the woman in "6 Inch" having "murdered everyone" in the club. Musically, Beyoncé concludes the song by echoing the backup singers' "Walk on," but she changes the lyric to "Come back." Repeating the call like an incantation, she might be heard to address an absent lover, but she could also be hailing other women—those voices in the background of the soul tradition, and in the backrooms of plantations. To come back and do what? One answer is, to help the community heal. Another is, to help burn shit down. These are not necessarily different.

The Punctuality of Erykah Badu

Speaking of unsung muses: Although she is seldom credited with being a precursor to Beyoncé and other contemporary artists, Erykah Badu's sonic experimentalism, Southern hipness, queenly persona, and innovative activism all prefigure the work Beyoncé does on *Lemonade*. Badu represented her own soul ethos of overcoming most dramatically in the false ending to her 2010 video for "Window Seat," where she staged her own JFK-style assassination and resurrection.[27] But that soul ethos has long shaped her approach to sampling and covering other artists' work.

Badu's presentist re-creations of her musical antecedents, and of her own artistry, help to explain her longevity vis-à-vis other neo-soul artists who launched careers at the same time she did, in the late 1990s (Jill Scott, Lauryn Hill, the long-absent D'Angelo). In 2015, for instance, Badu remixed Drake's "Hotline Bling" in an effort, she told Ryan Dombal of *Pitchfork*, to "communicate with [her son Seven's] generation."[28] The point wasn't just to connect with the kids by covering a cool song; it was, as Badu put it, to reboot her musical "hard drive": "My truth is relevant and my songs are relevant," she explained, "but I have to recalibrate myself and speed up my vibrations so that I can communicate with the voice of this generation."[29] Badu's concern with frequency and timing has shaped her work across two decades, from the retro-soul aesthetic of her debut album *Baduizm* to more local moments like the Madlib-produced track "The Healer," which honors J Dilla's mode of hanging just behind the beat.[30]

But Badu's just-in-timeliness (to recall her majestic track "Out My Mind, Just in Time") was never more salient than on *New AmErykah Part One*—an album that so brilliantly captured the miserable end of the George W. Bush years that several journalists traded their usual "best of the year" accolades for "best of the decade" claims. The album's lead track, "AmErykahn Promise," samples and remakes in Badu's image the Roy Ayers Musical Production song "The American Promise." RAMP released the song in 1977, at which point it served as a belated rejoinder to Lyndon B. Johnson's belated support for the civil rights movement. In the wake of the vicious attack on activists marching from Selma to Montgomery in March 1965, Johnson was moved to pass the Voting Rights Act, which, he said in a speech to Congress, would fulfill the "American promise" of democracy and the "full blessings of American life."[31] "We shall overcome," Johnson assured members of Congress as well as the American public, expressing his alliance with Martin Luther King and other activists.[32]

In RAMP's 1977 track, the American promise is made not to the people, but by them. Singers Sibel Thrasher and Sharon Matthews articulate the costs of citizenship in the form of their bodies and souls: "I'll give you my eyes / I'll give you my ears . . . I'll love you tooth for tooth and eye for eye."[33] The only possible resistance to this regime—alluded to via the Old Testament dictum of "an eye for an eye, a tooth for a tooth"—is self-destructive fragmentation, the obverse of Simone's loving, piece-by-piece reclamation of her body in "Life."

In Badu's version of the song, which displays the non-oppositional relationship to original recordings discussed in chapter 2, RAMP's track scores a monologue by Om'Mas Keith, who plays the role of a charismatic disc jockey/evil train conductor welcoming passengers (and the listener) to a capitalist dystopia where "we love to suck you dry."[34] Over the sound of a crying baby—another perverse throwback to soul-era productions such as Hathaway's "The Ghetto"—Badu and Keith outline the price of the ticket to the American dream. "All you have to do is make a promise," Badu says. "And stay on your grind," adds Keith. Then, elaborating the grind's shaming logic: "See what you can do with a little bit of work and effort, people?" With its dystopic imagery, sonic distortion, and outsized villains (Keith's response to one insurgent passenger is to extract "a brain tissue sample" from her), "AmErykahn Promise" is ripe for designation as an Afrofuturist work. But the song's most powerful effects are Afropresentist: Badu highlights RAMP's own futuristic sound and underscores the lasting relevance of the group's vision of American brutality. Badu's critique resides in the fact that, thirty years later, RAMP's song is still relevant. Just as RAMP had, in 1977, exposed the brokenness, or the inadequacy, of Johnson's 1965 promise, Badu highlights the present and ongoing failures of American policy to address the material, psychic, and spiritual costs of (black) American life.

Those costs include buying into patriarchy. Ever since her emergence as a neo-soul icon in the 1990s, Badu has carried the torch for a certain kind of black feminist politics, becoming what Zandria Robinson convincingly describes as a twenty-first-century blues woman singing to and for those on the margins.[35] But Badu has also played the role of conservative custodian of patriarchal black family values (a role that scholar Jason King noted as early as 1999).[36] She has publicly supported alleged rapist R. Kelly, applauded stricter legislation regarding girls' school dress codes, and released a healing "mixtape for the world" that was dominated by the songs of male artists—as was her own 2015 telephone-themed mixtape, *But You Caint Use My Phone.* That album featured Badu's remake of "Hotline Bling" as well as her covers of songs by New Edition, the Isley Brothers, Usher, and Tupac Shakur, and it included several male guest rappers to whom Badu played the gendered role of backup singer.[37] So it would be a mistake to imagine that Badu's—or any other artist's—Afropresentist art is necessarily more progressive than Afrofuturism. Unfolding as it does on the terrain of this world, Afropresentism is too enmeshed in present contradictions to transcend them. But Afropresentist works do defy progressive narratives that frame the present as the result of having overcome.

Janelle Monáe's Pop Afterlives

It is admittedly cheeky, if not downright perverse, to claim Monáe as an icon of Afropresentist art, since she has been the one woman consistently cited to prove that Afrofuturism is not a wholly male (though it is often framed as a male-dominated) tradition. By the time Monáe's album *The Electric Lady* was released, in 2013, the term *Afrofuturism* had become a shorthand for all things black and imaginative, and Monáe had established herself, with her android alter ego and high-tech concept albums, as a poster girl for the concept. The third installment in Monáe's Metropolis Saga, *Electric Lady* continues the postapocalyptic story of a rebellious android pop star (Cindi Mayweather) who falls in love with a human. But the album, which Monáe produced along with her Atlanta-based Wondaland Arts Collective, is less about androids and fantastic other worlds than it is about the unrealized futures that shape the present. "I'm tired of Marvin asking me what's going on," Monáe sings on "Q.U.E.E.N.," a song that features Badu and follows the elder artist in revealing the lasting relevance of soul-era critique.[38] If we are the beneficiaries of past struggle, Monáe suggests on the album, we are also the inheritors of long-deferred dreams.

The album's title turns a glorified object into a glorious subject, remaking the male fantasy theme park of Jimi Hendrix's *Electric Ladyland* into *The Electric Lady*, an agent who claims a term (*lady*) historically reserved for white women and seizes the creative power that electricity connotes. But the album title also evokes an era when *electric* became a keyword in American culture—when a nation emerging relieved from the 1970s energy crisis would create the "Electric Slide" and *The Electric Company* and raise a generation of kids with neon sneakers and astronaut dreams. Welcome to the future of the past.

On the first song, "Givin' 'Em What They Love," Monáe presents herself as the unlikely future or inheritor of a masculine musical past. She issues an outlaw's boast in the image of Hendrix's "Voodoo Child"; spins out a catalog of swaggering tropes, from Peter Tosh's "stepping razor" to Biggie's *Ready to Die*; and pays sonic homage to Lenny Kravitz and Led Zeppelin before showing off her guest artist, Prince. The last point merits pause, since the competitive Prince seldom played the role of guest artist to anyone. But the album moves right on from Prince to Monáe's collaboration with Badu, "Q.U.E.E.N." That song serves as a transition from Monáe's male-dominated rock overture to the rest of the album's woman-centered thrills. Before long, on the title track, the sonic middle ground that has been missing surges in like light through the album cover's red neon sign: "Electric Lady." "Electric lady you're a star / You got a classic kind of crazy / But you know just who you are . . . Y'all make me so proud," Monáe sings, as if conspiring to make irresistible a future of women celebrating other women—as, indeed, Beyoncé would later do on *Lemonade* and Monáe herself would do on her 2018 album, *Dirty Computer*.[39]

But this woman-centered celebration is not only a future projection; it is also an inheritance. Monáe's dense network of musical reference serves as a reminder that women have been cheering on, admiring, and seducing each other in black popular music ever since blues queen Bessie Smith sang about her "good jelly roll" in the 1920s.[40] Indeed, even "Givin' 'Em What They Love," with its in-your-face machismo, can be heard to pay tribute to women's work. The song's opening musical figure is a chain-gang grunt that echoes Grace Jones's *Slave to the Rhythm*, an album released a month before Monáe's birth, in 1985; and Monáe's gritty vocals can be heard to recall rock icon Betty Davis as much as any male star. But the most powerful shadow figure in Monáe's pantheon of genius black women is Lauryn Hill. Herself a child and student of soul, Hill has, to date, released only one studio album, *The Miseducation of Lauryn Hill* (1998), which Monáe evokes through the contralto vocal reaching and martial drums of "Victory," which recalls Hill's "To Zion," as well as through her reference to "marching to the streets" (on "Q.U.E.E.N."), which revives Hill's determination to "march through these streets like Soweto."[41]

Of all the genres Monáe has mastered, the R&B song of lost love—the ultimate sign of an unrealized future—might be her strongest suit. "No matter how the story's told," she sings along with a rising gospel choir, "We were like rock 'n' roll / We were unbreakable, I want you to know."[42] *Electric Lady*, with its record-correcting ambitions and long musical memory, reminds us that "Sally Ride," the title of one track, was a goad before it was a proper name—that the future once sounded like Wilson Pickett's "Mustang Sally" ("ride, Sally, ride") and like Aretha Franklin's bold sanctifying of that lyric in "Spirit in the Dark," before it looked like the first woman in space.[43]

With these histories in mind, one can hear *Electric Lady* as a field of unrealized futures. There is the aborted future of Hendrix, who died two years after releasing *Electric Ladyland*. There is the ambiguous future of Lauryn Hill in the decades since *Miseducation*. There is also the fractured promise (and increasingly fraught legacy) of Michael Jackson, whose work with the Jackson 5 is so palpable in the young striver's sound Monáe affects on "It's Code."[44] Monáe's investment in pop afterlives explains why her album ends with "What an Experience," a song indebted to 1980s synth-pop that references "Red Red Wine." Neil Diamond first released "Red Red Wine" in 1968, and UB40 made it a hit in the mid-1980s. The song's recording history therefore bridges the era of Monáe's birth with that of her mother. "You're the reason I believe in me," Monáe sings to her mother on the Stevie Wonder–inspired track "Ghetto Woman."[45] The 1968–84 trajectory of "What an Experience" asks what it means to "occupy the space," as Barack Obama writes in his first memoir, "where [your parents'] dreams have been"—or where your musical predecessors might have been heading.[46]

These issues of inheritance are urgent at a time when the most basic material gains of the civil rights and Black Power eras—economic mobility, voter enfranchisement, educational and residential equality—are mistaken as the goals of what was meant to be a long-term moral revolution. Even the material gains are, of course, under assault. And many black Americans are struggling to achieve yet more basic rights, such as the right to not be shot by police officers when their cars break down, or when they are playing with toy guns, or when they are at home asleep in their beds. In this context, Afropresentist art makes manifest what theorist Avery Gordon calls "the abolitionist imaginary": a "refusal to wait."[47] ("Stop shooting us," reads a sign in Beyoncé's video for "Formation.") Beyoncé, Badu, and Monáe all use soul citations to reconsider what dreamers of prior eras—those who boycotted buses, went to jail, started breakfast programs, rioted at Stonewall, and created the sound and meaning of soul—might have wanted. The basic question these artists ask, and that this book's revisitation of soul is meant to provoke, is this: If we are the future that past artists and activists dreamed of, how much freer were we all supposed to be?

NOTES

Introduction: Keeping On

Epigraph: Amiri Baraka, "Toni" (eulogy for Toni Cade Bambara, 1996), in *Eulogies* (New York: Agincourt Press, 2002), 232.

1 Gladys Knight and the Pips, "I've Got to Use My Imagination," comp. Gerry Goffin and Barry Goldberg, prod. Kenny Kerner, *Imagination*, Buddah, 1973.

2 Edward Patten, qtd. in James Johnson, "Gladys Knight and the Pips: A Day with Miss Knight," *New Musical Express*, June 2, 1973.

3 The group later sued Motown for "miscalculation of royalties and illegal management" ("Gladys Knight, Pips Sue Motown for $1.8 Million," *Philadelphia Tribune*, March 8, 1975).

4 Phyl Garland, review of *All I Need Is Time* by Gladys Knight and the Pips, *Ebony*, December 1973, 28.

5 See Ian Dove, "Gladys Knight Finding New Listeners for Soul," *New York Times*, November 9, 1973.

6 Mellonee Burnim shows how gospel songs themselves mimic the structure of traditional church services by moving "from the simple to the complex"; musically, this means "gradually adding layers of hand-claps, instrumental accompaniment, and/or solo voices" ("The Black Gospel Music Tradition: A Complex of Ideology, Aesthetic, and Behavior," in *More Than Dancing: Essays on Afro-American Music and Musicians*, ed. Irene V. Jackson [Westport, CT: Greenwood, 1985], 163).

7 Merald Knight, qtd. in Richard E. Prince, "Gladys Knight and the Pips," *Washington Post*, March 10, 1972. The group's longevity was especially unique, Prince wrote, "in an industry where the pressure of egos, finances and fickle public tastes make most groups last only long enough to take the money and run."

8 Gladys Knight, qtd. in B. J. Mason, "Gladys Knight and the Pips: It's a Family Affair," *Ebony*, June 1973, 178.

9 See, for instance, Knight's stated desire in Mason's *Ebony* profile to "be the example a young black woman can follow without destroying herself" or "going astray" (Mason, "Gladys Knight," 178), as well as the several images of the Pips as "family men" enjoying time with their wives and children (178, 179).

10 To argue for the prevalence and utility of this understanding of soul is not to deny other meanings. Other definitions include the spiritual life force expressed through black people's truthful "description of the world" (Amiri Baraka, "The Phenomenon of Soul in African-American Music," in *The Music: Reflections on Jazz and Blues*, ed. Amiri Baraka and Amina Baraka [New York: William Morrow, 1987], 273); "the cultural manifestations of the feelings, thoughts, and emotions of a black person's inner being, a spirit that had survived the Middle Passage, slavery, and Jim Crow, as well as apartheid" (Tanisha Ford, *Liberated Threads: Black Women, Style, and the Global Politics of Soul* [Chapel Hill: University of North Carolina Press, 2015], 6); and the insistence on being oneself (see Al Jackson Jr.'s remarks in Phyl Garland, *The Sound of Soul* [Chicago: Henry Regnery, 1969], 164).

11 I take Josef Sorett's point that, in the history of religious-aesthetic theory he traces, "church and spirit almost require each other" (*Spirit in the Dark: A Religious History of Racial Aesthetics* [New York: Oxford University Press, 2016], 8). The very claim to be "spiritual but not religious" manifests this interdependence, suggesting as it does the need to define spirituality in relation to more orthodox or organized ways of accessing the spirit.

12 Baraka, "Phenomenon of Soul," 270.

13 My sense of soul as a logic or cultural logic is informed by Wahneema Lubiano's work on black nationalism as a similarly pervasive, even unnamed, force in black life—see "Black Nationalism and Black Common Sense: Policing Ourselves and Others," in *The House That Race Built*, ed. Wahneema Lubiano (New York: Vintage, 1998), 232–52.

14 Gayle Wald, "Soul's Revival: White Soul, Nostalgia, and the Culturally Constructed Past," in *Soul: Black Power, Politics, and Pleasure*, ed. Monique Guillory and Richard C. Green (New York: New York University Press, 1998), 147.

15 See Portia Maultsby, "Soul," in *African American Music: An Introduction*, ed. Mellonee V. Burnim and Portia K. Maultsby (New York: Routledge, 2014), 277–98.

16 Maultsby, "Soul," 278.

17 Garland, *Sound of Soul*.

18 A. X. Nicholas, ed., *The Poetry of Soul* (New York: Bantam, 1971), xxii, xiii.

19 Nicholas, *Poetry of Soul*, xiii (italics in original).

20 Paul Gilroy, "Question of a 'Soulful Style'" (interview with Richard C. Green and Monique Guillory), in Guillory and Green, *Soul*, 251; Fred Moten, review of *Scenes of Subjection: Terror, Slavery, and Self-Making in Nineteenth-Century*

America by Saidiya V. Hartman and *Soul: Black Power, Politics, and Pleasure,* ed. Monique Guillory and Richard C. Green, TDR: *The Drama Review* 43, no. 4 (1999): 174.

21 Mark Burford, "Sam Cooke as Pop Album Artist—A Reinvention in Three Songs," *Journal of the American Musicological Society* 65, no. 1 (2012): 113–78; Daphne A. Brooks, "Nina Simone's Triple Play," *Callaloo* 34, no. 1 (2011): 176–97.

22 Maultsby, "Soul," 277–98; William L. Van Deburg, *New Day in Babylon: The Black Power Movement and American Culture, 1965–1975* (Chicago: University of Chicago Press, 1992), 192–247; Mark Anthony Neal, *What the Music Said: Black Popular Music and Black Public Culture* (New York: Routledge, 1994); Brian Ward, *Just My Soul Responding: Rhythm and Blues, Black Consciousness, and Race Relations* (Berkeley: University of California Press, 1998).

23 Monique Guillory and Richard C. Green, "By Way of an Introduction," in Guillory and Green, *Soul*, 3.

24 Geneva Smitherman, "Soul," in *Black Talk: Words and Phrases from the Hood to the Amen Corner*, rev. ed. (Boston: Houghton Mifflin, 2000), 266.

25 Zadie Smith, "*Their Eyes Were Watching God*: What Does *Soulful* Mean?," in *Changing My Mind: Occasional Essays* (New York: Penguin, 2009), 13.

26 James Baldwin, qtd. in Jane Howard, "Doom and Glory of Knowing Who You Are" (profile of James Baldwin), *Life*, May 24, 1963, 89.

27 Nikki Giovanni, conversation with the author, February 19, 2018.

28 Imani Perry, *May We Forever Stand: A History of the Black National Anthem* (Chapel Hill: University of North Carolina Press, 2018), 167, 166.

29 Martin Luther King Jr., "The American Dream" (1965), in *A Knock at Midnight*, ed. Clayborne Carson and Peter Holloran (New York: Warner, 2000), 97.

30 Fredric Jameson, *Valences of the Dialectic* (London: Verso, 2009), 532.

31 Jameson, *The Political Unconscious: Narrative as a Socially Symbolic Act* (Ithaca, NY: Cornell University Press, 1981), 19, qtd. in Kevin Honan, "The Political Conscious: 'A Further Round of Reflection' on Fredric Jameson's *Valences of the Dialectic*," *Field Day Review* 7 (2011): 98.

32 Mason, "Gladys Knight," 173.

33 Langston Hughes, "The Negro Speaks of Rivers" (1921), in *The Collected Poems of Langston Hughes*, ed. Arnold Rampersad (New York: Vintage, 1994), 23. See Amiri Baraka, "The Changing Same (R&B and New Black Music)," in *Black Music* (New York: Quill, 1967), 183; Larry Neal, "Some Reflections on the Black Aesthetic," in *The Black Aesthetic*, ed. Addison Gayle (New York: Anchor Books, 1972), 12–13; Julian Mayfield, "You Touch My Black Aesthetic and I'll Touch Yours," in Gayle, *Black Aesthetic*, 26; Ron Welburn, "The Black Aesthetic Imperative," in Gayle, *Black Aesthetic*, 131, 133.

34 Mayfield, "You Touch My Black Aesthetic," 26.

35 Jameson, *Valences of the Dialectic*, 532.

36 Alexandra T. Vazquez, *Listening in Detail: Performances of Cuban Music* (Durham, NC: Duke University Press, 2013), 27. For Vazquez, who engages Naomi Schor's 1987 work *Reading in Detail: Aesthetics and the Feminine*, the purpose of highlighting the feminization of this aesthetic category is to critique its "fetishistic deployment" by scholars who use analysis of the detail to display masculine prowess over Cuban music (Vazquez, *Listening in Detail*, 28). Vazquez hijacks the detail for the opposite purpose: to dispute the presumption that the music can be known.

37 Vazquez, *Listening in Detail*, 21.

38 I am grateful to Sarah Chihaya for this formulation.

39 *Ray*, dir. Taylor Hackford (Universal City, CA: Universal, 2004); James McBride, *Kill 'Em and Leave: Searching for James Brown and the American Soul* (New York: Spiegel and Grau, 2016), 31; *Muscle Shoals*, dir. Greg Camalier (New York: Magnolia Pictures, 2013).

40 *Standing in the Shadows of Motown*, dir. Paul Justman, prod. Paul Justman, Sandford Passman, and Allan Slutsky, written by Walter Dallas, Ntozake Shange, and Allan Slutsky (Van Nuys, CA: Artisan, 2002).

41 Thanks to Sean McCann for this concept.

42 Fredara Hadley, remarks at "Aretha's Amazing Grace: From Watts to Detroit" symposium, University of California, Los Angeles, March 25, 2019.

43 This feminist approach to soul should help remedy the problem that Daphne Brooks identifies when invoking a "black feminist soul genealogy that . . . remains under-theorized" in "Bring the Pain: Post-Soul Memory, Neo-Soul Affect, and Lauryn Hill in the Black Public Sphere" (in *Taking It to the Bridge: Music as Performance*, ed. Nicholas Cook and Richard Pettengill [Ann Arbor: University of Michigan Press, 2013], 190).

44 Trey Ellis, "The New Black Aesthetic," *Callaloo*, no. 38 (1989): 233–43; Greg Tate, "Cult-Nats Meet Freaky-Deke: The Return of the Black Aesthetic," *Village Voice Literary Supplement* (December 1986), 5–8, repr. in Greg Tate, *Flyboy in the Buttermilk: Essays on Contemporary America* (New York: Simon and Schuster, 1992), 198–209; Henry Louis Gates Jr., *Figures in Black: Words, Signs, and the "Racial" Self* (New York: Oxford University Press, 1987).

45 Bertram D. Ashe, "Theorizing the Post-Soul Aesthetic: An Introduction," *African American Review* 41, no. 4 (2007): 617.

46 Ashe, "Theorizing the Post-Soul Aesthetic," 617, 611.

47 Larry Neal, "The Black Arts Movement" (1968), in Gayle, *Black Aesthetic*, 257–74.

48 Ellis, "New Black Aesthetic," 234. The worst-case scenario I invoke is embodied by Touré's 2011 manifesto *Who's Afraid of Post-Blackness?*, in which Touré follows Thelma Golden's foundational definition of "post-black" art in rejecting "the idea that there is a correct or legitimate way of doing Blackness" but shifts the definition of post-blackness away from Golden's conception of collective artistic freedom and toward privatized consumer agency. See Touré,

Who's Afraid of Post-Blackness? What It Means to Be Black Now (New York: Free Press, 2011), 11. Richard Purcell develops a rigorous critique of Touré's work in "Trayvon, Postblackness, and the Postrace Dilemma," *boundary 2* 40, no. 3 (2013): 139–61.

49 Aretha Franklin, qtd. in Guillory and Green, "By Way of an Introduction," 1.

50 Margo Natalie Crawford, *Black Post-Blackness: The Black Arts Movement and Twenty-First-Century Aesthetics* (Urbana: University of Illinois Press, 2017), 2.

51 Toni Cade Bambara, "What It Is I Think I Am Doing Anyhow," in *The Writer on Her Work*, ed. Janet Sternburg (1980; New York: W. W. Norton, 2000), 160.

52 Gates, *Figures in Black*. I elaborate this point in chapter 1.

53 Ford, *Liberated Threads*; Ashley Farmer, *Remaking Black Power: How Black Women Transformed an Era* (Chapel Hill: University of North Carolina Press, 2017).

Chapter 1: From Soul to Post-soul

1 Lerone Bennett, "The Soul of Soul," *Ebony*, December 1961, 112.

2 Amiri Baraka, "The Phenomenon of Soul in African-American Music," in *The Music: Reflections on Jazz and Blues*, ed. Amiri Baraka and Amina Baraka (New York: William Morrow, 1987), 271, 272.

3 Bennett, "Soul of Soul," 114.

4 David Brackett, *Categorizing Sound: Genre and Twentieth-Century Popular Music* (Berkeley: University of California Press, 2016), 294.

5 See "James Brown Just 'Sings His Heart Out,'" *Chicago Defender*, September 4, 1965, in *The James Brown Reader: 50 Years of Writing about the Godfather of Soul*, ed. Nelson George and Alan Leeds (New York: Plume, 2008), 13. The lexical shift from blues and R&B to soul is staggered. As early as 1964, Berry Gordy tells the British press (with the soon-to-be-unnecessary disclaimer that it might "sound corny") that he "refers to the sound he is always striving for as 'soul'" (qtd. in Dave Godin and Norman Jopling, "A Great Visit to Hitsville U.S.A.," *Record Mirror*, September 4, 1964). On the other hand, as late as 1973, a writer for *Jet* describes Marvin Gaye's music not as soul but as "urban blues" (William Earl Berry, "Marvin Gaye: Inner City Musical Poet," *Jet*, February 1, 1973, 59).

6 Brackett, *Categorizing Sound*, 271.

7 Brian Ward, *Just My Soul Responding: Rhythm and Blues, Black Consciousness, and Race Relations* (Berkeley: University of California Press, 1998), 201. Ward notes that there was nothing new about soul's synthesis of sacred and secular idioms, which had informed African American musical practice across the twentieth century. What changed in the soul era was black listeners' widespread *embrace* of this mixture, theretofore a perennial subject of critique (191).

8   Amiri Baraka, "The Changing Same (R&B and New Black Music)," in *Black Music* (New York: Quill, 1967), 192.

9   Etta James, "Something's Got a Hold on Me," comp. Etta James, Leroy Kirkland, and Pearl Woods, *Etta James*, Argo, 1962.

10 Al Green with Davin Seay, *Take Me to the River: An Autobiography* (2000; Chicago: A Cappella Books, 2009), 90.

11 Nina Simone, qtd. in Phyl Garland, *The Sound of Soul* (Chicago: Henry Regnery, 1969), 184–85. Garland's profile of Simone ("Nina Simone: High Priestess of Soul") first appeared in *Ebony* in August 1969.

12 Ward, *Just My Soul Responding*, 192, 184.

13 See, among other sources, Chris Porterfield, "Lady Soul: Singing It like It Is," *Time*, June 28, 1968, 66; and Aretha Franklin with David Ritz, *Aretha: From These Roots* (New York: Villard, 1999), 150. We hear the truth of Franklin's claim in songs such as "Spirit in the Dark," where what Josef Sorett calls "an excess of spiritual powers . . . traverses popular oppositions (i.e., sacred and secular)" by "spilling out into the world in unpredictable ways" (*Spirit in the Dark: A Religious History of Racial Aesthetics* [New York: Oxford University Press, 2016], xii). Still, I maintain the term *secular* that Sorett might dispense with to mark my emphasis on performance that occurs outside the physical space of the church.

14 Jack Hamilton, *Just around Midnight: Rock and Roll and the Racial Imagination* (Cambridge, MA: Harvard University Press, 2016), 183.

15 Clayton Riley, "That New Black Magic" (review of *Soul!*), *New York Times*, May 17, 1970.

16 Garland, *Sound of Soul*, introduction (n.p.), 39.

17 Clarence Major, "Soul," in *Juba to Jive: A Dictionary of African-American Slang* (1970; New York: Penguin, 1994), 434.

18 I am grateful to Imani Perry for this insight.

19 Martin Luther King Jr., "I Have a Dream . . ." (1963), National Archives website, https://www.archives.gov/files/press/exhibits/dream-speech.pdf.

20 Green with Seay, *Take Me to the River*, 145.

21 Geneva Smitherman, "Soul," in *Black Talk: Words and Phrases from the Hood to the Amen Corner*, rev. ed. (Boston: Houghton Mifflin, 2000), 266.

22 David Ritz, *Divided Soul: The Life of Marvin Gaye* (1985; New York: Da Capo, 1991), 136; Carolyn Franklin, qtd. in David Ritz, *Respect: The Life of Aretha Franklin* (New York: Little, Brown and Company, 2014), 38.

23 I am thinking of how Akasha Gloria Hull glosses Toni Cade Bambara's understanding of "spiritual wisdom": as "first and foremost a force for transforming social and political ills" that "wear the very specific faces of racism, poverty, gender inequality, rampant capitalism, ignorance, and so forth" (Hull, *Soul Talk: The New Spirituality of African American Women* [Rochester, VT: Inner Traditions, 2001], 30). It is the soul era, in my view, that inaugurates the spiritual shift Hull dates to the new age movement of the 1980s.

24 Baraka, "Phenomenon of Soul," 270.

25 Anna Julia Cooper, *A Voice from the South* (1892; New York: Oxford University Press, 1990), 138.

26 W. E. B. Du Bois, *The Souls of Black Folk* (1903; Oxford: Oxford University Press, 2008), 8, 175.

27 Alain Locke, "Negro Youth Speaks," in *The New Negro*, ed. Alain Locke (1925; New York: Touchstone, 1997), 47.

28 Locke, "Negro Youth Speaks," 53.

29 James Baldwin, *The Fire Next Time* (1963; New York: Vintage International, 1993), 41–42.

30 Baldwin, "The Uses of the Blues" (1964), in *The Cross of Redemption: Uncollected Writings*, ed. Randall Kenan (New York: Pantheon, 2010), 59.

31 Godfrey Cambridge, qtd. in Porterfield, "Lady Soul," 66.

32 Porterfield, "Lady Soul," 64.

33 Baldwin, *Fire Next Time*, 33–34, 41–43 (italics in original), qtd. in Porterfield, "Lady Soul," 64.

34 Garland, *Sound of Soul*, 27.

35 Baraka, "Phenomenon of Soul," 272, 273; Baraka [LeRoi Jones], *Blues People: Negro Music in White America* (1963; New York: Perennial, 2002).

36 Baraka [Jones], qtd. in Porterfield, "Lady Soul," 62.

37 Ralph Ellison, qtd. in Porterfield, "Lady Soul," 65.

38 Ellison, "Remembering Jimmy" (1958), in *Living with Music: Ralph Ellison's Jazz Writings*, ed. Robert G. O'Meally (New York: Modern Library, 2001), 45.

39 Ellison, "What America Would Be Like without Blacks" (1970), in *The Collected Essays of Ralph Ellison*, ed. John F. Callahan (1995; New York: Modern Library, 2003), 586.

40 Ellison, *Invisible Man* (1952; New York: Vintage International, 1995), 580; "The Charlie Christian Story" (1963), in *Living with Music*, 36; "Richard Wright's Blues" (1945), in *Living with Music*, 103.

41 Langston Hughes, "The Negro Artist and the Racial Mountain," *Nation*, June 23, 1926; Baraka in fact argues that the very "notion of a middle-class [black] blues singer" is a contradiction (*Blues People*, 148).

42 Ellis Haizlip, qtd. in Gayle Wald, *It's Been Beautiful: Soul! and Black Power Television* (Durham, NC: Duke University Press, 2015), 64–65.

43 Sergeant Gerald Westbrook, "The Essence of Soul," *Negro Digest*, May 1964, 14.

44 Barbara Simmons, "Soul," in *Black Fire: An Anthology of Afro-American Writing*, ed. Amiri Baraka and Larry Neal (1968; Baltimore: Black Classic Press, 2007), 308. See Scott Saul for a convincing reading of Simmons's poem as expressing "an aesthetic that is at its best on the run" (*Freedom Is, Freedom Ain't: Jazz and the Making of the Sixties* [Cambridge, MA: Harvard University Press, 2003], 308–11).

45 Riley, "New Black Magic," 15.

46 Cameron Crowe, review of *Donny Hathaway Live, San Francisco Door,* April 13–27, 1972, available at the Uncool website, http://www.theuncool.com /journalism/donny-hathaway-live-review.

47 The Impressions, "Woman's Got Soul," comp. Curtis Mayfield, ABC-Paramount, 1965.

48 Sam and Dave, "Soul Man," comp. Isaac Hayes and David Porter, Stax, 1967.

49 Nikki Giovanni, "*The Sound of Soul,* by Phyl Garland: A Book Review with a Poetic Insert," in *Gemini: An Extended Autobiographical Statement on My First Twenty-Five Years of Being a Black Poet* (New York: Penguin, 1971), 114, 118.

50 Ford, *Liberated Threads,* 5–6.

51 Claude Brown, "Introduction to Soul," *Esquire,* April 1968, 79, qtd. in Hamilton, *Just around Midnight,* 179.

52 Brown, "The Language of Soul," *Esquire,* April 1968, 88. Despite its celebratory tenor, Brown's essay is a swansong for soul talk, which Brown believes is being abandoned by both radical and conservative black people: the "Ultra-Black" is "frantically adopting everything from a Western version of Islam," whereas the "semi-Negro" is "intent on gaining admission to the Establishment—even on an honorary basis," he writes (162).

53 William L. Van Deburg, *New Day in Babylon: The Black Power Movement and American Culture, 1965–1975* (Chicago: University of Chicago Press, 1992), 186.

54 Baraka, "Black Art" (1965), in *The LeRoi Jones/Amiri Baraka Reader,* ed. William H. Harris (1991; New York: Thunder's Mouth Press, 2000), 220.

55 Larry Neal, "Some Reflections on the Black Aesthetic," in *The Black Aesthetic,* ed. Addison Gayle (Garden City, NY: Anchor Books, 1972), 12, 15.

56 Baraka, "Changing Same," 199; Neal, "Some Reflections," 15.

57 Don L. Lee, "Toward a Definition of Black Poetry of the Sixties (after LeRoi Jones)" (1971), in Gayle, *Black Aesthetic,* 226, 232.

58 Notwithstanding Larry Neal's famous definition of the Black Arts movement as "the aesthetic and *spiritual* sister of the Black Arts concept" ("The Black Arts Movement" [1968], in Gayle, *Black Aesthetic,* 257, my emphasis)—as well as the fact that the theatrical and educational space Baraka established in Newark the year after founding the Black Arts Repertory Theatre/School in Harlem was called Spirit House—Josef Sorett's recent study is unique in noting that "the Black Arts constituted a set of *spiritual* practices that was intended to sustain black life" (*Spirit in the Dark,* 164, my emphasis). Discussions of soul and the Black Aesthetic therefore shared this spiritual orientation.

59 Charles Hughes, *Country Soul: Making Music and Making Race in the American South* (Chapel Hill: University of North Carolina Press, 2015), 103.

60 James Brown with Bruce Tucker, *James Brown: The Godfather of Soul* (1986; New York: Thunder's Mouth Press, 1990), 169.

61 Baraka, "Changing Same," 186–87.

62 Baraka, "Changing Same," 195.

63 I discuss these phenomena at greater length in chapter 3, as well as in *Donny Hathaway Live* (New York: Bloomsbury, 2016).

64 José Esteban Muñoz, *Cruising Utopia: The Then and There of Queer Futurity* (New York: New York University Press, 2009), 31.

65 Askia Touré [Roland Snellings], "Keep on Pushin': Rhythm and Blues as a Weapon," *Liberator* 5, no. 10 (1965), in *SOS — Calling All Black People: A Black Arts Movement Reader*, ed. John H. Bracey Jr., Sonia Sanchez, and James Smethurst (Amherst: University of Massachusetts Press, 2014), 89.

66 Neal, "Any Day Now: Black Art and Black Liberation," *Ebony*, August 1969, 54.

67 Neal, "Any Day Now," 56, emphasis in original.

68 Neal, "Any Day Now," 57.

69 Neal, "Any Day Now," 58, 62.

70 Neal, "Any Day Now," 62.

71 Riley, "New Black Magic," 15. The end of this passage is quoted in Wald, *It's Been Beautiful*, 105.

72 Clayton Riley, "On Black Theater," in Gayle, *Black Aesthetic*, 295.

73 "Who's Got Soul," *Esquire*, April 1968, 89.

74 Michael Haralambos, *Soul Music: The Birth of a Sound in Black America* (New York: Da Capo, 1974).

75 James discusses the feminist valence of this recording in Etta James (with David Ritz), *Rage to Survive* (1995; New York: Da Capo, 2003), 50.

76 Stevie Wonder feat. Shirley Brewer, "Ordinary Pain," comp. Stevie Wonder, *Songs in the Key of Life*, Tamla, 1976.

77 Ray Charles, "I Got a Woman," comp. Ray Charles and Renal Richard, Atlantic, 1954; Ray Charles feat. the Raelettes, "Hit the Road, Jack," comp. Percy Mayfield, ABC-Paramount, 1961; Ray Charles feat. the Raelettes, "You Are My Sunshine," comp. Charles Mitchell and Jimmie Davis, ABC-Paramount, 1962.

78 Nikki Giovanni, "Black Poems, *Poseurs*, and Power" (1969), in *Gemini*, 106.

79 Giovanni, "Black Poems," 106.

80 Giovanni, "Black Poems," 106–7.

81 *Gemini* includes early instances of Giovanni's (later reformed) heterosexism — see, e.g., "A Revolutionary Tale" (1968), in *Gemini*, 43.

82 Charles L. Sanders, "Aretha: A Close-up Look at Sister Superstar," *Ebony*, December 1971, 128, 130.

83 I owe this insight to Lynnée Denise (remarks at "Aretha's Amazing Grace: From Watts to Detroit" symposium, University of California, Los Angeles, March 24, 2019).

84 Peter Bailey, "Al Green: Apostle of Love," *Ebony*, November 1973, 108; Green with Seay, *Take Me to the River*, 108.

85 Shirley Brown, "Woman to Woman," comp. Homer Banks, Eddie Marion, and Henderson Thigpen, Truth, 1974; Betty Wright, "Clean Up Woman," comp. Clarence Reid and Willie Clarke, Alston, 1971.

86 Gladys Knight and the Pips, "If I Were Your Woman," comp. Gloria Jones, Clay McMurray, and Pam Sawyer, Motown, 1970.

87 Wald, *It's Been Beautiful*, 139.

88 Anthony Heilbut stresses the "crucial and fundamental" gay contribution to gospel itself and draws a fascinating connection between queerness and the language of soul. He tells how a record store clerk in Harlem informed him that Sam Cooke "liked men as well as women," stating, "Sure he's gay, how else could he have that much soul?" (*The Fan Who Knew Too Much: Aretha Franklin, the Rise of the Soap Opera, Children of the Gospel Church, and Other Meditations* [New York: Knopf, 2012], 43, 5).

89 Peter Guralnick, *Sweet Soul Music: Rhythm and Blues and the Southern Dream of Freedom* (1986; New York: Back Bay Books, 2012), 2. Guralnick excludes Motown from his conception of soul altogether by associating soul with "the uninhibited emotionalism of the church" (2).

90 Green with Seay, *Take Me to the River*, 227.

91 Mitchell Morris, *The Persistence of Sentiment: Display and Feeling in Popular Music of the 1970s* (Berkeley: University of California Press, 2013), 71, 82.

92 Ed Pavlić, correspondence with author, January 31, 2015.

93 Rotary Connection, "Respect," comp. Otis Redding, *Songs*, Cadet, 1969.

94 Nelson George's *The Death of Rhythm and Blues* (1988; New York: Penguin, 2004), for all its strengths, exemplifies this narrative.

95 Disco has long been cited as the death knell of soul and related social movements for both commercial and aesthetic reasons, as Hughes notes in *Country Soul* (178). Alice Echols has offered perhaps the most powerful challenge to this narrative, while exposing the homophobia and racial anxieties it encodes, in *Hot Stuff: Disco and the Remaking of American Culture* (New York: W. W. Norton, 2010). See, too, Echols's article "The Land of Somewhere Else: Refiguring James Brown in Seventies Disco" (*Criticism* 50, no. 1 [2008]: 19–41), which posits soul as the crucible for disco, not the victim of it.

96 Brown with Tucker, *James Brown*, 200, qtd. in Rickey Vincent, *Funk: The Music, the People, and the Rhythm of the One* (New York: St. Martin's, 1996), 79.

97 See Morris, *Persistence of Sentiment*, 72.

98 James Brown, qtd. in Ethel L. Payne, "James Brown Answers Emergency Call in D.C.," *New Pittsburgh Courier*, April 13, 1968.

99 Black communities' use of the word *soul* might have been "a spontaneous development," Ford notes, but the term was soon taken up by record executives who sought to market the "natural hairstyles, nonconformist fashions, political activism, and innovative musical forms" of such artists as Nina Simone, Miriam Makeba, and Odetta (*Liberated Threads*, 33). See Phillip Brian Harper's critique of the notion that soul's mass marketing compromises its "authentic" essence, in *Are We Not Men? Masculine Anxiety and the Problem of African-American Identity* (Oxford: Oxford University Press, 1996), 85.

100 Garland, *Sound of Soul*, 134–35.

101 Garland, *Sound of Soul*, 135.

102 Bennett, "Soul of Soul," 114.

103 Bennett, "Soul of Soul," 114.

104 Riley, "If Aretha's Around, Who Needs Janis?," *New York Times*, March 8, 1970.

105 Paul Gilroy, "One Nation under a Groove," in *Small Acts: Thoughts on the Politics of Black Cultures* (New York: Serpent's Tail, 1993), 38, qtd. in Mark Anthony Neal, *What the Music Said: Black Popular Music and Black Public Culture* (New York: Routledge, 1994), 29. For more on the relationship between commerce and the era's black freedom movements, see Mark Anthony Neal, "Trouble Man: The Art and Politics of Marvin Gaye," *Western Journal of Black Studies* 22, no. 4 (1998): 253; and Amy Abugo Ongiri, *Spectacular Blackness: The Cultural Politics of the Black Power Movement and the Search for a Black Aesthetic* (Charlottesville: University of Virginia Press, 2009).

106 Simone qtd. in Garland, *Sound of Soul*, 189.

107 Hughes, *Country Soul*, 89, 90.

108 Ward, *Just My Soul Responding*, 417.

109 Wilson Pickett, qtd. in Gerri Hirshey, *Nowhere to Run: The Story of Soul Music* (1984; London: Southbank, 2006), 314, qtd. in Ward, *Just My Soul Responding*, 358; Ward, *Just My Soul Responding*, 361. The economic viability of black nationalism was nowhere clearer than at Stax Records, where Al Bell literally capitalized on the allure of black militancy for black and white audiences alike, as Hughes explains in *Country Soul*, 102–3.

110 The Staple Singers, "I'll Take You There," comp. Al Bell, Stax, 1972.

111 Baldwin, *Fire Next Time*, 43.

112 Wald, *It's Been Beautiful*, 154, 151, 152; Richard Iton, *In Search of the Black Fantastic: Politics and Popular Culture in the Post–Civil Rights Era* (Oxford: Oxford University Press, 2008), 29.

113 Angela Davis, *Angela Davis: An Autobiography* (1974; New York: International, 2008), 161; Michele Wallace, *Black Macho and the Myth of the Superwoman* (New York: Dial, 1979); Cheryl Clarke, *After Mecca: Women Poets and the Black Arts Movement* (New Brunswick, NJ: Rutgers University Press, 2005); Audre Lorde, "Learning from the 60s" (1982), in *Sister Outsider: Essays and Speeches* (1984; Berkeley: Crossing Press, 2007), 134–44.

114 Ward demonstrates this point at great length in *Just My Soul Responding*, 369–80.

115 Toni Cade Bambara, "What It Is I Think I Am Doing Anyhow," in *The Writer on Her Work*, ed. Janet Sternburg (New York: W. W. Norton, 2000), 160.

116 Nelson George, *Buppies, B-Boys, Baps, and Bohos: Notes on Post-Soul Black Culture* (1992; New York: Da Capo, 2001), 1.

117 Eugene Robinson, qtd. in George, *Death of Rhythm and Blues*, 172.

118 Greg Tate, "Cult-Nats Meet Freaky-Deke: The Return of the Black Aesthetic," *Village Voice*, Voice Literary Supplement (December 1986), 5–8; Trey Ellis, "The New Black Aesthetic," *Callaloo*, no. 38 (1989): 233–43.

119 Ellis, "Notes on a Lifetime of Passing," *New Yorker*, September 22, 2017.

120 I would argue that it was this emergent professional class that formalized, systematized, and literally theorized the Black Aesthetic that had been such an unwieldy construction for Larry Neal, Stephen Henderson, and others. Whereas, in the late 1960s and early 1970s, the Black Aesthetic was a self-reflexive provocation, by the late 1970s, it was a program of professional inquiry and advancement. This is suggested, though perhaps not intended, by Houston Baker's 1984 call for a systematic academic mode of assessing those creative works inspired by the black aesthetic: "The defensive inwardness of the Black Aesthetic . . . made the new paradigm an ideal instrument for those wishing to usher into the world new and *sui generis* Afro-American objects of investigation. Ultimately, though, such introspection could not answer theoretical questions occasioned by the entry of such black, expressive objects into the world. In a sense, the investigator had been given—through a bold act of critical imagination—a unique expressive tradition but no distinctive theoretical vocabulary in which to discuss this tradition" (*Blues, Ideology, and Afro-American Literature: A Vernacular Theory* [1984; Chicago: University of Chicago Press, 1987], 86).

121 See Wald on the machinations of what Michael Omi and Howard Winant call "the racial state" (*It's Been Beautiful*, 184).

122 My account is informed by Mark Anthony Neal's *Soul Babies: Black Popular Culture and the Post-Soul Aesthetic* (New York: Routledge, 2002), 131–32, 169.

123 Ellis, "New Black Aesthetic," 235.

124 Ellis, "New Black Aesthetic," 240.

125 See Neal, *Soul Babies*; Lisa Jones, qtd. in Ellis, "New Black Aesthetic," 236–37, 240.

126 Jones, *Bulletproof Diva: Tales of Race, Sex, and Hair* (1994; New York: Anchor, 1995), 133.

127 Jones, *Bulletproof Diva*, 3.

128 Neal, *Soul Babies*, 103, 105. Neal develops the first account of not simply "post-soul" culture but "post-soul aesthetics," which for him describes a range of artistic responses (including satire, self-reflexivity, a diverse range of intertexts) to the specifically African American experience of post-1960s postmodernity—an era marked by heightened intraracial class divisions, a lapse of organizational energy in the wake of COINTELPRO, the commercialization of black popular culture, and an expansive sense of social possibility for middle-class beneficiaries of civil rights–era gains.

129 Bertram D. Ashe, "Theorizing the Post-Soul Aesthetic: An Introduction," *African American Review* 41, no. 4 (2007): 615.

130 Ashe, "Theorizing the Post-Soul Aesthetic," 614.

131 Ashe, "Theorizing the Post-Soul Aesthetic," 614, my emphasis.

132 Fred Moten, review of *Scenes of Subjection: Terror, Slavery, and Self-Making in Nineteenth-Century America* by Saidiya V. Hartman, and *Soul: Black Power,*

Politics, and Pleasure edited by Monique Guillory and Richard C. Green, TDR: The Drama Review 43, no. 4 (1999): 174.

133 Trey Ellis, "Straddling Black and White," *Los Angeles Times*, December 13, 2007, qtd. in Aldon Lynn Nielsen, "Foreword: Preliminary Postings from a Neo-Soul," *African American Review* 41, no. 4 (2007): 605.

134 Francesca T. Royster, *Sounding Like a No-No: Queer Sounds and Eccentric Acts in the Post-Soul Era* (Ann Arbor: University of Michigan Press, 2013), 9.

135 Editorial statement, *Billboard*, June 26, 1982, 3; Nelson George's remarks, *Billboard*, June 26, 1982, 43, 10, qtd. in Brackett, *Categorizing Sound*, 293, 294.

136 "Editorial: R&B Now Soul," *Billboard*, August 23, 1969, 3, qtd. in Brackett, *Categorizing Sound*, 271.

137 Brackett, *Categorizing Sound*, 294; Paul Taylor, "Post-Black, Old Black," *African American Review* 41, no. 4 (2007): 635.

138 Robin D. G. Kelley, *Yo' Mama's Disfunktional! Fighting the Culture Wars in Urban America* (Boston: Beacon Press, 1997), 25.

139 Kelley, *Yo' Mama's Disfunktional!*, 26.

140 Tate, "Cult-Nats Meet Freaky-Deke," 207.

141 Neal, *Soul Babies*, 114.

142 Lucille Clifton, "won't you celebrate with me" (1992), in *Collected Poems of Lucille Clifton, 1965–2010*, ed. Kevin Young and Michael S. Glaser (Rochester, NY: BOA Editions, 2012), 427. Several other historical, musical, and literary analyses—by James Smethurst, Margo Crawford, Aldon Nielsen, Amy Abugo Ongiri, Cynthia Young, Darieck Scott, Daphne Brooks, Gayle Wald, Tanisha Ford, and GerShun Avilez—have challenged what Wald calls "prevalent assumptions about the 1960s and 1970s nationalist political culture as a homophobic and patriarchal monolith" in the interest of recovering "the finely woven social textures" of these movements (Wald, *It's Been Beautiful*, 19). See James Smethurst, *The Black Arts Movement: Literary Nationalism in the 1960s and 1970s* (Chapel Hill: University of North Carolina Press, 2006); Margo Crawford and Lisa Gail Collins, *New Thoughts on the Black Arts Movement* (New Brunswick, NJ: Rutgers University Press, 2008); Crawford, *Black Post-Blackness: The Black Arts Movement and Twenty-First-Century Aesthetics* (Urbana: University of Illinois Press, 2017); Nielsen, "Foreword: Preliminary Postings," 601–8; Ongiri, *Spectacular Blackness*; Cynthia Young, *Soul Power: Culture, Radicalism, and the Making of a U.S. Third World Left* (Durham, NC: Duke University Press, 2006); Darieck Scott, *Extravagant Abjection: Blackness, Power, and Sexuality in the African American Literary Imagination* (New York: New York University Press, 2010); Daphne A. Brooks, "Nina Simone's Triple Play," *Callaloo* 34, no. 1 (2011): 176–97; Wald, *It's Been Beautiful*; Ford, *Liberated Threads*; GerShun Avilez, *Radical Aesthetics and Modern Black Nationalism* (Urbana: University of Illinois Press, 2016).

143 Thulani Davis, Portia Maultsby, Ishmael Reed, Greg Tate, and Clyde Taylor, "Ain't We Still Got Soul?," in *Soul: Black Power, Politics, and Pleasure*, ed. Mo-

nique Guillory and Richard C. Green (New York: New York University Press, 1998), 278.

144 Steven Drukman, "Introduction: On Black Power," in Guillory and Green, *Soul*, 8.

145 Baraka, "The Soul Brother" (eulogy for Ellis Haizlip, 1991), in *Eulogies* (New York: Agincourt Press, 2002), 190, qtd. in Wald, *It's Been Beautiful*, 213.

146 See David Smith, "Half-Century of US Civil Rights Gains Have Stalled or Reversed, Report Finds," *Guardian*, February 27, 2018.

Chapter 2: We Shall Overcome, Shelter, and Veil

1 "Nina Loves Porgy: Gershwin Tune Makes Singer-Pianist a Star," *Ebony*, December 1959, 169.

2 Amiri Baraka, "The Changing Same (R&B and New Black Music)," in *Black Music* (New York: Quill, 1967), 206–7.

3 Richard Dyer, *Stars* (1980; London: British Film Institute, 1982), 17. My approach resonates with that of Michael Awkward in his book *Soul Covers*. But whereas Awkward studies R&B covers less "as music" than as dramatic and poetic texts through which soul singers "(re)imagine, create, and develop their own artistic personae," I show how soul covers additionally advance artists' distinctly musical ideas about expressive possibility (*Soul Covers: Rhythm and Blues Remakes and the Struggle for Artistic Identity* [Durham, NC: Duke University Press, 2007], xviii–xix, 16).

4 Billed as "The American Tribal Love-Rock Musical," *Hair* premiered in 1967 and was staged at the Public Theater in New York in 1968. As the first "rock musical," the show itself constitutes an innovative hybrid theatrical form.

5 Nina Simone, qtd. in Phyl Garland, *The Sound of Soul* (Chicago: Henry Regnery, 1969), 189.

6 For two nuanced approaches to the subject of cover recordings and their various meanings and manifestations across the twentieth century, see Michael Coyle, "Hijacked Hits and Antic Authenticity: Cover Songs, Race, and Postwar Marketing," in *Rock over the Edge: Transformations in Popular Music Culture*, ed. Roger Beebe, Denise Fulbrook, and Ben Saunders (Durham, NC: Duke University Press, 2002), 133–60; and Sean Dineley, "Covers Uncovered: A History of the 'Cover Version,' from Bing Crosby to the Flaming Lips" (master's thesis, University of Western Ontario, June 2014).

Histories of popular music reveal ongoing debates about the origin of the term "cover." Dineley suggests it was "almost certainly crafted from the term 'coverage,'" as in the market reach a song achieved through multiple versions in the 1940s (56). But it might also have referred to the sheet music whose covers bore different artists' names or faces—a possibility that better accounts for why we came to speak of certain artists' cover versions of songs, not the geographic or market terrain the songs covered. (This alternative was suggested by Elijah Wald, who traces the term to the 1930s [correspondence with author, November 11, 2017]).

7 Awkward, *Soul Covers*, 20.

8 Simone with Stephen Cleary, *I Put a Spell on You* (New York: Da Capo, 2003), 26.

9 Simone with Cleary, *I Put a Spell on You*, 26–27.

10 Simone, qtd. in John S. Wilson, "The Two Faces of Nina Simone," *New York Times*, December 31, 1967.

11 Simone, qtd. in "Let Nina Simone Tell You About Soul Music," *New Journal and Guide* (Norfolk, VA), July 12, 1969.

12 Hollie I. West, "A Closer Look at the Styles of Aretha and Nina," *Washington Post*, March 22, 1970.

13 For the latter phenomenon, see Simone with Cleary, *I Put a Spell on You*, 117.

14 See Daphne A. Brooks, "Nina Simone's Triple Play," *Callaloo* 34, no. 1 (Winter 2011): 176–97.

15 Simone, "Love Me or Leave Me," *Little Girl Blue*, Bethlehem, 1958. See, too, her performance of the song on YouTube: Ninasimoneish, "Simone Style—Love Me or Leave Me—The Peach Voice. Nina Simone," March 5, 2012, YouTube video, 2:48, https://www.youtube.com/watch?v=0WHHW8PrF6Q.

16 Garland, *Sound of Soul*, 170.

17 Simone, qtd. in Arthur Taylor, *Notes and Tones: Musician-to-Musician Interviews* (1977; New York: Da Capo, 1993), 149.

18 Simone, qtd. in Taylor, *Notes and Tones*, 148.

19 Ruth Feldstein, *How It Feels to Be Free: Black Women Entertainers and the Civil Rights Movement* (Oxford: Oxford University Press, 2013), 88–89.

20 See *The Great Live Show in Paris*, Trip Records; although recorded in 1968, this album was not released until 1974. Simone's recording of "Life," while popular in the United States, was a bigger hit in England, where Simone had three albums on the British best-selling charts at once. Her decision to cover the song in 1968 was prescient—the following year, both the *Hair* original cast recording and the Fifth Dimension's recording of "Aquarius/Let the Sunshine In" would top their respective charts. Salamishah Tillet, "Strange Sampling: Nina Simone and her Hip-Hop Children," *American Quarterly* 66, no. 1 (2014): 120.

21 Brooks, "'I Ain't Got No, I Got Life': #OscarsSoWhite and the Problem of Women Musicians on Film," *Los Angeles Review of Books*, February 28, 2016.

22 Simone, qtd. in Edward Kossner, "To Nina Simone, Respect Means More Than Flattery," *Philadelphia Tribune*, April 11, 1961. For more on Simone's philosophy on audience-performer relations, see Simone with Cleary, *I Put a Spell on You*, 52.

23 Kathy Dobie, "Midnight Train: A Teenage Story," in *Trouble Girls: The Rolling Stone Book of Women in Rock*, ed. Barbara O'Dair (New York: Random House, 1997), 232, qtd. in Brooks, "Nina Simone's Triple Play," 176.

24 Simone with Cleary, *I Put a Spell on You*, 92–93.

25 Simone with Cleary, *I Put a Spell on You*, 94.

26 Robert Sherman, "Nina Simone Casts Her Moody Spells," *New York Times*, November 23, 1966.

27 West, "Closer Look."

28 Bernice Johnson Reagon, qtd. in Shana Redmond, *Anthem: Social Movements and the Sound of Solidarity in the African Diaspora* (New York: New York University Press, 2014), 207. Toni Morrison concurred, attesting in the wake of Simone's death that "she saved our lives" (qtd. in Stephen Holden, "A Younger Generation's Homage to a Soulful Diva," *New York Times*, June 24, 2004). Thanks to Salamishah Tillet for this reference.

29 See Alexis De Veaux's biography of Lorde, titled *Warrior Poet* (New York: W. W. Norton, 2006).

30 Ralph Ellison, "Flamenco" (1954), in *Living with Music: Ralph Ellison's Jazz Writings*, ed. Robert G. O'Meally (New York: Modern Library, 2001), 100.

31 For Franklin's reluctance to explicitly address politics in her music, see Aretha Franklin with David Ritz, *Aretha: From These Roots* (New York: Villard, 1999), 155. Franklin announced plans to pay $250,000 to bail Angela Davis out of prison and to play a benefit concert in Davis's honor, the latter of which Atlantic reportedly rejected (see Chester Higgins, "People Are Talking About," *Jet*, May 6, 1971, 42).

32 Valerie Wilmer, "Aretha—Lady Soul," *DownBeat*, August 8, 1968, 38.

33 West, "Closer Look."

34 Salamishah Tillet, remarks at "Aretha's Amazing Grace: From Watts to Detroit" symposium, University of California, Los Angeles, March 24, 2019.

35 Wexler and David Ritz, *Rhythm and Blues: A Life in American Music* (New York: Knopf, 1993), 212.

36 Chris Porterfield, "Lady Soul: Singing It Like It Is," *Time*, June 28, 1968, 62.

37 For Franklin's assessment of the story and its consequences, see Franklin with Ritz, *Aretha*, 123 (qtd. in Awkward, *Soul Covers*, 45). For more on Franklin's response to this article, see Awkward, *Soul Covers*, 42–54.

38 James Goodrich, "Aretha Returns with More Soul," *Jet*, November 12, 1970, 61.

39 Cecil Franklin, qtd. in David Ritz, *Respect: The Life of Aretha Franklin* (New York: Little, Brown, 2014), 43.

40 Franklin with Ritz, *Aretha*, 141.

41 Clayton Riley, "All Out for Aretha," *New York Times*, August 12, 1973.

42 Qtd. in C. Gerald Fraser, "Aretha Franklin 'Soul' Ignites Apollo," *New York Times*, June 4, 1971.

43 Qtd. in Fraser, "Aretha Franklin 'Soul.'"

44 West, "Closer Look."

45 "Aretha Franklin Cops Another Gold Record," *Chicago Daily Defender*, January 15, 1968.

46 Franklin, qtd. in Garland, "Aretha Franklin—'Sister Soul,'" *Ebony*, October 1967, 48.

47 Franklin, qtd. in "'Soul Is Part Gospel, Part Living,' Explains Aretha," *Baltimore Afro-American*, May 17, 1969.

48 Franklin, qtd. in "'Soul Is Part Gospel.'"

49 Craig Werner, *Higher Ground: Stevie Wonder, Aretha Franklin, Curtis Mayfield, and the Rise and Fall of American Soul* (New York: Crown, 2004), 182.

50 King Curtis, qtd. in Werner, *Higher Ground*, 182.

51 Etta James, qtd. in Ritz, *Respect*, 111, 112.

52 Franklin with Ritz, *Aretha*, 138; Jack Hamilton, *Just around Midnight: Rock and Roll and the Racial Imagination* (Cambridge, MA: Harvard University Press, 2016).

53 Eric Lott, *Love and Theft: Blackface Minstrelsy and the American Working Class* (Oxford: Oxford University Press, 1993).

54 Not everyone heard Franklin's "Eleanor Rigby" as an achievement. Hollie West thought Franklin's version, "although it is good for dancing, . . . misses the point of the tune entirely" ("Closer Look").

55 Merry Clayton released a similarly soulful, albeit less controlled, version of "Bridge" the same month as Franklin, in March 1971. A review of Clayton's *Gimme Shelter* suggests that Clayton's version appeared first: "Merry's version of 'Bridge over Troubled Water' is going to stand as the best to date until we hear from Aretha Franklin or Roberta Flack on the same subject" (Otis Troupe, "'Gimme Shelter' Gets High Rating," *Bay State Banner* [Boston], April 1, 1971).

56 Anthony Heilbut, *The Fan Who Knew Too Much: Aretha Franklin, the Rise of the Soap Opera, Children of the Gospel Church, and Other Meditations* (New York: Knopf, 2012), 124.

57 See Werner, *Higher Ground*, 183.

58 David Hinckley, "Legendary Singer Claude Jeter Dies," *New York Daily News*, January 8, 2009.

59 Franklin, "Bridge over Troubled Water," comp. Paul Simon, *Aretha Franklin's Greatest Hits*, Atlantic, 1971.

60 Chris Molanphy, correspondence with author, October 6, 2016.

61 Aretha Franklin, "Ain't No Way," comp. Carolyn Franklin, *Lady Soul*, Atlantic, 1968.

62 Emily J. Lordi, *Black Resonance: Iconic Women Singers and African American Literature* (New Brunswick, NJ: Rutgers University Press, 2013), 200–201.

63 Toni Cade Bambara, ed., *The Black Woman: An Anthology* (New York: Mentor, 1970).

64 Simone, qtd. in Garland, *Sound of Soul*, 183. She likewise told Hollie West three years later, "I wish that it had not been necessary to become socially and politically oriented. I don't want to be Jesus Christ. I don't know beans about politics—I mean technically. But I had to choose this way. My people were in

trouble" (Simone, qtd. in West, "Lady Doth Protest," *Washington Post*, October 28, 1972).

65 Sidney Barnes with Tom Wright, *Standing on Solid Ground: My Life and Struggles in the Music Biz* (Leicester, NC: BarVada Books, 2011), 384.

66 Barnes with Wright, *Standing on Solid Ground*, 357.

67 Barnes, correspondence with author, October 23, 2017.

68 Barnes with Wright, *Standing on Solid Ground*, 428.

69 Barnes with Wright, *Standing on Solid Ground*, 359; Barnes, correspondence with author, October 23, 2017.

70 Barnes with Wright, *Standing on Solid Ground*, 376. While Barnes suggests in his memoir that they connected equally well with the black audiences for which they performed—"I'm sure some of their lives were changed [by the experience]. We were different, we had succeeded, and we were black like them" (424)—he noted in private correspondence, "Most black crowds didn't understand what we were all about until the end of our career; then they were starting to catch on. Sort of like with Jimi Hendrix."

71 Garland, "Aretha Franklin—'Sister Soul,'" 47; Otis Redding, qtd. in Peter Guralnick, *Sweet Soul Music: Rhythm and Blues and the Southern Dream of Freedom* (New York: Back Bay Books, 2012), 332.

72 Barnes, correspondence with author, October 23, 2017.

73 Barnes, correspondence with author, October 23, 2017.

74 Aretha Franklin, interview with Anthony Mason, CBS *Sunday Morning News*, May 8, 2011.

75 Otis Redding, "Respect," *Otis Blue: Otis Redding Sings Soul*, Stax, 1965; Aretha Franklin, "Respect," comp. Otis Redding, *I Never Loved a Man the Way I Love You*, Atlantic, 1967.

76 Rotary Connection, "Respect," comp. Redding, *Songs*, Cadet, 1969.

77 *Merriam-Webster*, s.v. "recapitulate," accessed May 5, 2017, https://www .merriam-webster.com/dictionary/recapitulate.

78 Barnes, correspondence with author, October 23, 2017.

79 Minnie Riperton, qtd. in Chris Charlesworth, "Minnie Riperton," *Melody Maker*, April 12, 1975.

80 Garland, "Ebony Music Poll," *Ebony*, June 1976, 63, 64.

81 Eulaulah Hathaway, conversation with author, January 14, 2019.

82 Donny Hathaway, "Interview," WBLS (New York), 1973, on *These Songs for You, Live!*, Atlantic, 2004.

83 For more on Hathaway's cover recordings, see Lordi, *Donny Hathaway Live* (New York: Bloomsbury, 2016).

84 Edward Howard, qtd. in David Ritz, liner notes to *Donny Hathaway Live/In Performance*, Rhino, 2010.

85 See Hathaway's introduction to his cover of Stevie Wonder's "Superwoman (Where Were You When I Needed You?)," University of California, Los Angeles, May 1972, on *These Songs for You, Live!*.

86   Baraka, "Changing Same," 180–211.

87   Hathaway, "Jealous Guy," comp. John Lennon, *Donny Hathaway Live*, Atlantic, 1972; "Giving Up," comp. Van McCoy, *Donny Hathaway*, Atlantic, 1971.

88   Jerry Wexler and David Ritz, *Rhythm and Blues: A Life in American Music* (New York: Knopf, 1993), 260.

89   For Hathaway's performance of "Giving Up" at the Astrodome, see P. Stoychev, "Donny Hathaway—Giving Up (Live at the Astrodome)," February 1, 2009, YouTube video, 7:54, https://www.youtube.com/watch?v=kIdhzBFbmLU.

90   This reading reflects analysis of the song that appears in Lordi, *Donny Hathaway Live*, 38, 90.

91   Baraka, "Amiri Baraka: Ennobled by Coltrane," interview with Christopher Lydon (recorded 2007), *Open Source*, August 31, 2017.

92   Simone, qtd. in Wilson, "Two Faces of Nina Simone."

93   Simone, qtd. in Wilson, "Two Faces of Nina Simone."

94   Baraka, "Changing Same," 199.

95   Askia Touré [Roland Snellings], "Keep on Pushin': Rhythm and Blues as a Weapon," *Liberator* 5, no. 10 (1965), in SOS—*Calling All Black People: A Black Arts Movement Reader*, ed. John H. Bracey Jr., Sonia Sanchez, and James Smethurst (Amherst: University of Massachusetts Press, 2014), 89.

96   The Association, "Never My Love," comp. Donald and Richard Addrisi, *Insight Out*, Warner Bros, 1967.

97   Donny Hathaway, "Never My Love," comp. Donald and Richard Addrisi, *Never My Love: The Anthology*, Rhino, 2013.

98   Thelonious Monk, "Black and Tan Fantasy," comp. Duke Ellington, *Thelonious Monk Plays Duke Ellington*, Riverside Records, 1956; Lianne La Havas, "You Love Me," comp. Jill Scott, *Is Your Love Big Enough?*, Warner Bros/Nonesuch, 2012.

99   Along with Arrested Development's "Revolution," which it preceded in the closing credits, Franklin's "Someday" was the only song recorded for the soundtrack, which otherwise archived classic songs from Joe Turner's "Roll 'Em Pete" to Billie Holiday's "Big Stuff."

100   Franklin with Ritz, *Aretha*, 140.

101   Wexler, qtd. in Ritz, *Respect*, 112.

102   Arif Mardin, qtd. in A. Scott Galloway, liner notes to *Extension of a Man*, by Donny Hathaway, Atlantic, (1973) 1995, 5.

103   M. Cordell Thompson, "Aretha Is Rocking Steady Now," *Jet*, March 9, 1972, 61.

104   Aretha Franklin, "Someday We'll All Be Free," comp. Donny Hathaway and Edward Howard, *Malcolm X (Music from the Motion Picture Soundtrack)*, Warner Bros, 1992.

105   Wilton Felder, "Someday We'll All Be Free," *Inherit the Wind*, MCA, 1980. Many thanks to Mark Anthony Neal for directing me to this recording and Womack's.

106 Bobby Womack, "Someday We'll All Be Free," *Someday We'll All Be Free*, Beverly Glen Music, 1985.

Chapter 3: Rescripted Relations

1 Nina Simone, "Sinnerman," trad., *Pastel Blues*, Philips, 1965; see Otis Redding's performance of "Try a Little Tenderness" at the Monterey Pop Festival, comp. Jimmy Campbell, Reg Connelly, and Harry Woods, *Otis Redding: The Definitive Soul Collection*, Atlantic, 2006.
2 "An Interview with Audre Lorde," interview by Karla Hammond, *American Poetry Review* 9, no. 2 (1980), 8, qtd. in Elizabeth Alexander, *Power and Possibility: Essays, Reviews, and Interviews* (Ann Arbor: University of Michigan Press, 2007), 95.
3 Evelyn Harris, conversation with author, October 2013.
4 Aaron J. Johnson, "Lifted by the Audience: Audience Interaction in the Live Recordings of Donny Hathaway," paper presented at the Society for American Music Conference, Charlotte, NC, March 16, 2012, 5.
5 Samuel A. Floyd Jr., "Ring Shout! Literary Studies, Historical Studies, and Black Music Inquiry," *Black Music Research Journal* 11, no. 2 (1991): 275, qtd. in Johnson, "Lifted by the Audience," 3.
6 Sly Stone, qtd. in Les Ledbetter, "The New Sly Album: 'Music Feels Good,'" *New York Times*, April 20, 1973. Biographer Jeff Kaliss also reports that Stone was interested in buying one of Day's cars (see *I Want to Take You Higher: The Life and Times of Sly and the Family Stone* [New York: Backbeat, 2009], 115).
7 James Baldwin, "The White Problem" (1964), in *The Cross of Redemption: Uncollected Writings*, ed. Randall Kenan (New York: Pantheon, 2010), 78. The other "grotesque appeal to innocence" Baldwin cites is Gary Cooper.
8 Stone, qtd. in Ben Fong-Torres, "Everybody Is a Star: Travels with Sly Stone," in *Not Fade Away: A Backstage Pass to 20 Years of Rock and Roll* (San Francisco: Miller Freeman, 1999), 27.
9 Rickey Vincent, *Funk: The Music, the People, and the Rhythm of the One* (New York: St. Martin's, 1996), 93–94.
10 Dave Marsh, "Sly and the Family Stone," in *Fortunate Son: Criticism and Journalism by America's Best-Known Rock Writer* (New York: Random House, 1985), 56; Greil Marcus, *Mystery Train: Images of America in Rock 'n' Roll Music* (1975; New York: Plume, 1997), 70.
11 Vincent, *Funk*, 90.
12 Sly and the Family Stone, "Everyday People," comp. Sylvester Stuart, Epic, 1968. My sense of the band's personal and musical enactment of solidarity is informed by Bill Friskics-Warren's account—see *I'll Take You There: Pop Music and the Urge for Transcendence* (New York: Continuum, 2006), 193.
13 Marsh, "Sly and the Family Stone," 58, 59.

14 Marsh, review of Sly and the Family Stone's *Fresh, Creem*, September 1973.

15 See Marsh, review of *Fresh*.

16 Marcus, *Mystery Train*, 76.

17 Kaliss, *I Want to Take You Higher*, 111.

18 Sly and the Family Stone, "Que Sera, Sera," comp. Jay Livingston and Ray Evans, *Fresh*, Epic/CBS, 1973.

19 I owe this point about Rose's lyrical alteration to Enrico Bruno.

20 Stephen Davis, review of Sly and the Family Stone's *Fresh, Rolling Stone*, August 2, 1973.

21 Colleen Boggs, conversation with author, June 18, 2019. I am also grateful to Elizabeth Maddock Dillon and Eric Lott for conversations that helped me to think more about Rose in relation to Day.

22 Gladys Knight and the Pips, "If I Were Your Woman," comp. Gloria Jones, Clay McMurray, and Pam Sawyer, *If I Were Your Woman*, Motown, 1970.

23 Aretha Franklin, "Do Right Woman, Do Right Man," comp. Chips Moman and Dan Penn, *Never Loved a Man the Way I Love You*, Atlantic, 1967.

24 Nina Simone, "Be My Husband," *Pastel Blues*.

25 Simone's decision to cover a song originally sung by male convict laborers is fitting since, as Shana Redmond notes, Simone's voice on record constituted a uniquely queer "gender performance"; many listeners might not have known whether she was a woman or a man (*Anthem: Social Movements and the Sound of Solidarity in the African Diaspora* [New York: New York University Press, 2014], 208). But it is particularly through the ad-libs she performs that Simone queers the song's stated investment in heteronormative union.

26 "Rosie," Alan Lomax Collection, *Prison Songs: Historical Recordings from Parchman Farm, 1947–1948*, vol. 1, *Murderous Home*, Rounder, 1997.

27 Marisa Parham, *Haunting and Displacement in African American Literature and Culture* (New York: Routledge, 2009), 57.

28 Parham, *Haunting and Displacement*, 57.

29 Farah Jasmine Griffin, "Be My Husband," *Pitchfork*, May 15, 2017.

30 Simone recorded "Be My Husband" in May 1965, and *Pastel Blues* was released in October of that year. The Moynihan Report began to circulate internally in March 1965 and was leaked to the US public in July.

31 Simone with Stephen Cleary, *I Put a Spell on You* (New York: Da Capo, 2003), 117. Simone makes this statement while describing her motive in writing "Four Women" (1966).

32 Michael Awkward, *Soul Covers: Rhythm and Blues Remakes and the Struggle for Artistic Identity* (Durham, NC: Duke University Press, 2007), xxii.

33 Patricia Thompson, "Nina Simone Has College Crowd Sizzling with Hot African Dance," *Philadelphia Tribune*, October 17, 1964.

34 *Nina: A Historical Perspective* is available on the CD/DVD box set, *To Be Free: The Nina Simone Story* (Sony BMG, 2008).

35 Salamishah Tillet, "My American Dream Sounds Like Nina Simone," *NPR.org*, July 2, 2012.

36 Ruth Feldstein, *How It Feels to Be Free: Black Women Entertainers and the Civil Rights Movement* (Oxford: Oxford University Press, 2013), 103.

37 See David Ritz, *Respect: The Life of Aretha Franklin* (New York: Little, Brown, 2014), for Franklin's vexed relationships with other women in the industry. One famous exception: Franklin graciously offered her own Grammy Award to Esther Phillips in 1973.

38 Manny Tinsley, qtd. in Charles L. Sanders, "Aretha: A Close-up Look at Sister Superstar," *Ebony*, December 1971, 130.

39 Franklin with Ritz, *Aretha: From These Roots* (New York: Villard, 1999), 139.

40 Billy Preston, qtd. in Ritz, *Respect*, 235.

41 Aretha Franklin, "Dr. Feelgood," comp. Aretha Franklin and Ted White, *Aretha Live at Fillmore West*, Atlantic, 1971.

42 Wesley Morris, "Aretha Had Power. Did We Truly Respect It?," *New York Times*, August 16, 2018.

43 Sanders, "Close-up Look," 126.

44 Ann Powers, "Aretha Franklin," in *Trouble Girls: The Rolling Stone Book of Women in Rock*, ed. Barbara O'Dair (New York: Random House, 1997), 94.

45 Ntozake Shange, *for colored girls who have considered suicide when the rainbow is enuf* (1975; New York: Collier Books, 1989), 63.

46 Franklin, qtd. in Phyl Garland, "Aretha Franklin—'Sister Soul,'" *Ebony*, October 1967, 48.

47 Clayton Riley, "No Thing Quite Compares to Sister Aretha Franklin," *New York Times*, November 1, 1970.

48 Aretha Franklin, "Amazing Grace," comp. John Newton, *Amazing Grace*, Atlantic, 1972.

49 *Amazing Grace*, dir. Sidney Pollack (Al's Records and Tapes Production, 2018). For more on the film, see Emily J. Lordi, "'My Soul Is Satisfied': An Intimate New Documentary Explores the Source of Aretha Franklin's Power," *New Yorker*, April 5, 2019.

50 By reading delayed musical gratification as a method for heightening revolutionary energy, I provide an alternative to Robert Fink's intriguing analysis of soul teleology. Fink reads delayed rhythmic gratification in 1960s Motown productions as a means of training young listeners into "bourgeois values, especially goal direction, inhibition, and self-control"—and thus as advancing the project of upward mobility that Fink sees as the black neoliberal version of group uplift ("Goal-Directed Soul? Analyzing Rhythmic Teleology in African American Popular Music," *Journal of the American Musicological Society* 64, no. 1 [2011]: 186).

51 Albert Goldman, "Aretha Franklin: She Makes Salvation Seem Erotic," *New York Times*, March 31, 1968.

52 Donny Hathaway, "He Ain't Heavy, He's My Brother," comp. Bobby Scott and Bob Russell, *Donny Hathaway*, Atlantic, 1971; see, too, Hathaway's live recording of the song, on *These Songs for You, Live!*, Rhino, 2004.

53 Hathaway, "You've Got a Friend," comp. Carole King, *Donny Hathaway Live*, Atlantic, 1972.

54 See Hathaway, "The Ghetto," comp. Hathaway and Leroy Hutson, *Donny Hathaway Live*.

55 Hathaway, "Sugar Lee," comp. Hathaway and Ric Powell, *Everything Is Everything*, Atco, 1970; Ric Powell, liner notes to Hathaway, *Everything Is Everything*.

56 Hathaway, "The Ghetto."

57 Marcus, *Mystery Train*, 76.

58 *Report of the National Advisory Commission on Civil Disorders* (Washington, DC: US Government Printing Office, March 1, 1968), 1, qtd. in *New Thoughts on the Black Arts Movement*, ed. Lisa Gail Collins and Margo Natalie Crawford (2006; New Brunswick, NJ: Rutgers University Press, 2008), 2.

59 Powell, liner notes to *Everything Is Everything*. Hathaway's own liner notes to *Extension of a Man* (Atlantic, 1973) echo this point: he writes that the sequel to "The Ghetto," "The Slums," is "of the same idiom" as that song and is about "being happy, lively and reflecting on the joys of a people in a suppressed area." Hathaway also explains that he "recruited the entire Atlantic gang to rap some of that 'good ole alley talk' that has made the ghetto a haven (as well as a hell) shared by all included in the immediate area just around the corner from the suburbs!"

60 Dyana Williams, qtd. in *Donny Hathaway Unsung* (TV One, 2008).

61 Jerry Wexler and David Ritz, *Rhythm and Blues: A Life in American Music* (New York: Knopf, 1993), 259.

62 Leroy Hutson noted that "Hoss" was Hathaway's "pet name for [him]"—email message to author, November 2014.

63 Hathaway, "Voices Inside (Everything Is Everything)," comp. Richard Evans, Ric Powell, and Phil Upchurch, *Donny Hathaway Live*.

64 Eulaulah Hathaway, qtd. in Lordi, "Eulaulah Hathaway on Her Musical Marriage to Donny Hathaway," *New Yorker*, February 10, 2019.

65 Mayte Garcia, *The Most Beautiful: My Life with Prince* (New York: Hachette Books, 2017), 78.

66 Bonnie Allen, "Prince: What U See Is What U Get," *Essence*, November 1988, 72.

67 Allen, "Prince," 129.

68 "Prince: Premierpopartistisunderattack!!" *New Pittsburgh Courier*, July 12, 1986; Allen, "Prince," 72.

69 Susanna Hoffs, qtd. in Lauren Cochrane, "The Women behind Prince: 'The Respect He Showed Us Speaks Volumes,'" *Guardian*, April 24, 2017.

70 For one example of the demands Prince made of his women collaborators, Natalie Stewart tells how he brought her onstage for a Grammy after-party

performance and had her recite her poetry in double and then triple time. See Cochrane, "The Women behind Prince."

71 Prince, qtd. in "Rosie Gaines Joins Prince Following Audition," *Cleveland Call and Post*, October 18, 1990.

72 "Rosie Gaines," PrinceVault.com, last modified September 3, 2018, http://www.princevault.com/index.php?title=Rosie_Gaines.

73 Gavin Martin, review of "Prince and the New Power Generation: *Diamonds and Pearls*," *New Musical Express*, October 5, 1991.

74 Phil Sutcliffe, "Prince: The Entertainment Center, Sydney, Australia," *Q*, July 1992.

75 "Rosie Gaines," PrinceVault.com. According to Jason Draper, Prince was distracted from the Gaines project by his work with Carmen Electra; he let Gaines's solo debut album languish for years while refusing to release Gaines from her contract with Paisley Park Records (*Prince: Life and Times* [2008; New York: Chartwell Books, 2016], 115). When Prince's label folded in 1994, Gaines signed with Motown, releasing the album under the title *Closer Than Close* in 1995. She returned to work with Prince on later recordings and occasionally joined him in concert.

76 Gaines and Prince's live recordings of "Ain't No Way" and "Dr. Feelgood" are available on YouTube: Gary Mackey, "Rosie Gaines (with Prince)—Ain't No Way (Live)," August 28, 2011, YouTube video, 2:48, https://www.youtube.com/watch?v=FqIR8XGoB9c; https://www.youtube.com/watch?v=CDQonuneAng.

77 Chris Molanphy, "Le Petty Prince Edition," October 30, 2017, *Hit Parade*, prod. Chris Berube, podcast, 1:11:53, http://www.slate.com/articles/podcasts/hit_parade/2017/10/how_tom_petty_and_prince_led_parallel_careers.html.

78 "Nothing Compares 2 U," PrinceVault.com, last modified June 22, 2019, http://www.princevault.com/index.php?title=Nothing_Compares_2_U.

79 Jody Rosen, "Prince and Competition," *New York Times*, April 22, 2016.

80 Rosie Gaines, qtd. in Deborah Gregory, "Looking for a New Groove? Tune into the Eclectic Sounds of 'Alternative R&B'!," *Essence*, November 1995, 66. "What exactly is Gaines's sound? Straight-up soul with a twist of social consciousness and traditional reggae rhythms," Gregory noted—although, as Gaines put it, "In the final analysis . . . , music to me is just music" (66).

81 Prince feat. Rosie Gaines, "Nothing Compares 2 U," live version, comp. Prince, *The Hits/The B-Sides*, Warner Bros., 1993.

82 Prince feat. Rosie Gaines, "Nothing Compares 2 U," live version, accessed June 5, 2017, https://vimeo.com/140627358. PrinceVault.com lists this video as being "for promotional release only" and describes the live performance as being "intercut with footage from past videos"—Prince's common practice of filmic collage ("Nothing Compares 2 U," PrinceVault.com).

83 Mark Anthony Neal highlights this issue in *Soul Babies: Black Popular Culture and the Post-Soul Aesthetic* (New York: Routledge, 2002), 160–62.

Chapter 4: Emergent Interiors

1 Nathaniel Mackey, "Blue in Green: Black Interiority," in *Paracritical Hinge: Essays, Talks, Notes, Interviews* (Madison: University of Wisconsin Press, 2005), 199–200.

2 See Christopher Freeburg, *Black Aesthetics and the Interior Life* (Charlottesville: University of Virginia Press, 2017); Kevin Quashie, *The Sovereignty of Quiet: Beyond Resistance in Black Culture* (New Brunswick, NJ: Rutgers University Press, 2012).

3 Mackey, *Bedouin Hornbook* (1984; Los Angeles: Sun and Moon Press, 1997), 62. Mackey himself calls this reading into question when, later in the novel, his narrator imagines himself in a police officer's stranglehold and critiques himself for having aestheticized the brute fact of lynching into a poetic reading of vocal technique: "The prospect of a cop's arm around his neck reminded him that every concept, no matter how figural or sublime, had its literal, deadletter aspect as well. It seemed too easy to speak of 'alchemy,' too easy not to remember how inescapably real every lynching had been" (231).

4 Fred Moten, *In the Break: The Aesthetics of the Black Radical Tradition* (Minneapolis: University of Minnesota Press, 2003), 193–95; Michael Jarrett, *Soundtracks: A Musical ABC* (Philadelphia: Temple University Press, 1998), 228.

5 Chris Porterfield, "Lady Soul: Singing It Like It Is," *Time*, June 28, 1968, 64.

6 Moten, *In the Break*, 224.

7 Simon Frith claims that "there's no such thing as female falsetto," even though he acknowledges in a footnote that a female colleague has informed him this is a subject of "dispute among phoneticians": "How else would we describe what Minnie Riperton does with her voice on . . . 'Lovin' You?'" Frith asks. How else, indeed? (*Performing Rites: On the Value of Popular Music* [Cambridge, MA: Harvard University Press, 1996], 194, 324).

8 Although Solange does not cite Peebles as an influence, Solange's restrained vocals and relatively spare arrangements echo the lo-fi setup at Hi Records. Missy Elliott, whose self-produced work Solange does cite as an influence on her own, provides a different kind of historical link between Peebles and Solange. Elliott loops the opening line of Peebles's "I Can't Stand the Rain" through her breakout 1997 single "Supa Dupa Fly."

9 See, e.g., Peter Guralnick, *Sweet Soul Music: Rhythm and Blues and the Southern Dream of Freedom* (New York: Back Bay Books, 2012), 2.

10 Dorian Lynskey, "Ann Peebles: The Girl with the Big Voice," *Guardian*, February 20, 2014.

11 "Ann Peebles on 'I Can't Stand the Rain,'" Grammy Foundation, July 2, 2015.

12 According to Willie Mitchell, Peebles "was the girl with the big voice who could have really gone further. . . . But I don't think Ann . . . put as much energy into her career . . . as some of the rest of these people" (qtd. in Lynskey, "Ann Peebles"). Even Peebles admits, "I was happy the way I was. I still did a lot of

songs but at that point I was married, I had a child. . . . Knowing [that stardom] would take me away from what I was really like, it didn't bother me that much" (qtd. in Lynskey, "Ann Peebles").

13 The notion that Peebles was "the female equivalent of Al Green" was voiced in, among other sources, *Ebony*'s review of *I Can't Stand the Rain* (July 1974, 26). David Nathan hailed Peebles's belated emergence in a May 1974 issue of *Blues and Soul*: "All of a sudden, it seems like the whole world is talking about the talents of a magnificently soulful young woman and she puts it herself, 'I feel like I'm beginning to make it.' Her name is Ann Peebles and after what she describes as 'seven long, hard years,' she's achieving a goodly measure of the recognition that she's been working towards" (Nathan, "Ann Peebles: Hangin' On to Success," *Blues and Soul*, May 1974).

14 Ann Peebles, "I Can't Stand the Rain," comp. Ann Peebles, Don Bryant, and Bernard Miller, *I Can't Stand the Rain*, Hi, 1973.

15 Todd Everett reported in 1975, "Difficult though it may be to get Ann Peebles excited about any subject, she is happy enough to talk of her admiration for gospel monolith Mahalia Jackson. 'She's my idol,' states Ann with a slightly awe-stricken look in her eyes. 'And always will be. I must have every record Mahalia's ever made'" (Everett, "Ann Peebles . . . and the Hi Records Story," *Phonograph Record*, December 1975).

16 "It's like that end phrase on 'I Can't Stand the Rain.' We only got that after we'd fooled around with the song for a bit" (qtd. in Nathan, "Ann Peebles").

17 Phyl Garland, review of *Tellin' It* by Ann Peebles, *Ebony*, April 1976, 29.

18 Al Green with Davin Seay, *Take Me to the River: An Autobiography* (Chicago: A Cappella Books, 2009), 187.

19 Green with Seay, *Take Me to the River*, 239.

20 Green with Seay, *Take Me to the River*, 183. By using the word *blues* to refer to what would come to be known as *soul*, the album title also registers the uneven development of the latter term as a genre category, a phenomenon discussed in the first chapter.

21 Liner notes to Al Green, *Green Is Blues*, Hi Records, 1972.

22 Green with Seay, *Take Me to the River*, 248.

23 Green, "Summertime," comp. George Gershwin, *Green Is Blues*, Hi, 1969.

24 Claude Jeter qtd. in Anthony Heilbut, *The Fan Who Knew Too Much: Aretha Franklin, the Rise of the Soap Opera, Children of the Gospel Church, and Other Meditations* (New York: Knopf, 2012), 256.

25 Green, "Gotta Find a New World," comp. Carl Smith and Marion Oliver, *Green Is Blues*.

26 Peter Bailey, "The Greening of Al Green," *New York Times*, April 15, 1973.

27 Richard Wright, foreword to Paul Oliver, *Blues Fell This Morning: Meaning in the Blues* (Cambridge: Cambridge University Press, 1990), xiii.

28 Green conveyed interiority not only through his music but also through his quiet, deep-thinking persona. "He is complex and displays, even during

surface conversation, an exceptional degree of intelligence that makes him constantly question and search for the subtleties in life," according to William Earl Berry in *Jet*. "Easy answers to questions do not satisfy him. He is too complicated and erudite for that" ("Singer Al Green: Inventive Master of Rhythm and Blues," *Jet*, November 23, 1972, 55). Reporters often noted that Green lived alone in a massive ranch home in the Shelby Forest State Park outside Memphis, a place to which one would have to be led and could not be directed. The haven became a site of infamous trauma in 1974, when Green was attacked by a woman named Mary Woodson who poured boiling grits on him before killing herself.

29 Green's 1973 performance on *Soul!* is available on YouTube: TheChoke77, "Al Green SOUL! 1973 Love and Happiness," November 8, 2013, YouTube video, 7:50, https://www.youtube.com/watch?v=zSn-TTP7Egg.

30 Bailey, "Greening of Al Green," 105.

31 "Isaac was just cool as shit," according to drummer Willie Hall: "He was a great person, energetic, didn't do any drugs. He'd drink a little Lancers wine. And he would look up in the top of his head, the third eye, trying to come up with an idea—boom, it would come—perfect" (qtd. in Robert Gordon, *Respect Yourself: Stax Records and the Soul Explosion* [New York: Bloomsbury, 2013], 226–27).

32 Chester Higgins, "Black Moses of Today's Black Music," *Jet*, February 4, 1971, 58; Phyl Garland, "Isaac Hayes: Hot Buttered Soul," *Ebony*, March 1970, 82–91.

33 Although they recorded these hit songs at Stax, Sam and Dave were signed to Atlantic.

34 Hayes, qtd. in Rob Bowman, *Soulsville U.S.A.: The Story of Stax Records* (New York: Schirmer Trade Books, 1997), 182; "Black Moses: Isaac Hayes: A Self-Portrait," *Penthouse*, September 1973, 158.

35 Mark Anthony Neal incisively assembled these factors in a paper titled "Soul among the Ruins," delivered at the Association for the Study of African American Life and History Conference, Memphis, TN, September 27, 2014.

36 Hayes, qtd. in Hua Hsu, untitled paper presented at the American Studies Association meeting, Albuquerque, NM, 2008. For more on the impact of King's death on Hayes, see Hayes's remarks in the *Wattstax* commentary track (*Wattstax*, dir. Mel Stuart, 30th Anniversary Special Edition, 2004).

37 Hayes, qtd. in Bowman, *Soulsville U.S.A.*, 144.

38 Hayes, qtd. in Mark Anthony Neal, "The Blackest Moses: The Hot Buttered Soul of Isaac Hayes," *New Black Man in Exile*, June 27, 2017, http://www.new blackmaninexile.net/2017/06/the-blackest-moses-hot-buttered-soul-of.html; and in Bowman, *Soulsville U.S.A.*, 181.

39 Hayes, qtd. in Bowman, *Soulsville U.S.A.*, 181.

40 Terry Johnson, qtd. in Gordon, *Respect Yourself*, 71.

41 Guralnick, *Sweet Soul Music*, 369. According to Hayes himself, Stax seldom used strings due to budget considerations as well as label owner Jim Stewart's

desire "to keep that raw, funky sound" (Hayes, qtd. in Bowman, "The Stax Sound: A Musicological Analysis," *Popular Music* 14, no. 3 [1995]: 290). *Hot Buttered Soul* was perhaps the most dramatic exemplar of the departure from the "readily identifiable sound" that, according to Bowman, characterized Stax productions from 1961 to 1969 (285). Moreover, according to Bowman, the album was instrumental in establishing the LP as a viable format for R&B audiences (Bowman, *Soulsville U.S.A.*, 184).

42 Certainly Hayes was a key innovator of the "conceptual excess" that Zeth Lundy associates with 1970s popular music—double albums, long songs, and rock operas (*Songs in the Key of Life* [New York: Continuum, 2007], 11; see also 9–12 and 27–30). Yet Hayes's larger-than-life persona was so carefully cultivated that "largesse" might be a better descriptor than "excess." His gold chain suit itself was a deliberately multifaceted sign of pragmatism, glamour, and nationalist sentiment: a form of "air-conditioning" that helped him stay cool in the spotlight, it also signified the end of black "bondage" (Gordon, *Respect Yourself*, 237) and "a sex thing" ("Black Moses: Isaac Hayes: A Self-Portrait," 58).

43 Hayes, qtd. in Bowman, *Soulsville U.S.A.*, 182.

44 Garland, "Isaac Hayes," 84.

45 B. J. Mason, "Isaac Hayes: New Image, New Wife, New Career," *Ebony*, October 1973, 178.

46 "Black Moses: Isaac Hayes: A Self-Portrait," 154.

47 Several buildings in Watts were demolished and looted. But given that, according to Gerald Horne, "few homes, churches, or libraries were damaged," the events of August 11–16 appear to represent not a "mindless riot but rather a conscious, though inchoate, insurrection" (*Fire This Time: The Watts Uprising and the 1960s* [Charlottesville: University of Virginia Press, 1995], 3).

48 William Earl Berry, "How Watts Festival Renews Black Unity," *Jet*, September 14, 1972, 53.

49 Richard Iton, *In Search of the Black Fantastic: Politics and Popular Culture in the Post-Civil Rights Era* (Oxford: Oxford University Press, 2008), 97.

50 Mark Anthony Neal, *What the Music Said: Black Popular Music and Black Public Culture* (New York: Routledge, 1994), 88.

51 Horne, *Fire This Time*, 42.

52 Berry, "How Watts Festival Renews Black Unity," 54.

53 Mason, "Isaac Hayes," 178. "The money, the cars, all of it is just fringe, but Isaac Hayes is roots," Hayes told Mason (178). See also "Isaac Hayes Explains Why He Gave Talent and Time in Watts," *Cleveland Call and Post*, September 2, 1972. For more on Hayes's philanthropic work, see Chester Higgins, "Black Stars *Do* 'Give a Damn,'" *Ebony*, September 1971, 45–46.

54 Mackey, "Cante Moro," in *Paracritical Hinge: Essays, Talks, Notes, Interviews* (Madison: University of Wisconsin Press, 2005), 187.

55 Robert Duncan, qtd. in Mackey, "Cante Moro," 186.

56 Mackey, "Cante Moro," 184.

57 Bowman, *Soulsville U.S.A.*, 50.

58 Maureen Mahon, "They Say She's Different: Race, Gender, Genre, and the Liberated Black Femininity of Betty Davis," *Journal of Popular Music Studies* 23, no. 2 (2011): 147.

59 Farah Jasmine Griffin, notes toward essay to be titled "Songbirds and Wonderlove: The Ethereal Soul of Minnie Riperton, Syreeta Wright, Deniece Williams," draft paper presented at Black Feminist Sound Studies Workshop, Princeton University, January 26, 2013, 6.

60 Chris Charlesworth, "Minnie Riperton," *Melody Maker*, April 12, 1975.

61 Griffin, notes toward "Songbirds and Wonderlove," 6.

62 Charlesworth, "Minnie Riperton."

63 For more on Riperton's relationship to gospel, see Aaron Cohen, *Move on Up: Chicago Soul Music and Black Cultural Power* (Chicago: University of Chicago Press, 2019), 72; Lynn Norment, "'Perfect Angel' Leaves Legacy of Love," *Ebony*, October 1979, 96.

64 Riperton, qtd. in Penny Valentine, "Minnie Riperton: Perfect Angel in Flight," *Sounds*, April 12, 1975, qtd. in Cohen, *Move on Up*, 71–72.

65 Charlesworth, "Minnie Riperton."

66 Accounts of Riperton's range vary from five octaves to eight; Riperton herself reported her voice teacher's assessment that her range was five and a half octaves on the *Mike Douglas Show* on September 23, 1977 (MinnieRipertonChannel, "MINNIE RIPERTON Interview on Mike Douglas Show 1977," October 18, 2015, YouTube video, 2:54, https://www.youtube.com/watch?v=AnSjjCyxR-s). Virginia Dellenbaugh discusses the discourse of the angelic in relation to castrati and male pop singers in "From Earth Angel to Electric Lucifer: Castrati, Doo Wop, and the Vocoder," in *Popular Music Studies Today*, edited by J. Merrill, 75–83 (Wiesbaden: Springer VS, 2017).

67 Green with Seay, *Take Me to the River*, 252.

68 Riperton, qtd. in Cliff White, "Feminism Is, Uh, Like Skinning Cats . . .," *New Musical Express*, June 4, 1977.

69 This analysis of Riperton's politics of love challenges Mitchell Morris's reading of "Loving You" as sonically self-involved, even autoerotic. Comparing "Loving You" to Aretha Franklin's ecstatic address to a lover in "Natural Woman" ("Oh baby, what you done to me!"), Morris describes the former as a relatively "solipsistic, not to mention masturbatory" performance that, "for all its apostrophes to 'you,' is relatively unconcerned with the specifics of sexual transport" and instead offers "an exalted drift just above quiescence" (*The Persistence of Sentiment: Display and Feeling in Popular Music of the 1970s* [Berkeley: University of California Press, 2013], 82).

70 Riperton, qtd. in Vicki Wilson, "Minnie Riperton, On and Off Stage," *Philadelphia Tribune*, May 20, 1975.

71 Riperton, qtd. in Bob Lucas, "Minnie Riperton," *Ebony*, December 1976, 34, 40.

72 Riperton, qtd. in Lucas, "Minnie Riperton," 38, 40.

73 Riperton's sister Elaine Brumfield appears in *Minnie Riperton Unsung* (TV One, 2009).

74 Rudolph, qtd. in Robert E. Johnson, "Minnie's Husband Tells of Her Final Moments as They Listened to Stevie," *Jet*, August 2, 1979, 55.

75 Riperton, qtd. in Norment, "'Perfect Angel' Leaves Legacy of Love," 99.

76 The lyrics to Wonder's song are quoted by Rudolph in Johnson, "Minnie's Husband Tells," 54. The song title is cited in "Many Toasts Lifted to MR as She Rests in Peace," *Jet*, August 2, 1979, 15.

77 Rudolph, qtd. in Johnson, "Minnie's Husband Tells," 53.

78 Daphne Brooks, keynote conversation with Solange at Blackstar Rising and Purple Reign Conference, Yale University, January 26, 2017.

79 Brooks and Solange, keynote conversation.

80 "An Interview with Audre Lorde," interview by Karla Hammond, *American Poetry Review* 9, no. 2 (1980), 8, qtd. in Elizabeth Alexander, "'Coming Out Blackened and Whole': Fragmentation and Reintegration in Audre Lorde's *Zami* and *The Cancer Journals*," in *Power and Possibility* (Ann Arbor: University of Michigan Press, 2007), 95; Brooks and Solange, keynote conversation.

81 Doreen St. Félix, "In Solange's Room," *MTV.com*, October 5, 2016.

82 Brooks and Solange, keynote conversation.

83 Beyoncé, "Solange Brings It All Full Circle with Her Sister Beyoncé," *Interview*, January 10, 2017, https://www.interviewmagazine.com/music/solange.

84 Interview with Solange by Beyoncé, *Interview*.

85 Brooks and Solange, keynote conversation.

86 Rilke, qtd. in Mackey, "Blue in Green," 202.

87 Griffin, qtd. in Salamishah Tillet, "The Messenger," *Elle*, March 2017, 454.

88 Griffin, qtd. in Tillet, "The Messenger," 454.

89 Brooks and Solange, keynote conversation.

90 Brooks and Solange, keynote conversation.

Chapter 5: Never Catch Me

Epigraph: Clayton Riley, "All Out for Aretha," *New York Times*, August 12, 1973.

1 Amiri Baraka, "The Changing Same (R&B and New Black Music)," in *Black Music* (New York: Quill, 1967), 199.

2 James Brown, qtd. in R. J. Smith, *The One: The Life and Music of James Brown* (New York: Gothic Books, 2012), 149. Brown's definition of soul was subject to change according to his audience and mood. He told a white reporter in 1968, "Soul is when a man do everything he can and come up second. Soul is when a man make a hundred dollars a week and it cost him a hundred and ten to live.... Soul is when a man is nothin' because he's black" (qtd. in Mel

Ziegler, "James Brown Sells His Soul," *Miami Herald*, August 18, 1968, in *The James Brown Reader: 50 Years of Writing about the Godfather of Soul*, ed. Nelson George and Alan Leeds [New York: Plume, 2008], 46).

3 Robin James, *Resilience and Melancholy: Pop Music, Feminism, Neoliberalism* (Winchester, UK: Zero Books, 2015), 1–7.

4 Jackson calls Newport a "beer festival" in her memoir (written with Evan McLeod Wylie), *Movin' On Up* (New York: Hawthorn Books, 1966), 145. However, she elsewhere notes that she stopped singing at Newport simply because "people might not understand" ("'I Don't Swing,' Is Mahalia's Reply," *New York Amsterdam News*, July 16, 1960).

5 Mahalia Jackson, qtd. in "Mahalia Says She's Singing Only Gospels at Festival," *New York Amsterdam News*, July 6, 1957.

6 See "Didn't It Rain," *Mahalia Jackson: Live at Newport, 1958*, Sony, 1994. A film of Jackson's performance, drawn from Bert Stern's documentary *Jazz on a Summer's Day* (1960), is also available on YouTube: Loewenbach Fiul, "Mahalia Jackson—Didn't It Rain (Live Newport 1958)," June 22, 2013, YouTube video, 3:20, https://www.youtube.com/watch?v=90H486KOVBg.

7 Mellonee Burnim, "The Black Gospel Music Tradition: A Complex of Ideology, Aesthetic, and Behavior," in *More Than Dancing: Essays on Afro-American Music and Musicians*, ed. Irene V. Jackson (Westport, CT: Greenwood, 1985), 162. Burnim continues: "What appears as unsystematic and unstructured to the outsider is actually a well-conceived and well-executed concept of logically moving units within an organizational whole from one point in time to another" (162).

8 Jackson, qtd in Ralph Ellison, "As the Spirit Moves Mahalia" (1958), in *Living with Music: Ralph Ellison's Jazz Writings*, ed. Robert G. O'Meally (New York: Modern Library, 2001), 93.

9 Jackson, as told to Evan McLeod Wylie, "I Can't Stop Singing," *Saturday Evening Post*, December 5, 1959, 100. For a brilliant analysis of Jackson's modes of self-fashioning in relation to a variety of discursive networks (musical, religious, economic), see Mark Burford, *Mahalia Jackson and the Gospel Field* (New York: Oxford University Press, 2019).

10 Ralph Ellison, *Invisible Man* (1952; New York: Vintage International, 1995), 16. For more on the aesthetic and historical links between Jackson and Ellison, who reviews her performance at Newport in a 1958 *Saturday Review* essay titled "As the Spirit Moves Mahalia," see Emily J. Lordi, *Black Resonance: Iconic Women Singers and African American Literature* (New Brunswick, NJ: Rutgers University Press, 2013), 66–98.

11 "James Brown Finds Brown Capitalism Works," *New York Amsterdam News*, February 8, 1969.

12 Glenn Douglass, "Star-With-Power James Brown Breaks Apollo Record," *New Journal and Guide* (Norfolk, VA), November 27, 1965.

13 Smith, *The One*, 8.

14 "James Brown: The New Breed . . . Mr. Dynamite . . . Wears Many Hats," *New York Amsterdam News*, April 23, 1966.

15 Philip Gourevitch, "Mr. Brown," *New Yorker*, July 29, 2002.

16 The show is available on DVD (*TAMI Show: Teenage Awards Music International*, dir. Steve Binder [10 Spot, 2010]). Brown's performance can be viewed on YouTube: Afra Bass, "James Brown and the Famous Flames, Live on the T.A.M.I. Show 1964," May 5, 2016, YouTube video, 17:52, https://www.youtube.com/watch?v=6-EoX2JxCs4.

17 James Brown with Bruce Tucker, *James Brown: The Godfather of Soul* (New York: Thunder's Mouth Press, 1990), 152.

18 Smith, *The One*, 147–48.

19 Smith, *The One*, 148.

20 Brown with Tucker, *James Brown*, 153.

21 Bill Wyman, qtd. in Guy Stevens, "James Brown: The Stones Can't Stop Talking about King James," *Record Mirror*, December 19, 1964.

22 Brown, qtd. in Stevens, "James Brown," 149.

23 Smith, *The One*, 149.

24 Smith, *The One*, 150.

25 Brown reportedly curtailed his touring schedule in 1970, telling Ray Brack of *Rolling Stone* that he planned to "[cut] off about 85 percent of public appearances" by doing about thirty shows a year and "taking [his] music into movies and television" (Brown, qtd. in Brack, "James Brown: 'The Man' Vs. 'Negroes,'" *Rolling Stone*, January 21, 1970, in George and Leeds, *James Brown Reader*, 62–63).

26 "Doctor Says James Brown Collapse Is Caused by Overwork," *Pittsburgh Courier*, June 11, 1966. Brown's doctor reportedly instructed him to limit himself to four shows per day in lieu of the six he had been playing to accommodate crowds.

27 Gerri Hirshey, *Nowhere to Run: The Story of Soul Music* (1984; London: Southbank Publishing, 2006), 266.

28 Gertrude Sanders, qtd. in Hirshey, *Nowhere to Run*, 266.

29 See "James Brown Finds Brown Capitalism Works," 18. The actual numbers of Brown's entourage in the 1960s were fuzzy: "Nobody seems to know exactly how many people travel with the show," wrote one critic. "Or if they do know, they' re not sure if it mightn't be some kind of betrayal to reveal the exact number. So some say 40 and some say 50 and some just say 'a whole lot'" (Doon Arbus, "James Brown Is Out of Sight," *New York Herald Tribune*, March 20, 1966, in George and Leeds, *James Brown Reader*, 20).

30 Brown with Tucker, *James Brown*, 138.

31 "The Explosive Mr. Brown," *Ebony*, March 1965, 57.

32 Brown, qtd. in Smith, *The One*, 152.

33 For more on this innovation, see Harry Weinger with Alan Leeds, "It's a New Day" (liner notes to *Foundations of Funk*), in George and Leeds, *James Brown Reader*, 36.

34 Anne Danielsen uses this phrase to describe James Brown's grooves in such songs as "The Payback" (1973). See *Presence and Pleasure: The Funk Grooves of James Brown and Parliament* (Middletown, CT: Wesleyan University Press, 2006), 180, 184.

35 It was in fact Mahalia Jackson who offered one of the most damning critiques of labor conditions for black entertainers in these years. No stranger to grueling regimes (she embarked on a seventy-day, thirteen-thousand-mile tour of the United States the year after Newport), she issued a systemic diagnosis of Nat King Cole's death from lung cancer at age forty-five: "The wear and tear on Negro entertainers with these one night stands is unbelievable. They simply do not have time to have themselves checked out medically. So few of us out there make any real money. . . . The pressure is on us to keep working . . . to appear here, make a one night stand there. . . . We can't get TV shows; we can't get contracts to perform permanently anywhere. . . . I would think, wouldn't you, that America should pay tribute to its great artists like Cole, Duke Ellington, etc., . . . so that they would be relieved of financial pressures and worries" (Mahalia Jackson, qtd. in Chester Higgins, "'Nat Must Have Kept Going When He Shouldn't'—Mahalia," *Jet*, March 4, 1965, 22–23). If Jackson's infamous concerns with financial security motivated her own rigorous performance regime at the height of her fame, her determination to be justly compensated also moved her to resist overwork. At the close of a concert at New York's Town Hall in 1957, she reportedly obliged five curtain calls before she "marched back onstage, took Miss [Mildred] Falls by the hand and led her from the piano" (Alfred Duckett, "Mahalia Jackson Likes Applause [Beg Pardon] Amens at Concerts," *Chicago Defender*, June 1, 1957).

36 Robert Shelton, "Otis Redding Stars in 2 Park Concerts," *New York Times*, April 18, 1966.

37 Jonathan Gould, "In Memory of Otis Redding and His Revolution," *New Yorker*, December 10, 2017.

38 Gould, "In Memory of Otis Redding."

39 Gould, "In Memory of Otis Redding."

40 See Robert Shelton, "Otis Redding: A Major Loss," *New York Times*, March 3, 1968.

41 Otis Redding, "Ole Man Trouble," live version, comp. Redding, *Hollywood, Whisky A Go-Go*, April 10, 1966, Stax, 2016.

42 Brown with Tucker, *James Brown*, 176.

43 Brown with Tucker, *James Brown*, 176. As noted in chapter 1, Brown's politics were complicated, to say the least. Declaring in 1968 that "black power is what you can do for your people," he supported or founded several community

organizations geared toward black economic and educational empowerment (Brown, qtd. in John Lewis, "James Brown Talks on Blackness, Power," *Baltimore Afro-American*, March 16, 1968). But he also performed at Richard Nixon's inaugural festivities in 1968, despite having backed Nixon's opponent, Hubert Humphrey. He was perhaps the first black superstar to entertain soldiers in Vietnam in 1970, despite other black artists' resistance to the war.

44 Otis Redding, "Try a Little Tenderness," comp. Jimmy Campbell, Reg Connelly, and Harry Woods, *Complete and Unbelievable: The Otis Redding Dictionary of Soul*, Volt/Atco, 1966.

45 Jonathan Gould, *Otis Redding: An Unfinished Life* (New York: Crown Archetype, 2017), 392. That fall, a *Melody Maker* poll in the United Kingdom voted Redding the "world's number one male vocalist"—a category previously topped by Elvis Presley for the past ten years—and solidified Redding's reverse British invasion (see "Release Poll Data in Which Redding Overturned Presley," *Cleveland Call and Post*, September 23, 1967).

46 The Oslo performance of "Try a Little Tenderness," included on the *Stax/Volt Revue Live in Norway 1967* DVD (Stax, 2007), can be viewed on YouTube at: ReelinInTheYears66, "Otis Redding 'Try a Little Tenderness' Live 1967 (Reelin' in the Years Archives)," February 21, 2013, YouTube video, 6:18, https://www.youtube.com/watch?v=IQ9n2_5mbig.

47 Brown, qtd. in Smith, *The One*, 149.

48 Redding's performance of "Try a Little Tenderness" at the 1967 Monterey Pop Festival is included in D. A. Pennebaker's documentary *Monterey Pop* (Leacock-Pennebaker, 1968).

49 The performance of "Dr. Feelgood" I discuss is not the version of the song included on the album *Aretha Live at Fillmore West*. The March 6, 1971, performance of the song can be viewed on YouTube at Aretha Franklin on MV, "Aretha Franklin—Dr. Feelgood—3/6/1971—Fillmore West (Official)," September 24, 2014, YouTube video, 9:08, https://www.youtube.com/watch?v=V2x8zpoHkTU.

50 See Emmett G. Price III, "Singing the Sermon: Where Musicology Meets Homiletics," *Yale Journal of Music and Religion* 1, no. 2 (2015): 49. I am grateful to Matthew Morrison for directing me to this source and for other terminological assistance.

51 Audre Lorde, "Uses of the Erotic: The Erotic as Power" (1978), in *Sister Outsider: Essays and Speeches* (Berkeley: Crossing Press, 2007), 53–59.

52 Riley, "All Out for Aretha," 132.

53 Gaye, qtd. in Carlyle C. Douglas, "Marvin Gaye," *Ebony*, November 1974, 58.

54 Franklin's creation of a new zone of authority is almost comically apparent in her performance of "Spirit in the Dark" at the Fillmore. In a unique false ending captured on *Live at Fillmore West*, Franklin cajoles Ray Charles into coming onstage to reprise the song as a duet. Although it is immediately apparent that Charles doesn't know the words, the fact that Franklin isn't done singing

the song means that he's not either ("Spirit in the Dark," comp. Franklin, *Live at Fillmore West*, Atlantic, 1971).

55 Brent Hayes Edwards, "Notes on Poetics Regarding Mackey's 'Song,'" *Callaloo* 23, no. 2 (2000): 581.

56 Although there is not space to elaborate this point here, Gaye's 1976 album *I Want You* uses serial poetics less to examine the seriality of trouble than to explore the seriality of desire.

57 For Gaye and his accompanists' jazz training and commitment, see Ben Edmonds, *What's Going On? Marvin Gaye and the Last Days of the Motown Sound* (Edinburgh: Canongate, 2001), 103–6, 124–25; for other influences, including those of childhood hymns, see 154.

58 Gaye, qtd. in David Ritz, *Divided Soul: The Life of Marvin Gaye* (1985; New York: Da Capo, 1991), 132. While Gaye, like most other artists in this book, performed at benefit concerts for black causes, he was unusually candid about his disillusionment with the failures of US democracy: "I'm governed, ruled and manipulated and treated like cattle just like the rest of us," he noted, "But I'm apathetic toward our whole political system" (Gaye, qtd. in Vernon Gibbs, "Marvin Gaye May Not Be Goin' On," *Zoo World*, November 7, 1974).

59 See Phil Symes, "A Study of Marvin Gaye's Liberation," *Disc and Music Echo*, June 12, 1971.

60 Gaye, "Inner City Blues (Make Me Wanna Holler)," comp. Marvin Gaye and James Nyx Jr., *What's Going On*, Tamla, 1971.

61 For more on the technical process of splicing and reconstructing the tracks to create the album's continuous feel, see Edmonds, *What's Going On?*, 168.

62 Gaye's manner of harmonizing with himself, a technique popularized by Franklin on such songs as "Never Loved a Man" (1967), is yet another way of sounding black interiority. According to his former wife Janis Gaye, insofar as his overdubbed vocal sounds ("a sweet falsetto, a tender midrange, a sexual growl, a bottommost plea") represented different facets of Gaye himself, he hoped that by harmonizing them, he might "blend the differences in his own personality" (Janis Gaye with David Ritz, *After the Dance: My Life with Marvin Gaye* [New York: Amistad, 2015], 52).

63 Gaye, "What's Happening Brother," comp. Gaye and Nyx, *What's Going On*.

64 Steve Smith, qtd. in Edmonds, *What's Going On?*, 148.

65 Elgie Stover, qtd. in Edmonds, *What's Going On?*, 175.

66 Gaye, "Save the Children," comp. Gaye, Al Cleveland, and Renaldo Benson, *What's Going On*; Gaye, "God Is Love," comp. Gaye, Anna Gaye, Elgie Stover, and Nyx, *What's Going On*.

67 Gaye, "Mercy Mercy Me (The Ecology)," comp. Gaye, *What's Going On*.

68 Douglas, "Marvin Gaye," *Ebony*, 52.

69 Gaye, qtd. in William Earl Berry, "Marvin Gaye: Inner City Musical Poet," *Jet*, February 1, 1973, 60.

70 Gaye, qtd. in Stephanie Calman, "Marvin Gaye," *Ebony*, March 1981, 62.

71 Mark Anthony Neal, "Trouble Man: The Art and Politics of Marvin Gaye," *Western Journal of Black Studies* 22, no. 4 (1998): 255–56.

72 Neal, "Trouble Man," 258.

73 Neal draws on Paul Gilroy's analysis of gendered compensation in *The Black Atlantic: Modernity and Double Consciousness* (Cambridge, MA: Harvard University Press, 1993), 85.

74 Edmonds, *What's Going On?*, 218. The false endings of *What's Going On* are also complicated by the album format itself: when played on repeat, they might gain power or grow stale. While the same might be said of Franklin's live albums, Gaye's LP lacks the sound of an audience whose perpetual enthusiasm becomes part of the events that Franklin's Fillmore and *Amazing Grace* albums record.

75 Edmonds, *What's Going On?*, 201.

76 Kendrick Lamar has conducted many of his own innovative false endings, for instance by sonically "resurrecting" Tupac Shakur via sample for a long conversation at the end of Lamar's 2015 album *To Pimp a Butterfly*—after suggesting his own death via gunshot on the song "King Kunta." For a brilliant analysis of such moves, see Jade Conlee, "'Slow Motion for the Ambulance, the Project Filled with Cameras': The Voice of Kendrick Lamar as Already Dead," paper presented at MoPop Conference, Seattle, April 12, 2019.

77 Nate Patrin, review of *You're Dead!* by Flying Lotus, *Pitchfork*, October 6, 2014.

78 Lanre Bakare, "Best Albums of 2014: Number 9—*You're Dead!* by Flying Lotus," *Guardian*, December 2, 2014.

79 See Angela Y. Davis, *Freedom Is a Constant Struggle: Ferguson, Palestine, and the Foundations of a Movement* (Chicago: Haymarket Books), 2016.

80 Alice Walker, "My Friend Yeshi," in *Absolute Trust in the Goodness of the Earth: New Poems* (New York: Random House, 2002), 145.

Conclusion: "I'm Tired of Marvin Asking Me What's Going On"

1 Nelson George, *The Death of Rhythm and Blues* (1988; New York: Penguin, 2004).

2 *Teddy Pendergrass: If You Don't Know Me*, dir. Olivia Lichtenstein (Showtime, 2019); *The Two Killings of Sam Cooke*, dir. Kelly Duane (Netflix, 2019); *Mr. Soul: Ellis Haizlip and the Birth of Black Power TV*, dir. Melissa Haizlip and Samuel Pollard (2018); *Ain't Too Proud: The Life and Times of the Temptations*, dir. Des McAnuff, written by Dominique Morriseau, opened at the Imperial Theater on Broadway in March 2019; *Amazing Grace*, dir. Sydney Pollack, opened in wide release in April 2019.

3 Aaron Cohen, *Move On Up: Chicago Soul Music and Black Cultural Power* (Chicago: University of Chicago Press, 2019).

4 GerShun Avilez, *Radical Aesthetics and Modern Black Nationalism* (Urbana: University of Illinois Press, 2016), 10. See Wahneema Lubiano, "Black Nationalism and Black Common Sense: Policing Ourselves and Others," in *The House That Race Built*, ed. Wahneema Lubiano (New York: Vintage, 1998), 232–52.

5 Toni Cade Bambara, "What It Is I Think I'm Doing Anyhow," in *The Writer on Her Work*, ed. Janet Sternburg (1980; New York: W. W. Norton, 2000), 160, 163. Articulating an alternative tradition to white women writers such as Kate Chopin and Sylvia Plath, who "hawk despair, insanity, alienation, suicide" (163), Bambara exalts black figures such as Harriet Tubman, Paul Robeson, and her own grandmother, who insist that "lovers and combatants are not defeated" (162).

6 Bambara, "What It Is I Think I'm Doing Anyhow," 163.

7 Akasha Gloria Hull, *Soul Talk: The New Spirituality of African American Women* (Rochester, VT: Inner Traditions, 2001), 142–43.

8 Sylvia Wynter explores the complex ramifications of the relationship between "the Black Aesthetic movement of the 1960s" and black studies in "On How We Mistook the Map for the Territory, and Reimprisoned Ourselves in Our Unbearable Wrongness of Being, of *Desêtre*: Black Studies toward the Human Project," in *A Companion to African-American Studies*, ed. Lewis R. Gordon and Jane Anna Gordon (Oxford: Blackwell, 2006), 261–63.

9 Nathaniel Mackey, "Sound and Sentiment, Sound and Symbol," *Discrepant Engagement: Dissonance, Cross-Culturality, and Experimental Writing* (Tuscaloosa: University of Alabama Press, 1993), 244, 246. See also Mackey's invocation of "the limping eloquence or enablement of [West African god] Legba" several years later, in "Cante Moro," *Paracritical Hinge: Essays, Talks, Notes, Interviews* (Madison: University of Wisconsin Press, 2005), 194.

10 Paul Gilroy, *The Black Atlantic: Modernity and Double-Consciousness* (Cambridge, MA: Harvard University Press, 1993), 111.

11 Darieck Scott, *Extravagant Abjection: Blackness, Power, and Sexuality in the African American Literary Imagination* (New York: New York University Press, 2010), 11.

12 Christina Sharpe, *In the Wake: On Blackness and Being* (Durham, NC: Duke University Press, 2016), 22.

13 Greg Tate, Facebook post, September 27, 2016 (cited with permission of the author).

14 See this book's introduction, and citation of Portia Maultsby, "Soul," in *African American Music: An Introduction*, ed. Mellonee V. Burnim and Portia K. Maultsby (New York: Routledge, 2014), 278.

15 Amiri Baraka, "The Soul Brother" (eulogy for Ellis Haizlip, 1991), *Eulogies* (New York: Agincourt Press, 2002), 190, qtd. in Gayle Wald, *It's Been Beautiful: Soul! and Black Power Television* (Durham, NC: Duke University Press, 2015), 213.

16 This book was in production when I discovered that Julius B. Fleming had advanced his own theory of Afropresentism in his prize-winning essay, "Transforming Geographies of Black Time: How the Free Southern Theater Used the Plantation for Civil Rights Activism" (*American Literature* 91, no. 3 [2019]: 587–617). Fleming's definition of Afropresentism—as "a political, affective, and philosophical orientation toward enjoying and demanding the 'good life' in the here and now, in the present" (611)—is at once extremely valuable and quite different from my own articulation of the concept.

17 Mary Dery, "Black to the Future: Interviews with Samuel R. Delany, Greg Tate, and Tricia Rose," in *Flame Wars: The Discourse of Cyberculture* (Durham, NC: Duke University Press, 1994), 180.

18 D'Angelo and the Vanguard, "1000 Deaths," comp. D'Angelo and Kendra Foster, *Black Messiah*, RCA, 2014.

19 Donny Hathaway, "Little Ghetto Boy," comp. Earl DeRouen and Edward Howard, Atlantic, 1972; Dr. Dre, "Lil' Ghetto Boy," feat. Snoop Dogg and Daz Dillinger, *The Chronic*, Death Row, 1992; Wu-Tang Clan, "Little Ghetto Boys," *Wu-Tang Forever*, Loud/RCA/BMG, 1997. Thanks to Anthony Reed for the assist here.

20 My thinking here is indebted to Zandria Robinson.

21 I refer to Robin D. G. Kelley's *Freedom Dreams: The Black Radical Imagination* (Boston: Beacon Press, 2002).

22 Destiny's Child, "Survivor," comp. B. Knowles, A. Dent, and M. Knowles, *Survivor*, Columbia, 2001; Beyoncé, "1 + 1," comp. T. Nash, C-J Carter, C. Stewart, and B. Knowles, *4*, Columbia, 2011; *Cadillac Records*, dir. Darnell Martin (Sony, 2008). For a more thorough engagement of Beyoncé's aesthetic and ideological relationship to the soul tradition, see Emily J. Lordi, "Surviving the Hustle: Beyoncé's Performance of Work," *Black Camera* 9, no. 1 (2017): 131–45.

23 Beyoncé, *Lemonade*, dir. Beyoncé Knowles and Khalil Joseph (Parkwood/Columbia, 2016).

24 James McBride, *Kill 'Em and Leave: Searching for James Brown and the American Soul* (New York: Spiegel and Grau, 2016); *Nina*, dir. Cynthia Mort (RLJ Entertainment, 2016).

25 Beyoncé, "6 Inch," comp. A. Tesfaye, B. Knowles, D. Schofield, B. Diehl, T. Nash, et al., *Lemonade*, Parkwood/Columbia, 2016.

26 Isaac Hayes, "Walk on By," comp. Hal David and Burt Bacharach, *Hot Buttered Soul*, Stax, 1969.

27 "Window Seat: A Story by Erykah Badu," dir. Erykah Badu, co-dir. Coodie and Chike, Creative Control, 2010.

28 Erykah Badu, "Hotline Bling," comp. A. Graham, P. Jefferies, and T. Thomas, *But You Caint Use My Phone*, Motown/Control Freaq, 2015; Ryan Dombal, "Life on the Line: A Telephone Conversation with Erykah Badu," *Pitchfork*, December 10, 2015.

29 Dombal, "Life on the Line."

30 Erykah Badu, "The Healer," *AmErykah Part One (4th World War)*, Universal Motown, 2008.

31 Lyndon B. Johnson, "Special Message to the Congress: The American Promise," March 15, 1965. The speech can be viewed on YouTube: TheLBJLibrary, "Special Message to the Congress: The American Promise [on the Voting Rights Act], 3/16/65. MP506," June 24, 2013, YouTube video, 48:52, https://www.youtube.com/watch?v=5NvPhiuGZ6I.

32 Johnson, "Special Message to the Congress."

33 RAMP, "The American Promise," comp. E. Birdsong and Roy Ayers, *Come into Knowledge*, ABC Blue Thumb, 1977.

34 Erykah Badu, "AmErykahn Promise," comp. W. Allen, R. Ayers, and W. Birdsong, *New AmErykah Part One*.

35 Zandria Robinson, "'Gotta Sing on the Beats They Bring Us': Towards a Twenty-First-Century Blues Women's Epistemology," *Issues in Race and Society* 2, no. 1 (2014): 47–72.

36 Jason King, "When Autobiography Becomes Soul: Erykah Badu and the Cultural Politics of Black Feminism," *Women and Performance* 10, nos. 1–2 (1999): 211–43.

37 Erykah Badu, *But You Caint Use My Phone*.

38 Janelle Monáe feat. Erykah Badu, "Q.U.E.E.N.," comp. J. Robinson, K. Parker Jr., R. Irvin, et al., *The Electric Lady*, Wondaland Arts Society/Bad Boy/Atlantic, 2013.

39 Monáe, "Electric Lady," comp. J. Robinson, R. Irvin, N. Irvin III, and C. Joseph II, *The Electric Lady*.

40 Bessie Smith, "Nobody in Town Can Bake a Sweet Jelly Roll Like Mine," comp. Bessie Smith, Columbia, 1923.

41 Monáe, "Victory," comp. J. Robinson, R. Irvin, N. Irvin III, and C. Joseph II, *Electric Lady*; Lauryn Hill, "To Zion," comp. Lauryn Hill, *The Miseducation of Lauryn Hill*, Ruffhouse/Columbia, 1998; Monáe, "Q.U.E.E.N."; Hill, "Forgive Them Father," comp. Hill, *Miseducation*.

42 Monáe, "We Were Rock & Roll," comp. J. Robinson, R. Irvin, N. Irvin III, C. Joseph II, and K. Parker Jr., *Electric Lady*.

43 Monáe, "Sally Ride," comp. J. Robinson, R. Irvin, N. Irvin III, C. Joseph II, and K. Parker Jr., *Electric Lady*; Wilson Pickett, "Mustang Sally," comp. Mack Rice, *The Wicked Pickett*, Atlantic, 1966; Aretha Franklin, "Spirit in the Dark," comp. Aretha Franklin, *Spirit in the Dark*, Atlantic, 1970.

44 Monáe, "It's Code," comp. J. Robinson, N. Irvin III, C. Joseph II, and R. Gian-Arthur II, *Electric Lady*.

45 Monáe, "Ghetto Woman," comp. J. Robinson, N. Irvin III, and C. Joseph II, *Electric Lady*.

46 Barack Obama, *Dreams from My Father: A Story of Race and Inheritance* (New York: Three Rivers Press, 2004), 27.

47 Avery Gordon, *Keeping Good Time: Reflections on Knowledge, Power, and People* (Boulder, CO: Paradigm Publishers, 2004), x; Beyoncé, "Formation," dir. Melina Matsoukas (2016).

INDEX

Burnim, Mellonee, 129, 142, 165n6, 195n7
But You Caint Use My Phone (Badu), 160
"By the Time I Get to Phoenix," 111

call-and-response technique, 28, 53, 60,
    84, 94, 138–39
camaraderie, 4, 87, 94, 96
Cambridge, Godfrey, 23
capitalism, 34–35
"Change Is Gonna Come, A," 4, 29, 137,
    146, 151
Charles, Ray, 11, 30–31, 46, 56, 97, 198n54
Charlesworth, Chris, 66, 118
cheating songs, 32, 82, 84–86, 157
Chess, Leonard, 63
Chess, Marshall, 63, 64
Chess Records, 63, 67, 116, 117, 156
choirs, 72, 73, 91–92, 104
church, 60, 106, 129, 132, 147, 174n89;
    Franklin's connection to, 20–21, 92,
    140; representation of, 149. *See also*
    gospel
civil rights: activists and protesters, 20,
    54, 140; anthems, 32, 137; Johnson's
    support for, 159; material gains of, 2,
    41, 45, 163, 176n128; soul discourse
    and, 4, 9, 17, 19
classical music, 49, 50, 63
Clayton, Merry, 181n55
"Clean Up Woman," 32
Clifton, Lucille, 44
Cohen, Aaron, 151, 193n63, 193n64
Cole, Natalie, 88
Cole, Nat King, 33, 109–10, 135, 197n35
Coltrane, Alice, 148
Coltrane, John, 51, 68
Columbia Records, 57
Come to My Garden (Riperton), 117–18
commercialization, 35, 176n128. *See also*
    marketization
commodification, 34, 36
community, 12, 26, 51, 53, 149; belong-
    ing, 36, 37; building and breaking, 3, 6;
    conformity and, 14; divestment from,
    34, 39; investment in, 113–14, 123; soul

discourse and, 9, 44, 174n99; women
    and, 32, 82, 86
competition, 69, 71, 98–100, 133, 158, 161
Cooke, Sam, 3, 55, 56, 106, 135, 156,
    174n88; "A Change Is Gonna Come,"
    4, 29, 137, 146, 151
Cooper, Anna Julia, 22
covers, 11, 16, 33, 46–49; Badu's, 158–60;
    Franklin's notable, 47, 58–62, 71–73,
    88–92; Hathaway and the Asso-
    ciation's, 67–71; Hayes's, 111–12, 114;
    origin of term, 178n6; Rotary Connec-
    tion's, 63–64; Simone's notable, 10,
    47, 50–53, 179n20. *See also individual
    song titles*
"Cranes in the Sky," 123
Crawford, Margo, 14, 15
Creations, 105, 106
Crowe, Cameron, 26
Cuban music, 11, 168n36
cultural logic, 9, 10, 16, 19, 151, 166n13. *See
    also* soul logic
cultural production, 9, 13, 15, 16, 152
Curtis, King, 58, 68

dance, 86–87, 124, 133, 146–47
Dance to the Music (Sly and the Family
    Stone), 78
D'Angelo and the Vanguard, 155
Davis, Angela, 44, 54, 72, 140, 148, 180n31
Davis, Betty, 162
Davis, Miles, 101
Davis, Thulani, 44
Day, Doris, 76–77, 80–82, 184n6
delay tactics, 91, 186n50
Delfonics, 30
Dellenbaugh, Virginia, 193n66
Denise, Lynnée, 173n83
DeRouen, Earl, 95–96
Dery, Mark, 154
Diamond, Neil, 163
"Didn't It Rain," 128–30, 141, 195n6
Dillon, Elizabeth Maddock, 185n21
Dineley, Sean, 48, 178n6
disco, 34, 174n95

diva, 121; meaning, 58; Simone's reputation as, 86–87

diversity, 15, 17; aesthetic, 13, 34; black, 39, 42, 43–44; within unity, 25

documentaries, 12, 130, 150, 151. *See also* biopics

"Don't Touch My Hair," 124

"Do Right Woman, Do Right Man," 82–83

Dorsey, Thomas, 92, 128

Draper, Jason, 188n75

Dr. Dre, 155

"Dr. Feelgood," 76, 88–90, 99, 126, 138–40, 141, 145

Drukman, Steven, 45

Du Bois, W. E. B., 5, 22

duende, theory of, 114–15

duets: interracial, 33, 62, 64; male-female, 30, 76, 79–82, 97–100, 198n54

Duncan, Robert, 114

Dyer, Richard, 47

Dylan, Bob, 47, 48, 63

Ebony, 7, 19, 29, 190n13; Brown in, 133; Franklin in, 31; Green in, 108; Hayes in, 112; Knight and the Pips in, 2, 3, 166n9; Riperton in, 66, 121; Simone in, 46

eccentricity, 42–43

Echols, Alice, 174n95

Edmonds, Ben, 145, 200n74

Edwards, Brent, 141

"Eleanor Rigby," 46, 58, 181n54

Electric Lady (Monáe), 155, 161–63

Elliott, Missy, 189n8

Ellis, Trey, 13–14, 42, 44; "The New Black Aesthetic," 38–40

Ellison, Ralph, 17, 54; commentary on soul, 24–25; *Invisible Man*, 130

Ellison, Steven (Flying Lotus), 16, 128, 146–49, 154

encores, 127

erotics: ad-libs and, 74; Franklin's, 76, 89, 90–92, 140, 144; Hathaway's, 93; Prince's, 97; Redding's, 134

Errico, Greg, 78, 81

Esquire, 26, 30

Everett, Todd, 190n15

"Everyday People," 78

exhaustion, 5, 123, 145, 197n35

experimentalism/experimentation, 63, 96, 108, 110, 158

expression, artistic, 47, 53, 114–15, 178n3

Falls, Mildred, 128–29, 136, 197n35

false endings, 11, 16, 81, 126–28; Badu's, 158; Brown's, 132, 133–34, 138; death as, 146, 147; in Flying Lotus's "Never Catch Me" (video), 146–49; Franklin's, 138–40; Gaye's, 141, 143–45; Jackson's, 128–30, 195n4; Lamar's, 200n76; Redding's, 136–38; Simone's, 52

falsetto singing, 2, 5, 12, 16, 101–3; Black Power era and, 32; Gaye's, 143; Green's, 102, 105–7; Hayes's, 109, 111–12, 114–15; Peebles's, 104–5; popularity of, 33; Riperton's, 115–16, 117, 118–19, 121–22; Solange Knowles's, 123, 124–25

Famous Flames, 131

Farmer, Ashley, 15, 17

fashion, 30, 48, 174n99; Brown's, 131, 133; Green's, 31–32; Hayes's, 112–13, 192n42; Prince's, 97

feeling, depth of, 68, 69

Felder, Wilton, 72

femininity, 61, 66, 77, 82, 117

feminism. *See* black feminism

Fillmore West, 58–59, 76, 88–90, 138, 198n54

Fink, Robert, 186n50

Five Stairsteps, 30

Flack, Roberta, 46, 66, 71, 88, 93, 181n55

Fleming, Julius B., 202n16

Flying Lotus, 16, 128, 146–49, 154

Ford, Tanisha, 15, 17, 26, 35, 166n10, 174n99

"F.U.B.U. (For Us By Us)," 123, 125

"Four Women," 50, 185n31

improvisation, 75, 87, 90, 100. *See also* ad-
libs; false endings
individualism, 5, 45, 78–79
integration, 9, 13, 78, 137
interiority, 101–2, 123, 143, 199n62;
cool, 105; female, 16, 116, 118, 119,
122, 124–25; Green's, 108–9, 190n28;
Hayes's, 111
Iton, Richard, 37, 85
"I've Got to Use My Imagination," 1–3,
4

Jackson, Al, Jr., 166n10
Jackson, Mahalia, 16, 126, 127, 136, 140;
critique of labor conditions, 197n35;
Peebles's admiration for, 190n15; per-
formances at Newport, 128–30, 137,
141, 195n4, 195n6
Jackson, Michael, 162
James, Etta, 20, 30, 58, 156
James, Robin, 127
Jameson, Frederic, 9–10
Jarrett, Michael, 102
Jay-Z, 157
jazz, 12, 51, 75, 148; soul-, 19–20, 35
Jazz on a Summer's Day (1960), 130, 195n6
Jeter, Claude, 59, 107
Jet magazine, 55, 72, 145, 191n28
Jim Crow, 2, 151, 166n10
Johnson, Aaron, 75
Johnson, Lyndon B., 14, 159, 160
Jones, Booker T., 35, 109, 136
Jones, Lisa, 40–41
Jones, Uriel, 12

Kaliss, Jeff, 184n6
"Keep on Pushin': Rhythm and Blues as
a Weapon" (Touré), 28–29, 69
Keith, Om'Mas, 159–60
Kelley, Robin D. G., 44
Kerner Commission Report (1968), 95
King, Carole, 58, 92–93
King, Martin Luther, Jr., 9, 22, 54, 72,
110–11, 157, 159
Knight, Brenda, 2

Knight, Gladys, 1–4, 9, 82, 166n9. *See also*
Gladys Knight and the Pips
Knight, Merald, 2, 3
Knowles, Beyoncé, 16, 123, 124, 163; *Lem-
onade*, 155, 156–58, 162; Prince and, 98;
Super Bowl Halftime Show, 156
Knowles, Solange, 14, 16, 103, 122–25,
154, 189n8

Labelle, 32
labor, 10, 85, 86, 134; conditions, 135,
197n35; convict, 83, 185n25; overwork,
133, 145, 196n26; of performance, 51,
66, 70, 115
La Havas, Lianne, 71
Lamar, Kendrick, 146, 147, 200n76
language of soul, 10, 22, 30, 45, 174n88
Lee, Don L. (Haki Madhubuti), 27
Lemonade (B. Knowles), 155, 156–58, 162
"Let It Be," 58, 60–61, 69
"Life," 10, 47, 51–53, 159, 179n20
listening, method of, 11, 12, 16
Live at Fillmore West (Franklin), 88, 141,
198n49, 198n54, 200n74
Locke, Alain, 22–23
Lomax, Alan, 83
Lorde, Audre, 14, 22, 33, 38, 54, 121; on
defining oneself, 75–76; theory of the
erotic, 140
Lott, Eric, 58, 185n21
"Love and Happiness," 108
love songs, 33, 62, 70, 74, 120; Green's,
106, 108; laments, 114, 121; love tri-
angles, 157–58. *See also* cheating songs
"Loving You," 193n69
Lubiano, Wahneema, 151, 166n13

Mackey, Nathaniel, 101–2, 114–15, 152,
189n3, 201n9
Major, Clarence, 21
Malcolm X, 72, 73, 85, 155
Malcolm X (1992), 71, 72, 73, 140, 183n99
Marcus, Greil, 78, 94
Mardin, Arif, 71
marginalization, 22, 34, 100

patriarchy, 12, 32, 38, 92, 145, 160

Patrin, Nate, 148

Pavlić, Ed, 33

Peebles, Ann, 101, 103–5, 189n8; idols of, 105, 190n15; stardom, 189n12, 190n13

Perfect Angel (Riperton), 118–20, 193n69

performance style: Brown's, 126–27, 131–34, 135; erotic or sexual, 74, 89, 90–92, 93, 134–35; feminist politics and, 82, 86; Franklin's, 56–57, 87–92; Gaye's, 144–45; gospel, 20, 59–61; Green's, 31–32, 106–9; Hathaway's, 67–70, 93–94; Hayes's, 103, 113–15; Jackson's, 128–30, 197n35; power struggles and, 77; queer dynamics of, 4, 17, 30, 31, 32, 80, 81, 86, 185n25; Redding's, 134–38; Riperton's, 62, 65–66, 121; Simone's, 51–54, 84–85, 86–87, 185n25; Sly and the Family Stone's, 78–82

Perry, Edmund, 39–40

Perry, Imani, 9, 170n18

Pickett, Wilson, 36, 103, 138, 162

"Please, Please, Please," 131–32

police brutality, 39–40, 112–13, 158, 163

political organizations, 36, 72, 112

politics: Brown's, 197n43; culture and, 42, 44; Franklin's, 54, 180n31; Gaye's, 142, 145, 199n58; Hathaway's involvement, 72; protest, 146; racial, 133; Riperton's, 193n69; Simone's, 50, 62, 181n64; soul-era, 151. *See also* black feminism

popular culture, 32, 44, 176n128

popular music, 6, 15, 54, 58, 113, 139, 178n6; black women and, 156, 162; characteristics of 1970s, 192n42; fade-and-soar structure, 127; falsetto singing and, 32; heterogeneity of, 43

Porgy and Bess (Gershwin): "I Loves You, Porgy," 46, 48, 68; "Summertime," 106–7

Porter, David, 110

Porterfield, Chris, 23

post-soul, 17, 18; artists, 6, 13, 41, 43; scholarship, 41–42; term usage, 13, 38, 154; theory, 14, 16, 38, 43–44, 74

poverty, 39, 105, 134, 142

Powell, Ric, 95

power dynamics, 62, 108–9, 118, 152, 197n43; of the erotic, 140; gender, 12, 77, 80, 82, 135; racial, 137; Simone's, 51–52, 53

Powers, Ann, 90

Preston, Billy, 88

Prince, 14, 76, 161; albums, 97–98; background and mentors, 96–97; women collaborators, 97–100, 187n70, 188n75, 188n82

Proper Strangers, 63

protest songs, 50, 62, 137, 146. *See also* anthems

psychedelic rock, 33, 63, 69

Purcell, Richard, 169n48

"Q.U.E.E.N.," 161, 162

queer voices, 4, 5, 31–32, 34, 106, 185n25

"Que Sera, Sera," 76–77, 79–82, 83, 98–99, 106

race, 21, 45, 112, 134, 137–38; covering songs and, 48, 58, 61, 77; politics, 133, 156; record industry and, 35–36, 118, 122; signifiers, 3

racial memory, 10

racism, 39–40, 49, 113

rap, 152, 155, 160. *See also* hip-hop

Ray (2004), 11

Reagon, Bernice Johnson, 54

"Reasons," 119, 121

records labels, 34. *See also specific label*

Redding, Otis, 16, 72, 86, 103, 107, 148, 198n45; death, 110, 138; false endings, 126, 127, 136–38; performance style, 134–35; reaction to Franklin's "Respect," 64; "Try a Little Tenderness," 75, 135–38, 198n46, 198n48. *See also* "Respect" redemption, 2, 22, 150

Redmond, Shana, 180n28, 185n25

"Red Red Wine," 163

religion, 5, 20–22, 140, 166n11. *See also* church; spirituality

resilience: Black Power movement and, 27; the blues and, 23, 25; Brown's, 131, 133; community belonging and, 36; false endings and, 127; group, 16, 22, 25, 126; neoliberal narratives of, 14, 15, 127, 146; perpetual need for, 17, 133, 154; soul discourse and, 5, 9, 22, 26, 81, 130, 151; struggle and survival and, 3, 5, 54, 138, 154

"Respect," 33, 46, 48, 61–62, 64–66, 116, 138

response songs, 30

resurrection, 147, 158, 200n76

revival, 20, 81, 126, 129, 142, 151; of soul icons, 11–12, 156–57

rhythm and blues (R&B), 28, 57, 59, 86, 178n3; charts, 20, 43, 104, 118

Riley, Clayton, 21, 25, 30, 35, 37; on Franklin, 56, 90, 126, 127, 140, 148

riots, 6, 34, 94, 113–15, 192n47

Riperton, Minnie, 16, 63, 67; cancer and death, 120–21; *Come to My Garden*, 117–18; early life and musical training, 116–17; falsetto singing, 102–3, 118–19, 121–22, 189n7; *Perfect Angel*, 118–20, 193n69; Rotary Connection cover of "Respect," 33, 47, 62, 64–66; vocal range, 118, 123, 193n66

Robinson, Smokey, 31, 33

Robinson, Zandria, 160, 202n20

"Rolling in the Deep," 58

Rolling Stone, 80

Rolling Stones, 63, 117, 131, 132

"Roll with Me, Henry," 30

Rosen, Jody, 98

"Rosie," 83–85

Rotary Connection: interracial appeal, 64, 182n70; musical experimentation, 63, 116; *Songs*, 64; termination from

Chess label, 117; version of "Respect," 33, 47, 48, 62, 64–66

Roy Ayers Musical Production (RAMP), 159–60

Royster, Francesca, 42–43

Rudolph, Richard, 118, 120, 121

salvation, 92

Sam and Dave, 26, 110, 136, 150, 191n33

Sampha, 124

Sanders, Charles, 89

Sanders, Gertrude, 133

Saul, Scott, 171n44

Scott, Darieck, 152

Seat at the Table, A (S. Knowles), 103, 122–23, 125

self-trust, 75–76, 81

sensuality, 54; Baldwin's definition of, 23

serial poetics, 141, 143, 148, 199n56

sexual politics, 65–66, 107, 134, 193n69; Gaye's, 143, 145; of soul performance, 31–32. *See also* erotics

Shaft (1971), 145

Shange, Ntozake, 90

Sharpe, Christina, 152

Simmons, Barbara, 25, 171n44

Simmons, Will, 146–47

Simms, Bobby, 63, 64

Simon, Paul, 59

Simon and Garfunkel, 47, 59–61, 72

Simone, Nina, 36, 48; ad-libs, 76, 83–85; compared to Franklin, 54–56; dance style, 86–87; false endings, 52; feminist awakening, 85, 185n31; musical training, 20, 49; *Nina* biopic, 156; politics, 50, 62, 181n64; post-1960s exile, 34; reputation and virtuosity, 14, 50–51, 86

Simone, Nina, albums and songs: "Be My Husband," 76, 83–85, 89, 91, 100, 185n25, 185n30; *Emergency Ward*, 33; "Four Women," 50, 51, 185n31; "I Loves You, Porgy," 46, 48, 68; "Life," 10, 47, 51–53, 159, 179n20; "Love Me or Leave Me," 50; "Mississippi Goddam," 50,